THE POWER OF PERFORMANCE

ACTORS, AUDIENCES AND OBSERVERS OF CULTURAL PERFORMANCES IN INDIA

The Power of Performance

Actors, Audiences and Observers of Cultural Performances in India

Edited by

HEIDRUN BRÜCKNER
ELISABETH SCHÖMBUCHER
PHILLIP B. ZARRILLI

MANOHAR
2007

First published 2007

ISBN 81-7304-768-5

Published by

Ajay Kumar Jain for
Manohar Publishers & Distributors
4753/23 Ansari Road, Daryaganj
New Delhi 110 002

Typeset at

Digigrafics
New Delhi 110 049

Printed at

Lordson Publishers Pvt. Ltd.
Delhi 110 007

Contents

PART III: *THE OBSERVER*: RECONSIDERING THE CATEGORIES OF THE OBSERVER

Introduction

Heidrun Brückner and *Elisabeth Schömbucher*

The term 'performance' encompasses a wide range of cultural events, such as various theatrical performances and performing arts, the performance of oral texts, various kinds of political, religious and social rituals, and, eventually, any speech event. The inclusion of so many different events under a single concept of 'performance' is the result of a changing methodological approach in the social sciences. Emphasis has shifted from studying social institutions and texts to considering the actors and their creative potentiality. Since Milton Singer's (1972) often quoted statement about religious and cultural performances as 'the elementary constituents of the culture and the ultimate units of observation', the 'performance approach' has been further developed by various social scientists. Whereas some performance theorists such as Victor Turner (1982) and Richard Schechner (1985) take theatrical performances on stage and the theatrical potential of social life as their starting point, others, such as Bauman and Briggs (1990), apply the term performance in a linguistic sense to any speech event, whether artful and elaborated or just everyday verbal interaction. Both, the theatrical and the linguistic approaches, opened up new perspectives for the interpretation of culture. Cultural performances, such as rituals, ceremonies, carnivals and dramas, but also performances in the linguistic sense, so-called speech events, can be seen as interpretations of social life by the actors themselves and are then exhibited to the participants as well as to outsiders. However, it is not as easy for the outsider to read a public performance just like a text as, for instance, Geertz (1972) proposed.

The most crucial aspect in the performance approach, the shift from the study of texts 'to the analysis of the emergence of texts in contexts' (Bauman and Briggs 1990: 66), leads to another problem. Who is going to define 'context', what should be included, what can be excluded? An objective description of context is not possible. Contexts cannot be defined by observing and describing the natural environment of a performance. They rather 'emerge in negotiations between participants in social interactions' (ibid.: 68). This insight results in different perspectives which have to be taken into account by the observer rather than defining an 'objective' context. To avoid reifying 'context' by describing everything that surrounds a set of utterances, which seems adequate for selection by the analyst, Bauman and Briggs demand that language or rather speech should not only be seen in its referential or indexical function, but any use of language should be interpreted as 'social action' in which 'things are done with words' (cf. Austin 1962). With this shift from the study of context to the study of contextualization, an agent-centred view of performance is achieved. It enables the observer to show in which manner participants collectively construct the world around them (Bauman and Briggs 1990: 69).

Constructing social reality with words is a difficult endeavour. As Austin (1962) has shown, it is not sufficient to make an utterance. For an utterance to be convincing, meaningful, 'felicitous', a number of preconditions have to be fulfilled. What is valid for an utterance can also be applied to any performance. Performances based on words, images or one's body can be powerful, convincing, authentic, or they may fail. It came to be postulated that cultural performances attempt to communicate meaning, and that they are of a reflexive character in which life is interpreted, identity is created and individual crisis is explained and mastered. More recently, yet another aspect of agency has been stressed: cultural performances are not only said to communicate meaning but also possess the potential to transform the status of the participants. They are events where different versions of culture can be negotiated and even social critique might be expressed. The transformative power of a performance becomes even more obvious when successful performances are compared with those which failed. Quite a few examples of 'failed' performances indicate that performances neither automatically have an impact on the participants or audience, nor that they merely enact a certain cultural text (Flueckinger 1988; Brückner 2001). Failed performances show that a successful performance must have a number of features which enable the transformation of its participants. The meaning of a performance cannot be found solely in its corresponding text. If we understand language as social action, the power of any performance, be it aesthetic or ritual, cannot be a product of its linguistic content but reveals itself in the communicative processes taking place between the performer and the audience in the course of a performance.

The present volume aims at examining the transformative power of performances. It is the outcome of a panel discussion at the sixteenth European Conference on Modern South Asian Studies held in Edinburgh in September 2000. Following Schieffelin's dictum that '[t]he central issue of performativity, whether in ritual performance, theatrical entertainment or the social articulation of ordinary human situations, is the imaginative creation of a human world' (1998: 205), our notion of performance obtains a different quality. It is no longer the *mise-en-scène* with its poetic and aesthetic qualities that is emphasized. Instead, other aspects of 'constructedness', such as efficacy in healing rituals or the creation of divine presence in ritual and theatre are taken into consideration. How does the 'imaginative creation' work? How is social reality constructed? How is efficacy obtained? What makes a performance powerful? All the contributions to this volume are concerned with the power of performance in one way or the other. They comprise different kinds of performances such as rituals, dance, theatre and martial arts, without any further distinctions of genres, because in many instances no sharp borderline can be drawn between ritual and theatrical performances. It has been shown that the dichotomy between theatre and ritual is a European construct that cannot be applied to the South Asian context (Fischer-Lichte 2000: 17ff; Rao and Köpping 2000: 11ff). Instead, the articles revolve around three perspectives: the perspective of the performer, of the audience and of the observer. The notion of performance as an event where structure and process come together results in a multi-perspective approach. An actor's performance is determined not only by normative structures, but also by his individual intentions and the expectations of the audience. Actors, participants and the audience interpret performances according to their own differing cultural and personal concepts. Therefore, performances cannot be perceived as monolithic events but gain their meaning and transformative power on different levels. This volume wants to do justice to these different perspectives.[1]

In the four contributions of Part I, different rituals are studied from the perspective of the performers, their physical enactment and their techniques of empowering a performance and creating presence. An agent-centred view of performance usually takes the role of the actor/performer as its starting point. How does he act? What makes his performance meaningful, true and efficient? How does he empower a performance? Is it words, action, charisma, merging the individual personality with the enacted character? Does the performer stick to the rules or rather transgress them when necessary? Where is the borderline between the authentic and the unauthentic, between the meaningful and the meaningless?

The three papers in Part II of the book switch over to the perspective of the audience. For quite some time, the 'classical' perspective in performance studies has focused on the role of the performer. More recently, other participants and especially the audience have been taken into consideration. Realizing that there is not one privileged or authoritative perspective from which to look at a performance has opened up a different access to the power of performance. The meaning and the impact of power cannot be derived from the actor alone. The audience, too, is an important constituent in any performance. It is not only the performer, but the audience as well, who empowers a performance. The decision about the authenticity of a performance or about its failure is to a large extent taken by the audience. The contributions of Part II show that oral texts are not simply texts performed orally but texts composed while being performed. The actual version of the 'text' performed is influenced by the audience. Its members do not have to accept what is performed for them, they might voice criticism or even leave the performance (Flueckinger 1988). There might be an objective meaning in a performance, but it is also subjectively made by each listener. Taking into consideration the 'listeners' it becomes obvious that 'text' is not the ultimate feature of a performance. What is 'heard' does not always correspond to what has been said. Things unsaid might have been heard, according to the individual conditions of the participants and audience.

In the five contributions forming Part III, problems of cultural translation and representation are dealt with taking the perspective of the outside observer. In analogy to Lévi-Strauss' dictum that there cannot exist a common analysis of religion by a believer and by a non-believer (Lévi-Strauss 1965), we argue that there cannot be a common perspective between participants and observers of performances. Assuming that actors, participants and the audience understand a performance in accordance with their respective cultural and personal backgrounds, it becomes essential to consider the observer's perspective. We have to face the question whether any cultural translation is possible without desacralization? How shall we cope with the case of an icon being perceived by some as a manifestation of divinity and as a piece of art with symbolic cultural meaning by others? Or with the case of a devadasi being perceived as a deity's vessel by some and as a role-impersonator by others? Or with a singer of oral epics considered by some to create divine presence and by others to present cultural symbols or images? These questions force us to reconsider such categories as text, image and voice. Most recently, some scholars have demanded that not observing and describing, but acting oneself is the way to obtain new insights into how power of performance is obtained. This has resulted in another approach: observers learning to be performers themselves. Such scholars-cum-performers gain new insights into what exactly empowers a performance, what it means to give up one's own individual personality, what it means to taste emotions and make the audience taste them as well.

With the emphasis on the three different perspectives of actor, audience and observer we want to overcome the dichotomy between observing and describing, text and performance, actor and audience. How actors and participants are able to empower or rather disempower a performance is shown in Marzia Balzani's paper on a kingly ritual in present-day Jodhpur, Rajasthan. The durbar (courtly audience) used to be centred on the figure of the maharaja as the pivot of the state and the source of political, religious and economic authority. A traditional durbar enacted and embodied the hierarchical relations between different groups and individuals within the state. At an ideal durbar, a specific seating plan and an order of presenting coins (*nazar*) to the maharaja reflects the subtle distinctions of status and rank between the participants. In modern India, the maharajas are no longer recognized as rulers by the Indian states. A durbar of today is simultaneously a private ritual, a cultural performance and a means of ensuring that the traditional authority of the maharaja in India remains a part of the living knowledge of those who take part in or witness the durbar. A modern durbar also displays elements of a folkloric spectacle taking place in the five-star palace hotel with tourists present. Despite these changes a successful durbar today requires that everyone present be attired in accordance with his status and perform his allotted role at the appropriate time. The fact that participants have the power to undermine the success of this kingly ritual was shown at the 1989 durbar, when the Maharaja of Jodhpur had changed the seating order. Because of the impact of this change on the third generation descendants of the royal family, the affected guests protested and threatened to stay away from the durbar altogether. The maharaja had to rearrange the seating plan as well as the order of presenting offerings. This example shows that although the context of the performance had changed significantly, its symbolic meaning still was of political importance. Authority on the part of the maharaja is not guaranteed but must be re-established and negotiated upon at these public ritual events. The example also shows that participants, although of a lower status, are able to make the ritual fail. Because of their refusal to play their part in an altered procedure it was necessary to re-order the ritual in ways which might radically undermine the position of the ruler. It is this very position the ritual is designed to (re-)establish and publicly proclaim before the assembled audience who also plays the part of ritual performers.

Another example of re-ritualization in an altered historical context is presented in Hanne de Bruin's paper on the female-dominated rural devadāsī tradition in Tamil Nadu. Rural devadāsīs used to be dedicated to the village goddess and incorporate her during festivals. The few remaining devadāsīs describe themselves as 'living embodiment of the goddess' or as 'belonging to the goddess'. Sacred power and divine presence was created by the devadāsī's own body with the practice of 'showing hands' in which the devadāsī and the goddess mirror each other. In contrast to performers of rural theatre, devadāsīs did not perceive themselves as 'playing a role', but as 'an integral part of the goddess'. Devadāsīs cannot be portrayed as ritual performers without considering the wider cultural context, especially the impact of modernization which changed social and religious values and strengthened the Brahmanic view of sacred power. The conceptualization of sacred power as an organic force represented by the sexually active goddess and her devadāsīs has been marginalized in favour of a more male-oriented, ritualistic, and ascetic Brahmanical view. Non-Brahman village rituals directed at the invocation and representation of sacred power as a live and embodied presence acquired a negative connotation. The social disapproval of the devadāsī tradition resulted in a loss of influence, prestige, honour and status on the side of the devadāsīs. Therefore they had to resort to different performances. Devadāsīs became full-fledged actresses and owned commercial theatre companies performing songs and dance or even Puranic plays during festivals. But even as rural actors, they seem to be unable to escape social stigmatization. Since rural devadāsīs today have discontinued incorporating the goddess de Bruin attempts to explore their subjective reality through interviews. She is able to illustrate the performers' own understanding of their performances, and the way they experience social reality.

Balzani's and de Bruin's contributions cope with the gap between the lived-in reality of the subjects of their study and the reality of our academic reflections on it by adopting the perspective and conceptions of the actual performers. At first sight, such an approach does not appear to be open to Karin Steiner who discusses the meaning of an ancient Vedic ritual documented and transmitted in a complex set of texts in her 'How to Attain Heaven: The Vājapeya Sacrificial Ritual'. They comprise texts to be recited and sung during the performance of the ritual by various priests and by the patron, as well as meta-texts containing detailed prescriptions for performance and explanations of the meaning of ritual elements. Steiner views the sacrificial rituals (śrauta rituals) as 'elementary constituents' (M. Singer) encapsulating the Vedic culture. For the first time, she attempts to access these texts by means of a performative approach based on Bauman's notion of performances evoking an imaginative reality and bringing about an altered awareness of the spectators and the protagonist. The Vedic ritual studied by Steiner is one of the most dramatic and spectacular ones, namely the Vājapeya, or 'power drink'. Its theme and purpose is the patron's attainment of heaven. This is symbolically enacted in several dramatic sequences of the ritual featuring the ascent to heaven and the safe return. The central scene is the patron and his wife climbing the sacrificial pole and succeeding to descend back to earth. By way of this enactment the power of performance becomes manifest. Steiner analyses the structure of the central scene in terms of van Gennep's model of passage rites as reformulated by Turner and in the light of the latter's concept of liminality that permits her to grasp emotional and performative aspects of the Vājapeya. By performing the central scene the patron's status elevation is enacted and legitimated and his agency is expanded.

Bozena Sliwczynska provides a comprehensive description of the regular first public performance (*araṅṅēṟṟam*) of a young actor of the Cākyār community in Kerala's traditional Sanskrit theatre (*Kūṭiyāṭṭam*). This performance precedes the initiation ritual of investiture with the sacred thread (*upanayanam*) for Cākyār boys in general and is conducted irrespective of their future profession. Those who actually take to acting later have another debut in speech-oriented performance (*Kuṭṭu*) in due course. Sliwczynska's account blends the information provided by acting manuals, earlier descriptions, conversations with experts, and her own observation of a performance demonstration in January 2000. In this manner, a complete picture is provided, although today's practice has taken to shortcut versions. The author emphasizes the ritual character of the initial performance in terms of a *rite de passage*. She argues that it appears to be essential to establish 'Cākyārhood', because even those young Cākyārs who do not become actors perform their *araṅṅēṟṟam*. She also points out that several sequences of the latter will be repeated as regular preliminary rites before every stage performance of the actor all through his career. The *araṅṅēṟṟam* further comprises basic narrative techniques of this theatre such as the *nirvahaṇa* flashback. It is of special interest that in his first performance the actor appears in the role of the *Sūtradhāra*, the stage director of Sanskrit drama whose presence is restricted to the prologues of the plays. The performer presents the opening verse of the *Bālacaritam* (ascribed to Bhāsa). In contradistinction to the other elements of the *araṅṅēṟṟam*, this character's role is no regular feature on the Kūṭiyāṭṭam stage. Under the impact of a changing social and political reality, the ritual character of the first performance as traditionally given by a Cākyār in a temple theatre may also be put into question. What happens to it when the theatre leaves the temples and members of other communities, including foreigners, are initiated into the art?

Actors are, of course, of foremost importance in empowering a performance, since they provide the basis of every performance. However, the actual interpretation and communication in each performance depends as much on the audience as on the actors. Joan Erdman's paper on 'Empowering Performance: The Choreographic Techniques of Uday Shankar' shows us how Uday Shankar was able to enchant not only an Indian audience but also Western and Far Eastern ones. Without a dance education in the traditional sense, Uday Shankar got into contact with Indian dance only in the West. After initial performances with Western dancers he went back to India in the 1920s and 1930s where he perfected his modern techniques for Indian dance, enabling him to establish an overall company style, and to teach this style and his repertoire to new company members. He opened the Uday Shankar India Culture Centre in Almora, in northern India. There he not only trained his company dancers, but changed Indians' notions about their own dance culture which has been further developed since then. Between 1931 and 1937, his innovations and creative choreographic techniques were staged in 800 performances in 26 countries. What made his choreographies authentic to an Indian as well as a European audience? According to Erdman, his new dance techniques were a bricolage of experience, cultural knowledge and the genius of creative power and imagination. His dance movements were based on temple sculptures and traditional paintings on India's mythological themes. This alone did not make him an authentic translator of Indian culture. He was also able to cater to the beliefs and prejudices of the contemporary audience. Western audiences of his time perceived spiritualism as authentic Indian culture. He was authentic for them because he was Indian by birth. In the West, Shankar embodied the exotic other in a perfect way. He had personal charisma and elegance and he was the erotic, divine dancer, beautiful like a god, embodying possession and ecstasy.

Mirella Lingorska's paper 'Between Performance and Competence: Exploring the Idea of Audience According to Indian Classical Views' considers the role of the audience in the Sanskrit classical court play. Critical of the drift of performance studies to try and assemble ritual, devotional, and classical drama performances under a single head of 'cultural performance', Lingorska reminds us of distinctions that should not be ignored. She claims a separate aesthetic domain for 'dramaturgical events' as discussed in ancient Sanskrit treatises and not affected by the medieval spread of devotionalism. Her argument for the purely aesthetic, an 'artlike art' takes its clues from her analysis of the classical concept of audience. On the basis of the Nāṭyaṣāstra, the ancient Indian treatise on dramaturgy, and of Abhinavagupta's famous commentary, Lingorska is able to show that the classical Sanskrit drama needed qualified spectators in order to display its complex meanings. This necessity resulted in a theory of audience in which desirable qualities and appropriate behaviour are described. Audience is not seen as a homogeneous body but as consisting of members of different social groups and classes. This results in multiple perspectives, each group bearing a specific response to the dramatic presentation. A major distinction is made between the common public and the expert members of the audience. The ideal audience of a Sanskrit play consists of people with thorough knowledge of the contents and the technical intricacies of the stage performance. On the assumption that an audience is a heterogeneous body of persons with different preconditions, the impact of text in performance has to be reconsidered. The genuine emotive charge of the dramatic speech cannot be treated as text in terms of classical speech act theory. In the context of the present volume, Lingorska's analysis of a classical Indian theory of audience and aesthetic experience also points to the limitations of modern notions of performativity.

Elisabeth Schömbucher's contribution on 'The Power of Listening: Giving Meaning to Divine Words in Possession Performances' also aims at a theory of audience. She considers the conditions of listening as essential in evaluating the textual content of an oral performance of possession. Comparing the divine speech as uttered by a medium in a state of possession with what was heard by the audience and narrated to the author, shows that the listener not only gives voice to the speaker but also reveals how he or she gives meaning to an oral text. A performance of possession is not just a product of enacted speech, but also a product of listening. The performer and the audience are equally agents in the process of interpreting and giving meaning to utterances during states of possession. An analysis of what was heard by the listener provides information of what exactly is heard in oral texts and what is omitted. In her account of what she heard, the professional listener doesn't distinguish between cultural knowledge, her associations, her own memories of past events and actual components of the divine talk. In fact, only a few passages of the spoken and heard words are congruent. In her analysis, Schömbucher distinguishes three parts in every divine discourse: panegyric passages, narrative elements and directive passages. In the panegyric passages, the power of the gods is praised. These passages are highly standardized and consist of formulaic elements in which cultural knowledge is presented. No need was felt to narrate these passages to the researcher, since everybody knows how powerful the gods are. By means of the narrative portions, the gods (or rather the mediums) refer to the past. These passages are passed on by the professional listener, although she refers to a large extent to her own version of what happened in the past. The differences between the divine memory and the listener's memory are of no significance. Most important are the directive passages which are developed in the dialogue between the god and his audience. Instructions about the worship of the gods and making the offerings are passed on in great detail. The comparison of the spoken and the heard versions of an oral text shows that effectiveness is not based on speaking alone, but that it is listening as well which provides an oral text with illocutionary force.

The contributions in the third part of this volume deal with methodological problems and offer new approaches to the study of performances. Saskia Kersenboom's paper on 'The Faculty of the Voice' addresses the question of representation of performances. She demands radical methodological changes in order to grasp human culture in all its complexities. She shows that despite Saussure's differentiation between langue and langage, the phenomenon of langage was never thoroughly conceptualized nor solved. Although speech, embodiment and the relationship of the 'speaking body' to the world were discussed by various French sociologists and anthropologists, bringing us closer to the approaches now termed performative, all theorists offer theories, concepts and abstractions, but what is lacking, according to Kersenboom, is a solid 'methodology of praxis' that enables us to deal with the very concrete nature and dynamics of performance. She is searching for a suitable method and technique that can identify, follow, describe, analyse and interpret performance, the speaking body in its relationship to the world, and the word embodied in praxis.

Kersenboom perceives culture as a performance with the body as the most important means through which culture is presented in words, sound and image. Reversing Ricoeur, she states that action should not be considered as text, but that text should be considered as action. Performances of human culture can be captured in full only by multi-media devices. In this way, not only verbal utterances, but also non-verbal messages such as sound and (moving) image can be considered. Her reflections lead her to consider the faculty of the voice in order to find out what empowers a performance. What does the human voice speak of while in performance? How does it formulate its verbal and non-verbal messages, what are these messages capable of effecting and to which purpose? The spoken word cannot be translated into written word. Non-verbal expressions cannot be put on paper. Any performance of human culture can only be captured in full by multi-media devices.

Kersenboom formulates yet another methodological demand. In trying to find out what gives authority and empowerment to a performance, she stresses the role of practitioners. Along with words they transport meaning through sound, image, smell, taste and touch. To grasp all these particularities, mere observing is not sufficient. Kersenboom demands participant participation instead of participant observation. Being a performer of Indian classical dance herself, she gets other insights into such performances than she would have obtained by mere observation.

Heike Moser's paper 'To Enjoy Playing with Play' deals with *Kūṭiyāṭṭam*, the only surviving regional variety of classical Sanskrit theatre in India, and has implemented the demand for participant participation. Her paper is about the inner process of learning how to perform and becoming a *Kūṭiyāṭṭam* performer herself. *Kūṭiyāṭṭam* came out of the temple compounds by the middle of the twentieth century and was confronted not only with a new audience, not versed in Sanskrit and gesture-language, but also with pupils from other castes. This step was, and still is, a big issue among conservative actors. For them, *Kūṭiyāṭṭam* is a ritual theatre, primarily performed for the deity of the temple and never in front of an audience lower in rank than Brahmans, nobles and castes of temple servants. Herself a pupil of lower rank and from another culture, Moser describes the interplay between her teacher and herself as pupil. How could she understand the nine *rasas*, and how could she make the audience feel these most subtle emotional impulses? How could she write about something which is not only put in words but mostly communicated through imitation. Although her paper naturally is a meta-discourse, she is nevertheless able to pass on to the reader the essentials of the interplay between a pupil and a teacher. How can a pupil taste the face of the teacher, his mood, his play with emotions (and later the audience, the face of the performer)? Although in *Kūṭiyāṭṭam* there is a text which is recited by the performer, this recitation, when textualized, has only a very limited meaning. Its meaning has to be performed by the actor with hand gestures, eye movements, facial expressions and voice. Constant repetition, improvement and refinement result in gradually understanding the *rasas*. Body memory remembers not only the recited text, but the recitation combined with gestures. Voice, body, costume, audience and 'heart' add to the meaning of *Kūṭiyāṭṭam*. The ultimate goal of any performer, be it pupil or master, Moser had to learn, is not embodying sentiments (*bhāva-rasa*) but playing with them.

A similar yet different experience is described by Phillip Zarrilli in his contribution about 'Embodying the Lion's Fury'. Zarrilli analyses the state of 'fury' (*raudra*) as it is represented, and embodied, in three forms in Kerala: *Kathakali* (the traditional dance-drama), *kalarippayattu* (the traditional martial art), and *kīrti-mukhas* (the leonine 'faces of glory' that protect thresholds of temples). Himself a performer, too, it took him years of training in Kerala's martial art to be able to experience from the inside the single-minded state of transforming fury which he had observed at first from the outside and which frightened him tremendously. After he had seen the lion's furious gaze for the first time as performed to him by his teacher he had no appropriate language to express what he had witnessed. The fluidity and virtuosity of the performance was breathtaking because it manifested the power and danger of the fury which was enacted. He felt that the terror and fury enacted could have done harm to the other. At the same time, it was completely controlled. The difference between watching and performing became obvious to him several years later. It was through the never-ending circle of repetition, correction and reflection in the process of learning how to perform that the author was able to perceive the potential within any particular pattern of movement. According to his experience, each movement has an inner life which must be exhibited by the performer. It is the process of repetition and correction which leads to intuitive embodiment where the body is able to respond, like an animal immediately to stimuli in the environment. According to Zarrilli the actor 'becomes' the character he is embodying and he becomes one with his original qualities. Regarding terror and fury it is the ambivalence that gets enacted by the master performer. Its power might protect as well as destroy the counterpart.

In his article on 'Creating Presence: Performing the Oral Narrative of Devnārāyaṇ' Aditya Malik reconsiders central categories with which oral epics are perceived by outside observers. He compares the notions of text and performance as derived from the researcher's own cultural framework with the notions within the framework of the culture described. He argues that within the narrative tradition of Devnārāyaṇ, a 'folk-deity' worshipped in Rajasthan, there exist meta-level concepts such as verbal narrative, visual narrative, performance and performer, which need to be taken seriously. The narrative of Devnārāyaṇ is performed in a ritual context by singer-priests in front of a long, elaborately painted cloth scroll that depicts the deity together with other characters and scenes from the narrative. The purpose of the performance is to evoke the presence of Devnārāyaṇ. His presence is never given, rather it needs to be manifested, evoked, generated through the performance. Malik examines the categories of performance, remembrance and memory, song and declamatory chant, repetition, dialogue and reported speech. Each of these features forms the context for the communicative act of telling and listening to the oral narrative. Taken together they are able to elicit the presence of Devnārāyaṇ. He shows that the focus is not on the text as such, but on the scroll, which is an icon of the deity and of the text. The scroll is not self-explanatory. It is not sufficient to look at it, it needs to be read and rendered meaningful by a specialist, the singer. Another category, the image, needs to be reconsidered as well. Images on the scroll are not icons in the sense of being traditionally conceived visual representations of religious themes, but they are the iconic and visual presence of characters and scenes from the narrative. Especially Devnārāyaṇ's presence in the image on the scroll is as real as the divine manifestation in *mūrtis* in Hindu temples. Malik shows that the singer's work in reciting an oral epic is not simply to sing, rather it is to mediate between the narrative and the audience. With this dialogic interaction the singer aims at establishing and testifying to Devnārāyaṇ's divine presence. The nature of this interaction, as a fundamental feature of performance, reveals how presence together with knowledge about divinity and community is constituted and created.

The study of ritual and theatre has seen a huge number of new and important contributions. Since the 'performative turn' in the nineties, categories such as theatrical, ritual, performative, have been deconstructed and disposed of their Western origin. The consideration of texts has developed into considering texts in their context and even further into perceiving context rather as a process of contextualization. Due importance has been given to the audience besides the performer. Despite all these achievements we still have to cope with the contradictions inherent in the process of cultural translation. How can performances be studied from a perspective based on principles radically different from those assumed by the participants? The contributions in this volume attempt an approximation to the meaning and power of performance by considering them from various perspectives.

NOTE

1. It should be noted that this distinction is made by the editors only for analytical purposes. In fact, each article refers to all three perspectives which cannot be separated from each other. But, in each contribution one of the three perspectives is emphasized.

REFERENCES

Austin, John L., 1962, *How to Do Things with Words*, Oxford: Oxford University Press.

Bauman, Richard and Charles L. Briggs, 1990, 'Poetics and Performance as Critical Perspectives on Language and Social Life', *Annual Reviews of Anthropology* 19: 59-88.

Brückner, Heidrun, 2001, 'Fluid Canons and Shared Charisma: On Success and Failure of Ritual Performance in a South Indian Oral Tradition', in Vasudha Dalmia, Angelika Malinar and Martin Cristof (eds.), *Charisma and Canon: Essays on the Religious History of the Indian Subcontinent*, New Delhi: Oxford University Press, pp. 313-27.

Fischer-Lichte, Erika, 2000, 'Theatralität und Inszenierung', in Erika Fischer-Lichte and Isabel Pflug (eds.), *Inszenierung von Authentizität.* Tübingen and Basel: Francke, pp. 11-27.

Flueckiger, Joyce Burkhalter, 1988, 'He Should Have Worn a Sari: A "Failed" Performance of a Central Indian Oral Epic', *The Drama Review* 32 (1): 159-69.

Geertz, Clifford, 1972, 'Deep Play: Notes on the Balinese Cockfight', *Daedalus* 101:1-37.

Hughes-Freeland, Felicia, 1998, 'Introduction', in F. Hughes-Freeland (ed.), *Ritual, Performance, Media,* London: Routledge.

Rao, Ursula and Klaus-Peter Köpping, 2000, 'Die "Performative Wende": Leben—Ritual—Theater, in Klaus-Peter Köpping and Ursula Rao (eds.), *Im Rausch des Rituals: Gestaltung und Transformation der Wirklichkeit in körperlicher Performanz,* Münster: LIT, pp. 1-31.

Lévi-Strauss, Claude, 1965, 'The Bear and the Barber', in William A. Lessa and Evon Z. Vogt (eds.), *Reader in Comparative Religion: An Anthropological Approach,* 2nd edn., New York: Harper and Row, pp. 289-97.

Schechner, Richard, 1985, *Between Theater and Anthropology*, Philadelphia: University of Pennsylvania Press.

Schieffelin, Edward L., 1998, 'Problematizing Performance', in F. Hughes-Freeland (ed.), *Ritual, Performance, Media,* London: Routledge, pp. 194-207.

Singer, Milton, 1972, *When a Great Tradition Modernizes: An Anthropological Approach to Indian Civilization*, London: Pall Mall Press.

Turner, Victor, 1982, *From Ritual to Theater: The Human Seriousness of Play*, New York: Performing Arts Journal Publications.

PART I

The Performer: Power and Presence in the Enactment of the Performer

1

Spectacle and Power in the Organization of Kingly Ritual: The Case of Jodhpur, Rajasthan

Marzia Balzani

This paper considers a ceremonial ritual which takes place on an annual basis in contemporary Jodhpur, Rajasthan, a former princely state and now part of the democratic nation state of India. This ritual, called the durbar, has a long history throughout India and was a standard court and imperial ceremony which focused on the maharaja or ruler as the pivot of the state and centre of all authority in his domain. Durbars are formal court ceremonies, 'combining the place for the ceremonial drama of the principality, the acts and formal relation of that ceremonial, and the ruler who was . . . the chief actor in that ceremonial' (Haynes E.S. 1990: 461). All durbars consist of symbolic gestures and symbolic placements of those involved. In relation to the Mughal durbar Fisher writes:

> The symbols used in the Mughal court, including ritual gestures of greeting, appropriate location in court with respect to the Emperor and other notables, substances and words presented or received, and formalities of departure, all held significance. In addition to the incorporation of symbols representing the sacred, these rituals also constituted a political message. Thus, all parties—Mughal and foreign, Asian and European—recognized that the symbolic meetings between the Mughal court and the representative of another power expressed and affected the relationships between the states represented. (Fisher 1990: 425)

All those present in the durbar were ranked in relation not only to the maharaja but also to each other. To be successful the durbar had to incorporate all the groups making up the state without causing conflict within the durbar itself and also without having to recognize publicly the existence of alternative structures of authority which may have coexisted with that of the ruler. Inevitably, in a short paper much of the detail of the ethnography in what follows has had to be omitted and only a few elements and categories of participants in the durbar have been discussed.

In Milton Singer's terms, the durbar would clearly constitute a 'cultural performance', that is to say, one of the 'concrete observable units of Indian culture, the analysis of which might lead to more abstract structures within a comprehensive cultural system' (Singer 1972: 64). For Singer, Indians 'thought of their culture as encapsulated in these discrete performances, which they could exhibit to visitors and to themselves. The performances became [for Singer] '. . . the elementary constituents of the culture and the ultimate units of observation. Each one had a definitely limited time span, or at least a beginning and an end, an organised program of activity, a set of performers, an audience, and a place and occasion of performance . . .' (Singer 1972: 71). While agreeing that the durbar has elements which can be understood in performative terms and while certainly agreeing with Singer that such cultural events can encapsulate values and represent in condensed form significant aspects of the culture under study, there are some limitations to a performance model for understanding social action. Before outlining what happens during a durbar I would like to mention some of the problems as well as the advantages involved in viewing social action as performance. A major difficulty in the notion of social action as performance is that it implies, to a Western audience raised on theatre and film traditions, that there is something inauthentic, staged or put on in any performance (Schieffelin 1998: 200). For those in other societies the performance model may be no more than an ethnocentric imposition which distorts more than it reveals (Schieffelin 1998: 200-1). For some, performing in a ritual or behaving in a ritualized manner may be the point at which they are most truly themselves (Hughes-Freeland 1998). Certainly, as far as the contemporary durbar in Jodhpur is concerned, the ceremony may be viewed as a performance by the Western tourists who stumble across it and watch from the upper east gallery overlooking the hall where it takes place, but for the members of the nobility who take part in it, what is going on has more to do with a proclamation of kinship, identity and personhood revealed in their position and place in the durbar than any straightforward or simplified Western notion of performance might suggest.

One of the standard approaches to the analysis of 'cultural performances' has been to try to read them as one would a text, to look for the often hidden meanings in the symbols and language manipulated in the rituals under scrutiny (e.g. Geertz 1973). While useful and fruitful in many respects, this approach has tended to overemphasize the cognitive aspects of ritual performances and to underplay their emotional, aesthetic and fundamentally embodied aspects (Schieffelin 1985). The point about attending a durbar is not that it is a part of the tradition of the nobility in Jodhpur, something which is known intellectually, but that it is a part of what one does and feels if one belongs to the appropriate social group. To adapt Marrett's famous dictum on primitive religion that 'religion is not so much thought out as danced out', one might say that rituals are not so much thought out as played out. As Bailey writes: 'The model of cultural performance contemplates conduct that is profoundly disintellectual. As modelled, the performance is not, even when it purports to be, an invitation to be rational, to doubt, to ask questions even-handedly. It is an enticement directly to feeling, to unquestioning belief; an implantation of values and in that respect a form of diseducation. It is designed to make people not think, not question, not calculate, only to feel and ultimately to act on the "truth" that is presented to them' (Bailey 1996: 5). This is achieved, precisely, by the form and pattern of the ritual: the chanting of the priests, the splendour of the surroundings, the colour of the outfits worn, the majesty and pomp of the proceedings. The durbar works, while it is in progress, not by drawing the participants into a 'willing suspension of disbelief' (Coleridge) as happens in the theatre. In the durbar the experience is real, which is not to say that it is in any straightforward way a representation or creation of reality as it exists outside the durbar in the wider society. If all is going well, the thinking about, discussing and rationalizing the durbar happens before and after the ceremony, not during it. There is, to continue with the drama analogy, often said to be a 'script' or text for performances which can be 'read' by analysts of performances. However, 'the character of performance as accomplishment, together with its interactive quality and element of risk, make it easy to differentiate it from the notion of "text" . . . performance can never be text, and its unique strategic properties are destroyed when it is considered as, or reduced to, text . . . it is precisely the performativity of performance for which there is no analogue in text. . . . Performances are a living social activity, by necessity assertive, strategic and not fully predictable. While they refer to the past and plunge towards the future, they exist only in the present' (Schieffelin 1998: 198). 'A ritual is not a text with a pre-established structure of meanings, but something which emerges as participants bring together bits and pieces of knowledge in the performance: it creates reality and selves experientially. Performance, then, whether in the context of ritual or theatre, despite all framing and formality, . . . remains fundamentally risky and interactive' (Hughes-Freeland 1998: 15).

In preparation for the durbar, for example, seating plans are prepared by the Jodhpur palace staff, invitations are sent and arrangements made. The actual performance of the durbar, however, cannot be reduced to this 'text'. Evidence for this comes partly from the disputes over the durbar which arose in 1989 when the pre-arranged plans for the durbar and the controversy this aroused meant that the plans/'script' and the actual performance of the durbar were two quite different matters and one in no way reflected or acted as a representation of the other. Beyond the distinction of text and performance, one needs also to bear in mind that 'individual participants may experience a ritual differently on different occasions, . . . or the acceptable constituent parts of a spectacle may change over time . . . or between groups . . . or between cases. . . . Such performative diversity, however, is not unfettered agency but creativity contingent on a structure or field of preconditions which constitutes a set of references: . . . the shared understanding of what is a traditional performance . . . . Without such preconditions to act against or play with, creativity would not emerge' (Hughes-Freeland 1998: 7-8).

The Durbar

Let me now turn to my ethnographic example. An ideal and somewhat idealized durbar would have had the maharaja raised above all others present, on a throne, and surrounded by representatives of all groups in the state, from the highest nobles to the lowest-ranking eligible members of the different government offices. These men would be seated or standing, according to their status, on plain sheets meant for the lowliest to costly carpets and cushions meant for the most noble. Each of those present would be placed at an appropriate distance from the maharaja, again depending on their status, with the highest-ranking closest to the body of the ruler and the lowliest the most distant from him. All would be dressed in formal clothes with turbans of auspicious bright colours and those whose position and rank entitled them would be carrying swords with decorated hilts. In the formal setting of a state room each man present, again starting with the highest-ranking, would move with precision and as much dignity as possible towards the maharaja to offer him homage in the form of coins (known as *nazar* and *nichrawal*),[1] symbolic of his loyalty and allegiance to the throne. By accepting the offering of coins the maharaja publicly acknowledged the place and legitimacy of the man making the offering and incorporated him into the hierarchical order of the state. Different ranks of people and individuals with special honours would be greeted differently by the maharaja, thus making fine distinctions of status visible to the audience/participants (Kathuria 1987: 307; *Rajputana and Ajmer List of Ruling Princes, Chiefs and Leading Personages* 1939: 102-3). Coming close to the body of the maharaja and viewing him also conferred blessings on the man so honoured, in the manner in which viewing the idol of a god in a temple also conferred blessing and enhanced the spiritual well-being of the viewer. The durbar was also the place where public announcements of formal honours given to some of those present were made. When each man had walked up to the maharaja, made his offering, had darshan (auspicious view) of the ruler and returned to his original place in the hall, the ceremony was over.

Those present during the durbar collectively served to enact a public performance of an idealized microcosm of the state with the ruler at its centre and each man, summoned from all corners of the state and from all walks of life, annually reaffirming allegiance to the ruler and receiving public recognition of his legitimacy from the ruler, having his darshan and returning, thus enhanced, to take up his role in the state for the coming year. During pre-Independence times attendance at a state durbar was obligatory and absences were noted and pursued by the palace bureaucracy with potentially negative repercussions for those who failed to attend without good cause (BSAR, 48 C/3/1 II; BSAR, C/1/1 V-B).

The durbar currently held on the birthday of the former Maharaja of Jodhpur (henceforth H.H. Jodhpur) is only one of a series of rituals beginning with various *pujas* (worship) performed by the pandits and *purohits* of the Jodhpur royal family. Most of those who attend the durbar never see any of these preparatory but necessary rituals taking place and some are unaware of their existence or their details. While the priests conduct the pre-durbar rituals H.H. Jodhpur and his son first have darshan of various goddesses, gods and saints at the Jodphur fort and then pay their respects to their ancestors at Jaswant Thara (the royal cremation ground near the fort). In this way the cosmological blessings of gods and approval of the ancestors are sought for the day's proceedings and the levels of the divine and the deceased are integrated into the practices of the present. H.H. Jodhpur, enhanced by having darshan[2] at the fort temples and blessed by his ancestors, becomes the mediator between the divine and human worlds and the various groups which make up the state and becomes the one whose darshan is sought during the durbar, for '[i]n his person, partly through his participation in ritual observances, the king symbolize[s] abundance and prosperity and [is] an auspicious sight (darshan), properly fitted out, for his subjects to view' (Price 1989: 563).

The desire for order and the need for each man to be in his rightful place in the hierarchy are reflected in the attention paid to the arrangements for the seating plans, regulations about the appropriate dress, and the number of people put in charge of particular groups in the durbar (UBP 1987-9). Everyone, from the gods and goddesses (*kul* and *isht devis)* of the Jodhpur royal family to the garden staff, has his or her part to play.[3]

Even during pre-Independence times, however, there were difficulties in accommodating some of those in the state into the durbars and the periodic disputes and misunderstandings which arose led to compromises which worked with more or less success to mask the problems faced in the public performance of the durbar ritual. The groups which could be incorporated only with difficulty into the durbar included British officers and personnel of the Jodhpur state. Such men could not publicly offer obeisance to the maharaja of Jodhpur because they were subjects first and foremost of the British monarch. The British male employees of the maharaja of Jodhpur were expected to attend the durbar but did not present *nazar* or *nichrawal* (BSAR 1948 C/3/1). In this way they were part of the ceremony and yet fell short of being fully incorporated into the symbolic hierarchy of the court. The allegiance of the English was to their own king or queen and so it could not also be to the maharaja of an Indian state. The British officers were also, in this respect, in a delicate position, being members of the Jodhpur state service and also owing primary allegiance to the British monarch. They could not take their places in the durbar of the maharaja as his subjects and yet could not simply ignore the ritual occasions of the court. The problem of where to place the British in the durbar and its proposed solution are the topics of a letter dated 20 June 1941 written by the Chief Minister of Jodhpur state to the Deputy Chief Minister. The letter reads:

> I have spoken to His Highness recently on the subject of ceremonials to be observed on the occasion of the birthday of the Bada Maharaj Kumar. As you are aware, some misunderstanding has been caused by the absence of all British officers from the celebration recently.
>
> I suggested to His Highness that the present position, in which British officers are omitted from attendance at the Palace on the occasion of His Highness's birthday, might give rise to a feeling that British officers are unwilling to attend. As I know that this is not the case, and also because I think that it is more proper that British officers in Jodhpur service should be included to some extent in the annual celebrations, I propose that on the occasions of the birthdays of His Highness and the Bada Maharaj Kumar Sahib all British officers should be required to be present at the Palace, etc., at a stated hour; they might then either be introduced to His Highness by name, by the senior officer present, and [then should] bow and shake hands [with His Highness] or His Highness might walk down the ranks, greeting each officer in turn. After this simple ceremony, the officers would be permitted to leave. . . .
>
> His Highness seems to agree with me that something like the above would be a good idea and I am quite sure that British officers would welcome the order. (BSAR 1939-41 C/1/1).

With the British officers a compromise ceremonial arrangement was reached which satisfied their honour and yet did not bring the irreconcilable differences of alternative authority structures and hierarchies into the open. In 1961 when the Queen of England paid a visit to India she asked to be present at a durbar. So a durbar was arranged at Jaipur, the state capital of Rajasthan, in which princes and *jagirdars* (possessors of estates granted by rulers) were present but no member of the Government of India attended. The Queen was formally received by the Indian Government in a separate ceremony. Here, again, the two authorities, that of the maharaja with his court and that of the elected Government of India could not be present in the same ceremony without one having publicly to submit to the other. Mutual avoidance was the only solution (Hurtig 1988: 156).

In the late 1980s and early 1990s this basic pre-Independence pattern continued in the Jodhpur court with those who were content to be part of the Indian-style durbar attending it and formally presenting their *nazar* in the, more or less, traditional way, and those who could not or would not attend the durbar taking part in the informal British-style refreshment party which was also held by H.H. Jodhpur. The former occasion is held on the birthday of H.H. Jodhpur based on the Indian calendar and the latter on his birthday based on the European calendar.

Another category of men known as Rao Rajas[4]—men born of, or descended from, maharajas and their concubines—found that their right to make their offerings to the maharaja after the sons (and their descendants) of maharajas had been challenged during the first half of the twentieth century. The position of the Rao Rajas was anomalous in the court and caste system of Rajasthan. As a result of the 'seed' these Rao Rajas inherited from their fathers they were considered to have royal blood in their veins (cf. Dube 1986). As with all the offspring of Rajputs, legitimate or otherwise, the Rao Rajas are considered to have the Rajput *ansa* (essence) in them (Srivastava 1994: 592).[5] In durbars they had *tazimi* honours (which the maharaja publicly displayed by enacting particular standardized gestures of greeting and bidding farewell in the durbar to show fine distinctions of status and rank) and were often given positions of administrative importance in the state. However, because of the status of their mothers they were not permitted to intermarry with other Rajputs or ever inherit the throne of Marwar. In fact, when recalling the status and position of Rao Rajas one of the maharajs[6] of a certain age I interviewed stated, 'in previous years, in my childhood, we never used to sit with the Rao Rajas to eat our meals—we did not take drink out of his [*sic*] glass or we didn't take water out of his glass. They were treated as a lower caste as their mothers were not Rajputs and the marriage was not legal marriage—it was just that maharaja took a fancy to a girl or woman and he just kept her.'

The Rao Rajas had in the past to defend against what they considered to be attacks on their honour and rights in the durbar. As is clear from the above, each group in a durbar is hierarchically ranked and each group presents its *nazar* in a set order, with the heir-apparent presenting first and the state employees (prior to 1947) last. Early in the century it appears that attempts were made effectively to demote the Rao Rajas from their position as those who gave *nazar* following the maharajs to a lower position where they gave *nazar* after the *sirayats* (collateral descendants of the maharajas of Jodhpur).

Technically, the Rao Rajas were closer to the ruler by virtue of their father (or FF or FFF) but were somewhat lower in status because of their mother's (or MM's or MMM's) status. Other nobles were further from the throne in a genealogical sense but had mothers of the same caste as their fathers and who were legally married to their fathers. The conflict which arose was in part due to an increasingly 'British' world view among the elites in India in which the very existence of concubines became harder and harder to accept and which led to the introduction of notions of propriety which had no room for the institutionalization in public of such practices as concubinage and their consequences.[7] Although some individual Rao Rajas held important posts in the state, the conflict was also, in part, to do with a shift in power away from the Rao Rajas as a group. The visible change of position and status, had it succeeded, would have been displayed for all present to see in the durbar. This helps to explain the strength of the protest of the Rao Rajas and their decision in 1916 to write to the Resident, Western Rajputana States, protesting the slight to their honour and seeking redress. Part of their letter is as follows:

> We beg to bring to your kind notice that the Regency Council Raj Marwar Jodhpur has interfered in our rights and honour which we enjoy from

ancient times. By this interference we have sustained heavy loss in our rights and nobility. We do not understand why the Regency Council has introduced such a rule against the rules in force from ancient times.
We all Rao Rajahs belong to the family of H.H. the Maharaja Sahib of Jodhpur and from ancient times it is the custom that we make *nazar* after all the Maharajahs and this procedure in force till now and our *Tazim* number comes to that of Maharajahs. No change was made in this system till the Darbar held when His Excellency Lord Minto and the ceremony of present H.H. enthronement. The Record of our *nazar* and rank and *Tazim* is still on file at the Residency.
At the time of the Durbar held on arrival of H.H. the Maharaja Sahib from England recently, the Regency Council raised the question that our *nazar* should be taken after that of other Thakurs. Upon this we requested you by wire to consider our case and we were allowed to make *nazar* as usual. But the Council has again now issued an order that in the durbar which is to be held on arrival of His Excellency Lord Hardinge we should make *nazar* after the Thakurs which is against the rules and we are therefore compelled to submit this application and request you to consider the case and decide the question before the arrival of His Excellency the Viceroy and the Regency Council may be ordered not to interfere in such a system in force from ancient times and to withdraw the orders already passed. . . . (IOL R2 Pt. 2, 184368 - 1916)

The Rao Rajas were here using the conservative language of past precedence, 'ancient rights' and their claim to 'nobility' to maintain the status quo in the face of attempts to change the durbar order of *nazar* presentation. They felt the situation was serious enough to ask the British to intervene in a matter of Jodhpur court ceremonial. Where the Rao Rajas were correct to state that the past practice had indeed favoured them, the contemporary situation was changing and the Rao Rajas could not be sure that their situation was secure. According to non-Rao Raja informants who remember state times, the solution to the 'problem' of when the Rao Rajas could present *nazar* was solved by removing the Rao Rajas from some durbars altogether.[8] The Rao Rajas were asked to attend durbars on the same day as all other maharajs and sardars (nobles) but to do so earlier than the others and in a separate room. Here they were given the opportunity to present their *nazar* to the maharaja before all others but with none present whose relative status might lead to a conflict over the status of the Rao Rajas. According to some maharajs the Rao Rajas were permitted to re-enter the main durbars about

60 years ago. However, the letters and files from the 1930s which list the seating arrangements sometimes explicitly include the Rao Rajas and generally place them behind the maharajs.

Creative compromises of the sort outlined above were not unusual as a means of dealing with conflicts over what might appear from an early twenty-first century position to be a great deal of fuss over ceremonial niceties in a context in which the very basis for monarchical rule was to be increasingly questioned and was finally brought to an end in the decades that followed. And yet, what was at stake for the participants was a sense of honour without which no man could hold his head up in a gathering and without which it became harder, for example, to arrange appropriate marriage alliances for one's children and take care of one's dependents. This was a system in which economic wealth was not a primary factor in the assessment of a man's worth and it was not unusual for *sirayats* to have considerably greater honour and lower incomes from their *jagirs* (estates) than Thakurs of lesser status.[9] 'Quite generally, "mere economic" power, and especially "naked" money power, is by no means a recognized basis of social honour. Nor is [economic] power the only basis of social honour. Indeed, social honour, or prestige, may even be the basis of political or economic power . . .' (Weber 1946: 180). This astute observation not only applied to the position of the nobility in pre-Independence times but may very well continue to play a part in contemporary politics in South Asia with those who can legitimately claim past membership with a positively valued status group, drawing on this for their own contemporary political advantages. Those who do not possess 'honour' and 'status' based on lineage may create it by replicating the (adapted) forms of the rituals of those with status and honour. Being present for all to see in the right place in the durbar is an essential part not only of performing one's status and role but of actually making manifest that one has the status and position which entitles one to be present at the durbar in an appropriate status-related place.

The noblemen more distantly related to the maharaja but born of parents who were of the same caste and legally married argued that their legitimacy entitled them to make their offerings to the maharaja before the Rao Rajas. Such disputes clearly show that the durbar was a significant social and political ritual which made manifest the rank and order of members of society and where one's honour, status and prestige could be enhanced or undermined by changes in the seating order and order of precedence. Such disputes also reveal the changing and contested nature of the ritual despite the somewhat idealized notion that the ritual was traditional and unchanging over long periods of time. Changes in the durbar reflected changes in the power of particular groups and their political manoeuvrings outside of the durbar ritual itself. In Victor Turner's terms inclusion in the durbar for the nobility of Jodhpur was to participate in a 'star-group' where 'only those who feel strongly about their membership in such a group are impelled to enter into relationships with others which become fully "meaningful", in the sense that the beliefs, values, norms, and symbols "carried" in the group's culture become so internalized in a member that they constitute a major part of what s/he might regard as his/her identity, what makes that member a specific person' (Turner 1987b: 46).

The difficulty in understanding the relationship of the durbar to the wider social world is not an issue just for the present when rulers no longer have legal powers and monarchy has been abolished in India. Even in state times the durbar served to construct a reality which never existed in the form in which it was presented. 'The great paradox of cultural performance is that the reality that is celebrated and asserted is an imagined reality, and its creators have a freedom of invention that is denied to positive reality. Victor Turner's Ndembu [for example] proclaim their essential commonality, their belonging together . . . but they do so only because there is a structured reality, which concerns power and conflict, and features backbiting and malice and is itself what drives the Ndembu to celebrate their imagined unity. . . . This imagined community . . . carries with it an uneasy awareness of its own falsity, an awareness that it is not only imagined but also imaginary' (Bailey 1998: 13).

Since 1947 India has been an independent nation state and the former rulers have been removed from political office (save for those who stood for democratic election and won political power on this basis). In 1971 the Deregulation of Princes Act formally deprived the rulers of their titles and privileges. Given this, the fact that H.H. Jodhpur chooses to continue to hold a durbar at the time of his birthday each year in his palace, which is now also a five-star hotel primarily for international tourists, is worthy of anthropological attention and discussion. H.H. Jodhpur is no longer a ruler of state by virtue of his birth and at the time of my fieldwork (1988-90) he had not been elected to political office. Given the dramatic changes in political context since 1947 the ritual durbar ceremony can no longer function to bring together and symbolically represent all aspects of the state of Jodhpur. Indeed, politicians and members of government departments pointedly do not attend the contemporary durbars, as to do so would imply that they are submitting themselves to an aristocratic social order which would undermine their position as democratically elected politicians or government officials in a democratic state.

The durbar as it occurs at present can officially be no more than a private ritual organized by H.H. Jodhpur and his staff. It is, however, a private function with media presence in that it is advertised in the local press so that the men who do not receive individual invitations may attend it if they so wish. In this way it becomes a ritual open to a limited and appropriately behaved and attired male public. Despite the dramatic change in context the form of the ritual recalls the political and ritual legitimacy of the past maharajas of Jodhpur and evokes, in those who attend it, memories of a traditional form of rule which, partly because it no longer exists, can be favourably compared to the current shortcomings of the state and national governments. In this sense the cultural performance of the durbar may be 'reflexive—in the sense that the performance is often a critique, direct or veiled, of the social life it grows out of, an evaluation (with lively possibilities of rejection) of the way society handles history' (Turner 1987a: 22).

While not being advertised or ever described as a political ritual, this durbar can serve in informal ways to achieve politically-oriented goals. This is done through a range of means and strategies, not all of which need be consciously manipulated by the palace but which, when taken together, create the persona of a maharaja based on traditional values and respect and which can, in other fora, be utilized to political effect. Those who attend witness and share in the display of what Bourdieu calls 'symbolic capital'. 'Symbolic capital, in the form of prestige and renown, is possibly "the most valuable form of accumulation" because it can be converted into political and economic benefit' (Bourdieu 1977: 179 quoted in Barnes 1996: 31). Particularly for those who were members of the aristocracy such annual events may revive in palpable, embodied and emotional form knowledge about their history and past glories and so promote solidarity among participants and help to maintain boundaries around their groups. However, because rituals make things happen and because they are essentially social and interactive there is always the risk that far from uniting groups they may act to reveal differences and exacerbate factionalism. 'Everything (in ritual . . .), from the observance of the correct procedures to the resonance of the symbolism, the heightening of emotion, the sense of transformation, all depend on whether the performers and other participants can "bring it off". It is always possible the performance may fail. Thus "performance" is always inherently *interactive*, and fundamentally *risky*. Amongst the various people involved (who often have different agendas) there is always something aesthetically and/or practically at stake, and something can always go wrong' (Schieffelin 1998: 198).

In this light the durbar of 1989 was a memorable one for the controversy it sparked among members of the aristocracy in Jodhpur. In performance terms what happened constituted one of Turner's social dramas (1982: 10-11, 1987b: 34-5). The social drama began with a 'breach' which occurred when H.H. Jodhpur tried to change the rationale for the durbar seating plans and those who felt that they were being penalized in the reorganization protested, causing a crisis. The 'critics of crisis' (Turner 1982: 10) then sought to restore peace and to resolve the situation before the breach within the Jodhpur nobility became public by the non-performance or non-attendance at the durbar of a significant section of the Jodhpur nobility. A compromise was reached and the durbar went ahead with some rather unusual variations in the order in which groups rose to make their *nazar* presentations. What is interesting from the performance perspective is that, despite the vehemence of the protests and the hectic negotiations which took place behind the scenes between the issuing of the printed invitations and the durbar itself, the actual durbar went ahead without a hitch. Those who did not already know of the dispute would never have been able to guess, from the ritual itself, what had been going on. The public performance of the durbar and the offerings of *nazar* proceeded as though the unusual seating order of the 1989 durbar was perfectly normal and ordinary. The genuine emotions and distress caused by the proposed changes in the seating plans did not, in the end, undermine the actual spectacle and show of the durbar itself.

The traditional Jodhpur durbar placed the maharaja at the centre with sons of maharajas (maharajs) seated to his left and descendants of the brothers of the first ruler of Jodhpur (nobles known as *sirayats*) to his right. This line of aristocrats looked out at the prominent citizens who sat, again in rank order, facing them. The order for rising to pay homage to the maharaja was—first heir-apparent, then sons of maharajas and their descendants (maharajs) followed by the descendants of the brothers of the first ruler of Jodhpur (*sirayats*). When all the nobles had taken their turn to make their offerings to the maharaja, the citizens, starting with the most distinguished, would rise to make their offerings (see diagram 1).

In December 1989 the Maharaj Kumar, the son of H.H. Jodhpur and heir-apparent, was told by his father, and contrary to the position as set out in the printed invitations (diagram 2), to sit in the first position among the prominent citizens and not with the nobility at all (diagram 3). This put him in the position of sitting opposite all the members of the aristocracy and was an extremely unorthodox seat for him to take. In effect H.H. Jodhpur was publicly demoting his only son to a position inferior to that of all former nobles and royal family members in the durbar. This was not, however, meant as a slight to his then teenage son but as a rebuke to the refractory maharajs who were refusing to accept the palace's decision to end the titles of maharajs after three generations and therefore remove them from the section of the durbar reserved for maharajs. What this meant was that in 1989 the grandsons of Jodhpur maharajs could continue to sit to the left of H.H. Jodhpur and keep the title maharaj but great-grandsons of Jodhpur maharajas would lose their titles and be required to sit with prominent and honourable, but not titled, citizens. They would also, therefore, be expected to present their *nazars* after the collateral descendants of the rulers and not before them as the maharajs do.

The maharajs objected strongly to such a change arguing that maharajs of the third generation would continue to sit in their usual place while their sons, their own blood, would be forced to accept lower status than their fathers' and sit opposite them in the durbar.

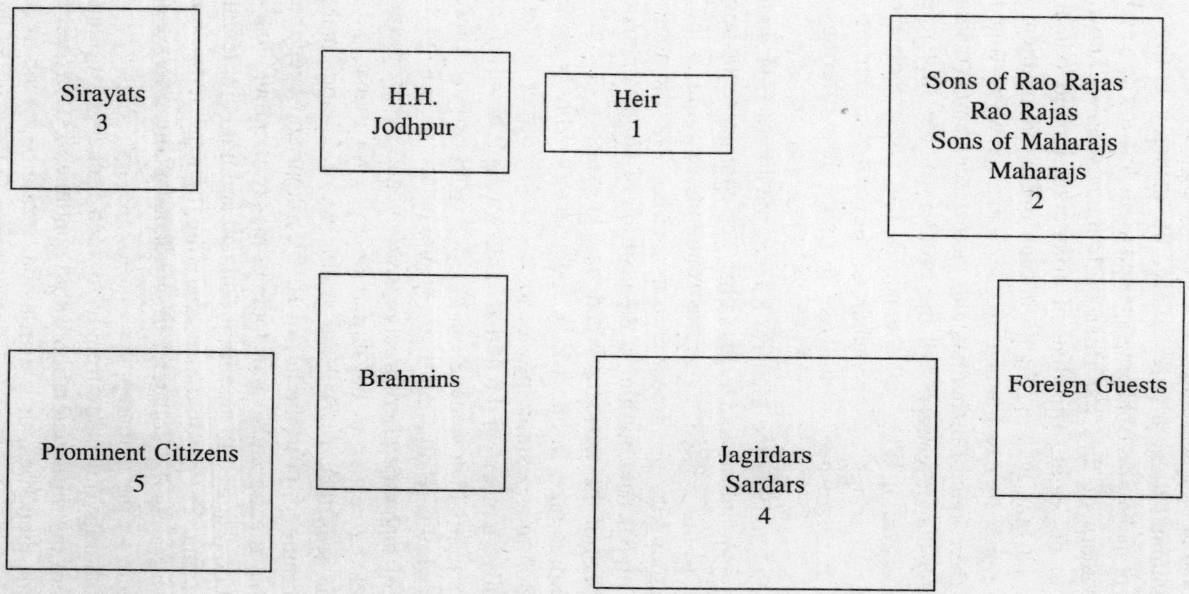

Diagram 1. 'Standard' Durbar. (Numbers in the diagrams refer to the order in which *nazar* was/should have been presented.)

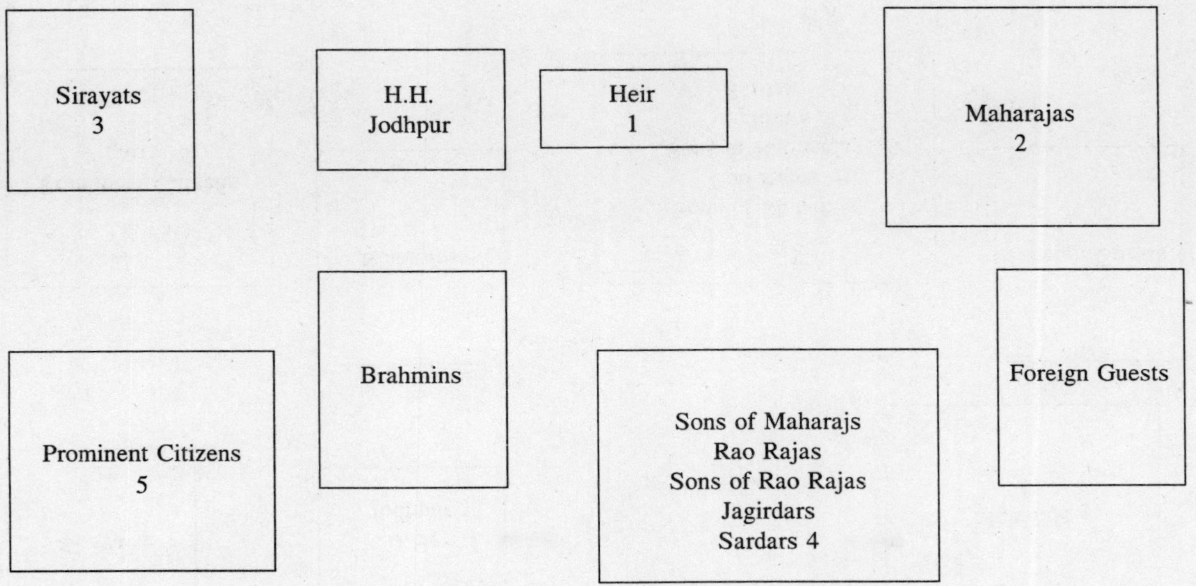

Diagram 2. Planned Durbar.

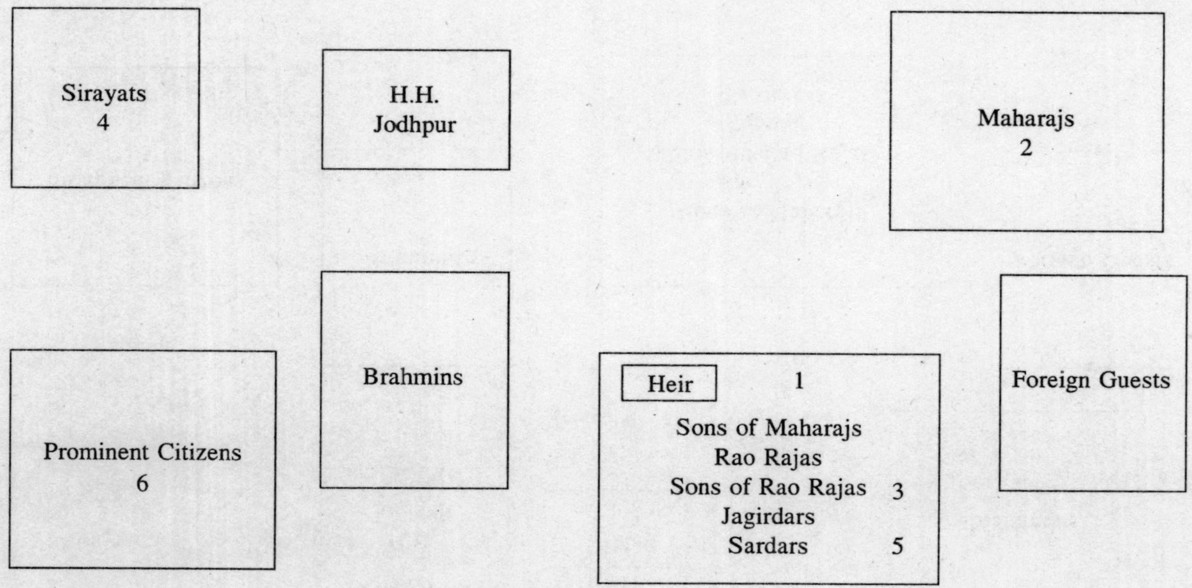

Diagram 3. Actual Durbar.

This would effectively divide families and produce an unbearable and excessive hierarchical distinction between fathers and sons in the durbar.[10]

Some of the maharajs were so upset by the proposed change that they threatened not to attend the durbar at all and so leave the section for maharajs empty. This, had it happened, would have been a very public rebuke to H.H. Jodhpur. H.H. Jodhpur was reported to have said that as the printed invitations had already been sent out there was no possibility of changing the seating arrangements for the coming durbar but that, as a concession, the sons of maharajs seated with prominent citizens would be permitted to present their *nazars* to H.H. Jodhpur before his collateral descendants. With this compromise the maharajs agreed to attend the durbar. The somewhat unorthodox result was that, according to the 1989 layout, the Maharaj Kumar (heir-apparent) sitting below both maharajs and collateral descendants (*sirayats*) offered his *nazar* first and was followed by the maharajs, then came the sons of maharajs, then Rao Rajas and only after this did the collateral descendants present their *nazars* to H.H. Jodhpur.

When I returned to Jodhpur in 1994 I obtained a printed durbar invitation for that year which shows that the situation has returned to its pre-1989 position and in this instance it appears that the maharajs have, for the time being, resolved the situation to their own advantage as the palace has decided to permit the title of maharaj to continue for five generations, so allowing all current maharajs to be seated to the left of H.H. Jodhpur in the durbars.

The question of whether or not the maharajs kept their titles and for how long affected not only their relative honour and status in the durbar but also relationships among kin. Some of the maharajs in the third generation who would not have been directly affected by the proposed changes nonetheless objected strongly because of their position within their own extended families. As Maharaj Sajjan Singh put it:

> It did not hurt me because I belong to the third generation but I had to accompany my brothers because if I die, which I will, they will take me to the cremation ground. So I've got to keep my relationship, not only by death but also by marriages, by any good auspicious occasion . . . I can't leave my kith and kin—does not matter if I was not affected . . . my sons,

even at that point my nephews, my grand-nephews they were affected, therefore, I was affected (18/1/90).

The attempt by the palace to re-institute the system of having titles lapse after three generations was perceived by those it affected as a threat not only to their current position but also to future marriage relations and to general networks of reciprocity among kin.[11] More immediately and specifically, one privilege which was threatened was the right to be cremated on Jaswant Thara. This is a cremation ground near the Jodhpur fort reserved for the cremation of rulers and maharajs but not of Rao Rajas. If the title of maharaj disappears so too would the right to use this royal cremation site.

Ultimately, the dispute about where a small group of men sat in a durbar which had no official political standing in the 1990s became a matter in which not only the honour but personhood and rights and duties of kin well beyond the confines of the durbar hall were at stake (cf. Davies 1998).

So much for the aristocracy who attend the durbar, but what of all the other non-noble men who attend? What does the annual ceremony to greet H.H. Jodhpur on the auspicious occasion of his birthday mean for them? For some it appears to be no more than a prestigious day out at the palace, a place which is effectively off-limits to the local Indian population.[12] For others the durbar has political and economic implications. Some of those attending had been given charitable donations for various purposes by H.H. Jodhpur and so attendance was felt to be a show of respect and gratitude. For others, there were connections with the royal family dating back to state times, and as some had not been able to attend the durbars while they were employed as government officials they now attended after their retirement. Yet others had business contacts with the palace and chose to attend on the basis of this. For the foreign guests of H.H. Jodhpur and the tourists who now watch the durbar the ritual is viewed as a spectacle which is seen to be 'authentic' and 'traditional' unlike some of the more clearly tourist-oriented cultural performances which are available for international visitors to Rajasthan. This inclusion, albeit limited, of tourists into the durbar suggests the incorporation of new elements of spectacle and theatricality within the ritual performance. This transformation may be interpreted as the move towards new or expanded ritual ends, or, since the present H.H. Jodhpur's role in the local and national tourist industries is a significant one, as the legitimation and consolidation of traditional ideas of power in new forms. This change in, or transformation of, tradition also raises the issue of the nature of interpretation and communication in performance, since there is clearly a distance between what the tourist audience understands of the ritual and its presence as part of ritual efficacy for the indigenous participants.

The durbar is also, despite official claims in the palace to the contrary, a form of political action. Before very briefly outlining a few examples of why this is so, it is worth considering Parkin's discussion of Abner Cohen's contribution to the study of performance and ritual as a form of political action: 'power and symbolism [are] distinct variables in distinct relation with each other as when religious belief (kinship, etc.) becomes the medium through which people control others or when people's attempts to influence others become expressed and legitimized through an appeal to religion or kinship. Cohen described the transformative qualities of these two dimensions with the example of the symbolic or cultural becoming political and vice versa. The reverse case is when political movements lose their strategic qualities but remain ceremonially important, perhaps later to assume new political or economic functions .... In 1969 Cohen proposed the concept of power as not only immanent and comprising economic and political directives, but also presentable to people in such a way that they would gladly submit themselves to social rules and authorities to the extent even of regarding them as desirable' (Parkin 1996: xv).

The durbar in Jodhpur is a form of political ritual, firstly, because the ritual begins by reaffirming the authority of the central actor in both religious and ancestral terms by virtue of which H.H. Jodhpur is symbolically claiming, on traditional grounds, a legitimacy which no contemporary Indian politician could ever hope to equal. Secondly, the very form of the durbar and its history, which is known to all Indians, enacts an alternative hierarchical system of power and authority which, for all the protestations that this is a private gathering of family and associates to celebrate a birthday, is clearly opposed to the forms of government in any democratic state. It shows that alternatives have existed to the current political system and that there are those who still have the knowledge and ancestry to be able to continue such practices. Thirdly, and this is a level at which it is hard to gauge in any empirical terms the extent to which the durbar is political, those men who attend are granted the opportunity to mingle with and meet each other during the refreshments that are served after the durbar (cf. Barnes 1996: 34-5). The opportunities for networking, making contacts, re-establishing personal links with men who are all assembled in one place at one time may be very significant indeed. H.H. Jodhpur is a rich and locally powerful man, he has many business interests and is the trustee of many local charities. This is the 'paradox of cultural performance: it is real in its effects but, because imagined, gives its creators and their audience a freedom of invention and interpretation which does not exist with regard to structured or positive reality. Politics and its representation are both aspects of reality but they play on our consciousness in quite distinct ways' (Parkin 1996: xxi). While not wishing to suggest that the durbar is in any way part of a strategy towards gaining political or other forms of power or that all those present are there for the same reason and experience the ritual in the same way, it is one of the many ways in which H.H. Jodhpur maintains a public profile in Jodhpur. He organizes and attends many local ritual, social and charitable functions. The durbar is one of these and one which proclaims one of the aspects of royalty adapted for the modern world. H.H. Jodhpur, a central figure of authority who ritually unites into one coherent body all those within his domain. Even on a purely ritual level this is no mean feat given the recent communal history of violence in India and one which may prove advantageous in the wider political realm (cf. Barnes 1996: 20).

H.H. Jodhpur continues to live and work and perform his ritual functions in Jodhpur, and it might be as well to mention in conclusion that in 1990 he became an independent member of parliament, Rajya Sabha, from Rajasthan, and in 1994 the Chairman of the Rajasthan Tourism Development Corporation. The Umaid Bhavan Palace where the durbar takes place continues to be Jodhpur's most prestigious hotel complex. As a result of his ancestry and by his actions, H.H. Jodhpur has chosen to embody a modern form of kingship and his 'performance' in rituals such as the durbar outlined above serves to reinforce his connections to both past and present, tradition and modernity; it communicates through multiple media complex messages in a context where apparently insignificant changes in past ritual practices can make the fragility of the continued performance of the rituals, based as they are on the support and compliance of those who take part, manifest in the social dramas that result.

NOTES

1. Mayer describes the offering of *nazar* and *nichrawal* during durbars in Rajasthan in the following manner:
   First men entered the durbar hall in reverse order of precedence, and left it in order of precedence, so that the structure of the court was made manifest; then homage was made to the Ruler-on-the-*gaddi* in the form of obeisance (*mujra*); then a coin was circled clockwise in front of H.H. in a movement known as *nichraval*, the aim being to keep the evil eye away, such coins being accepted and distributed to H.H.'s retainers; then a further coin (*nazar*) was offered, this being accepted as a token of homage (and placed in the state treasury) on major occasions such as the durbar following the *abhiseka*, but otherwise returned with the word 'excused' (*maf*). . . (1982: 145).
2. On the importance of darshan and the need to both see and be seen, see Babb 1981, where the gaze of the ordinary mortal upon the guru or god enhances the ordinary mortal and may raise the level of spiritual perception and knowledge above its mundane state. Power may be transmitted by seeing and being seen and as a corollary to be blind is to be without power and therefore debarred from positions of power. Blindness may also be equated with impotence and ought normally to disqualify a man from becoming a king. Presumably, the powerful seeing a king is capable of may equate with his enhanced potency. One maharaj informant told me that in his father's time there were many people who did not have their daily meal until they had had their darshan of the maharaja because the maharaja was 'the representative of god' and so the ruler had to keep a set time free each day when any 'public man could go and have his darshan and then leave.' Interview 18/1/90. Cf. Burghart, '[J]ust as the Hindus of Nepal visit the temple in order to behold (darshan) the gods and receive their blessings (*asis*), so also they visit the palace gate or royal parade ground on auspicious

occasions in order to behold (darshan) the king and to receive his royal blessings (*asis*)' (1978: 528).

3. Cf. Geertz 1980: 13.
4. The title of Rao Raja was bestowed on an entire group dating from the reign of Maharaja Takht Singh (r.1843-73). In some states in Rajasthan this category of men were known by titles such as 'Bhaba'. Maharaj Prem Singh in a letter dated 24/7/81 to Maharaj Prahlad Singh writes that Rao Rajas, descended not from the ruler but from his brothers were known as Bhabas in Jodhpur. Shri Parasmal Khinswara stated that the title Rao Raja was instituted on 22 September 1836 by Maharaja Takht Singh, and that prior to this the Rao Rajas had been known as Bhabas (interview 13/6/89). Given that Maharaja Takht Singh's rule did not begin until 1843 this date is unlikely to be correct.
5. Cf. The position outlined by Srivastava who describes the position of the children produced by Rajputs and concubines at a social level below that of the rulers of state. He writes of the Darogas who call themselves Rajputs but whose claim to this status is denied by others. Others are considered to be of low caste. 'The Ravanna Rajputs are included in the list of the Other Backward Classes' (Srivastava, 1994: 591). The following quote from Srivastava although not specifically about the Jodhpur Rao Rajas may shed some further light on their position in the Jodhpur court.
   'The terms *gola* (and feminine *goli*) are used for the children of the concubines from their Rajput masters. In the present context, both these terms are pejorative, and this perhaps derives from the practice, extant in some parts of the erstwhile western Rajasthan princely kingdoms, of sending *golas* and *golis*—as servants and concubines and maid-servants respectively—as part of the dowry of the full-legitimate daughter of a Rajput couple. The rigidity of the marriage choices observed at the level of the full-legitimate children lapsed into laxity at the level of the half-legitimate progeny; in other words, the marriage rules for the progeny of concubines were, quite expectedly, less clear' (ibid. 592-3).
6. The title maharaj is used in Jodhpur for the sons of maharajas who do not inherit the throne and for their sons for a number (3, 5 or 7) of generations.
7. See also Marglin 1985, for a similar situation in relation to the devadasis.
8. Individual Rao Rajas who held administrative posts would attend durbars in which, for example, British officials were present as part of the maharaja's retinue. In this instance it was their official post rather than their nobility which took precedence (although they were probably chosen for these posts on the basis not only of aptitude but also of

status). In one instance for 17 January 1914 relating to an exchange of visits between the Maharaja and the Resident the following note is found in the files: 'As a rule the Residency Vakil is seated amongst the State officers [i.e. on the side of the maharaja and the nobility] but on the present occasion as some dispute is going on between Sardars and Rao Rajas with regard to the question of precedence of seats he was seated with the staff of the Resident considering his status as the Rao Raja of Maharaja Regent Sahib' (BSAR 1918, 5 IV). The Rao Raja in this instance was Rao Raja Narpat Singh.

9. Cf. Price's analysis of the relative and shifting *mariyatai* (honour) as opposed to *antastu* (wealth related position) in south Indian *zamindari* courts where the former was fluid and where actors shared in ruling authority but the latter was an absolute status 'held by virtue of the influence which wealth brings' (Price 1996: 135ff).
10. Cf. Geertz 1980: 123, '("Where do you sit?" is the standard request for status identification) [and] was the axis around which the public life of society revolved.'
11. There appears to be a fair amount of discrepancy about how long titles are supposed to last—three generations seemed the most often stated, although one maharaj told me that this was the case until the reign of Maharaja Umaid Singh when it was extended to seven generations because the latter's wife had relatives in the fourth generation who stood to lose their titles unless the number of generations eligible to keep the titles was increased. At this point the length of time the titles lasted was made seven generations using the argument that death pollution affects relatives up to seven generations and that those interrelated for seven generations are forbidden to marry.
12. Local people are strongly discouraged from entering the palace save on clearly regulated and delimited grounds. The cover charge for the cafe in the palace was, in 1994, more than the monthly rent I was paying for a two-bedroom flat in a middle-class suburb of Jodhpur just a few years earlier. Palace staff make local Indians feel unwelcome and uncomfortable when visiting the palace.

REFERENCES

Babb, L.A., 'Glancing: Visual Interaction in Hinduism', in *Journal of Anthropological Research*, 1981, vol. 37, pp. 387-401.

Bailey, F., 'Cultural Performance, Authenticity, and Second Nature', in *The Politics of Cultural Performance*, D. Parkin, L. Caplan and H. Fisher (eds.). Oxford: Berghahn Books, 1996.

Barnes, S., 'Political Ritual and the Public Sphere in Contemporary West Africa', in *The Politics of Cultural Performance*, D. Parkin, L. Caplan and H. Fisher (eds.). Oxford: Berghahn Books, 1996.

Bourdieu, P. 1977. *Outline of a Theory of Practice*, Cambridge: Cambridge University Press.

Burghart, R., 'Hierarchical Models of the Hindu Social System', in *Man* 1978, vol. 13, pp. 519-36.

Davies, C.A., 'A oes heddwch?: Contesting Meanings and Identities in the Welsh National Eisteddfod', in *Ritual, Performance, Media*, Hughes-Freeland, F. (ed.), London: Routledge, 1998.

Dube, L., 'Seed and Earth: The Symbolism of Biological Reproduction and Sexual Relations of Production', in *Visibility and Power: Essays on Women in Society and Development*, L. Dube, E. Leacock and S. Ardener, (eds.), New Delhi: Oxford University Press, 1986.

Fisher, M.H., 1990, 'The Resident in Court Ritual, 1764-1858', *Modern Asian Studies*, 24/3: 419-58.

Geertz, C., *The Interpretation of Cultures*, New York: Basic Books, 1973.

———, *Negara: The Theatre State in Nineteenth-Century Bali*, Princeton: Princeton University Press, 1980.

Haynes, E.S., 1990, 'Rajput Ceremonial Interaction as a Mirror of a Dying Indian State System, 1820-1947', *Modern Asian Studies*, 24/3: 459-92.

Hughes-Freeland, F. (ed.), *Ritual, Performance, Media*, London: Routledge, 1998.

Hurtig, C., *Les Maharajahs et la Politique dans L'Inde Contemporaine*. Paris: Presses de la Fondation Nationale des Sciences Politiques, 1988.

Kathuria, R.P., *Life in the Courts of Rajasthan*, New Delhi: S. Chand, 1987.

Marglin, F.A., *Wives of the God-King: The Rituals of the Devadasis of Puri*, New Delhi: Oxford University Press, 1985.

Mayer, A.M., 'Perceptions of Princely Rule: Perspectives from a Biography', in T.N. Madan (ed.), *Way of Life: Householder, King, Renouncer*, New Delhi: Vikas Publishing House, 1982.

Parkin, D., 'The Power of the Bizarre', in *The Politics of Cultural Performance*, D. Parkin, L. Caplan and H. Fisher (eds.), Oxford: Berghahn Books, 1996.

Price, P., 'Kingly Models in Indian Political Behaviour', *Asian Survey*, 1989, vol. 29/6, pp. 559-72.

———, *Kingship and Political Practice in Colonial India*, Cambridge: Cambridge University Press, 1996.

Rajputana and Ajmer List of Ruling Princes, Chiefs and Leading Personages, Simla: Government of India Press, 1939.

Schieffelin, E., 'Performance and the Cultural Construction of Reality', in *American Ethnologist*, 1985, vol. 12/4, pp. 707-24.

———, 'Problematizing Performance', in *Ritual, Performance, Media*, Hughes-Freeland, F. (ed.), London: Routledge, 1998.

Singer, M., *When a Great Tradition Modernizes*, Chicago: Chicago University Press, 1972.

Srivastava, V.N., 'The Rathore Rajput Hero of Rajasthan: Some Reflections on John Smith's *The Epic of Pabuji*', *Modern Asian Studies*, 1994, vol. 28/3, pp. 589-614.

Turner, V., 'Social Dramas and Stories About Them', in *From Ritual to Theatre: The Human Seriousness of Play*, New York: PAJ Publications, 1982.

———, 'Images and Reflections: Ritual, Drama, Carnival, Film and Spectacle in Cultural Performance', in *The Anthropology of Performance*, New York: PAJ Publications, 1987a.

———, 'Social Dramas in Brazilian Umbanda: The Dialectics of Meaning', in *The Anthropology of Performance*, New York: PAJ Publications, 1987b.

Weber, M., 'Class, Status, Party', in *From Max Weber: Essays in Sociology*, H.H. Gerth and C.W. Mills (eds. and trans.), New York: Oxford University Press, 1946.

MANUSCRIPTS

(BSAR: Bikaner State Archives, IOL India Office Library, UBP Umaid Bhavan Palace)

BSAR 1918, *5 IV Ceremonials: Appointment of Resident, etc.*

BSAR 1948 C/3/1 File Cover: *Presentation of Nazars and Neochhrawar to H.H. Maharaja Sahib Bahadur by Sardars, Mutsaddis, etc., of Different Status.*

BSAR, 48 C/3/1 II File Cover: *Information asked for by the Minister-in-Waiting, Government of Jodhpur.*

BSAR, C/1/1 V-B *Ceremonials: Birthdays of His Highness from 1939 to 1941.*

IOL 1916 *R2 Crown Representative's Records—Indian States R2, Pt. 2, 184/368.*

UBP *His Highness's Household: Auspicious Birthday of H.H. the Maharaja Sahib Bahadur of Jodhpur, Dec. 1987-Jan. 1989.*

2

Devadāsīs and Village Goddesses of North Tamil Nadu[1]

Hanne M. de Bruin

This essay focuses on the rural devadāsī tradition in north Tamil Nadu.[1] It forms part of a larger exploration into the history and interconnectedness of popular rural theatre and dance forms in the region. These forms include all-night theatre performances in *Kaṭṭaikkūttu* style and in a style locally known as 'Drama' or '*Nāṭakam*', and dance and theatre performances by rural devadāsīs. Furthermore, the essay looks into the problematic relationships between the devadāsī tradition and the dominant perceptions of contemporary Indian culture and religiosity. I propose that the 'inner conflict' of Hindu tradition (Heesterman 1985: 10-25), and the way in which Hinduism and Indian society have reacted to the impact of modernity, could help to explain and better understand the stigmatization of the devadāsī in particular and of rural professional performers in general. The inner conflict of tradition involves two interactive domains characterized by processes of exchange and juxtaposition: on the one hand, normative Hinduism representing, ideally, an ultra-mundane transcendental order, which has suppressed or sublimated violence and strife, and, on the other hand, the mundane lived in world characterized by potentially violent sacrality, conflict, and interdependence. It is the latter 'social' world in which the village devadāsīs live(d) and with which they, and their descendants, had and have to cope.[2]

Introduction

Tirumati M. Dhanammal (Ta. Taṉammāḷ) is about sixty-five years old. She wears a yellow cord from which hangs a black and golden pendant around her neck, a red dot on her forehead, and a string of jasmine flowers in her well-oiled hair. In outward appearance she is just like any other married Hindu woman in rural Tamil Nadu whose husband is alive, in spite of the fact that the 'father of her children' died several years ago.

At an early age Dhanammal was dedicated to Puliyattāmma(n̲) or 'Tiger Lady', the Goddess of the village of Veḷḷambi,[3] in fulfilment of a vow made by her mother and father. In a ceremony presided over by a Brahmin priest and attended by all her relatives, she was formally married to a ritual sword (*katti*) placed against her left shoulder and decorated with a protective thread and a turban. A paternal aunt tied the *poṭṭu*, the marriage pendant worn by the goddess and the devadāsī, but not by 'ordinary' married Tamil women, who wear a differently shaped ornament called a *tāli*. The expenses of the ceremony were borne by the patron (colloquial Tamil *nēmiccāḷ*) selected by her family, with whom Dhanammal began living together 'as husband and wife'.

After the ceremony Dhanammal became the official village devadāsī of Veḷḷambi. In return for rendering services during the annual festivals in honour of Puliyāttamman̲, Dhanammal held a *mirācu* entitling her to a fixed share (*ari* or *vilakku*) of the harvest produce. Dhanammal gave up her performance rights in 1973, long after the Devadāsī Act had come into force. Asked about the reason why, she explained in an interview recorded on video that:

> My son got married. My daughter-in-law and her female relatives were all wearing a *tāli*. If there's a woman in the house like me, some think badly of it. They don't like it. They believe it affects their status. That's why I relinquished it totally. (de Bruin and Rajagopal 2000)[4]

Dhanammal must have been one of the last practising village devadāsīs in the northern parts of Tamil Nadu. She said not to know of any other girl having been dedicated to a village goddess after her own dedication, a statement that was confirmed by other rural informants. Her biography testifies to the fact that modern society failed to provide a category for devadāsī women who, through their alliances with their patrons, defied the caste system and the idealized picture of the Hindu domestic woman.[5] Academic discourse and popular politics have sensationalized the question of whether the devadāsī was, or was not, a prostitute, in addition to being a dramatic and ritual performer. While the 'sexual content' of the devadāsī tradition, and the way it reacted to the impact of modernity, needs further investigation, the equation of the devadāsī with a prostitute is clearly an oversimplification and an inadequate explanation of the stigma that came to be attached to her person and her profession.[6] Her stigmatization not only disqualified the devadāsī from full social acceptance, it also made her reluctant to let her female relatives enter into the same profession and adopt her life-style.[7] According to Dhanammal the devadāsī tradition has become extinct, because

> . . . in the present, degenerate time my children and their families-in-law think it is indecent: 'Our girl-children will be labelled the granddaughters of a devadāsī. It's offensive. We don't want to be associated with it.' That's the reason. My own children don't want to have any connection with this profession. (de Bruin and Rajagopal 2000)

Through the process of stigmatization modern society thus effectively accomplished the devadāsī's disinheritance of her own tradition, her economic and ritual disempowerment, and the disappearance of her person and performance from the rural stage.

The 'Unspeakability' of the Tradition

I do not know whether Dhanammal's life story is representative of that of other village devadāsīs who were her predecessors or near contemporaries. Yet all informants I was able to trace shared the same reluctance to talk about their own or their relatives' connection with the tradition. Attempts to explore the rural devadāsī practice at the level of persons who were actually involved in it confronts one with the realization that contemporary Tamil society has suppressed important aspects of the tradition. These aspects, concerning both devadāsī praxis and social conventions, were relegated to the 'unspeakable' domain of remembered, collective culture, and history. The active role played by the rural devadāsīs as female ritual specialists in the handling of sacred power, their economic self-sufficiency, their relative independence from a male 'head of the family', and their mixed or inter-caste descent, in particular, appear to have become the focus of controversy. Changing perceptions of the devadāsī custom that were stimulated by both reform and revival movements emerging from the wider colonial context and the regional political arena, resulted in the devaluation of the social and religious status of the devadāsīs and their descendants.[8] These social reform and revival movements coincided with the gradual erosion of local systems of hereditary rights and obligations which had until then provided the economic support basis for the ritual and dramatic tasks performed by the devadāsīs and other rural performers (de Bruin 1999: 144-5). As a consequence of these social, political and economic changes, the devadāsī lost not only her 'honour' derived from her ritual association with the deity, but also her bargaining power towards potential patrons who wished to be associated with her as a form of social prestige (Srinivasan 1985: 1869-70).

Furthermore, the 'unspeakability' of the devadāsī tradition has been facilitated by the fact that the generation, whose members possess(ed) first-hand knowledge of the custom, has become almost totally extinct. In fact, this essay describes the remnants of a phenomenon that must have been widespread and flourishing in the countryside of north Tamil Nadu about seventy or eighty years ago, but which today resists public recollection.[9]

Descendants with a devadāsī background admit that they have been trying to wipe out all traces of their connection with the tradition to the extent that their grandchildren have no knowledge about it. Their most forceful instrument to accomplish this has been to ensure that their marriage alliances followed the dominant marriage pattern of Tamil society. Marriage partners were chosen from among potential candidates of the caste to which the devadāsī descendants managed to get access after they abandoned 'inter-caste' relationships. These relationships were an integral aspect of the devadāsī *muṟai*. They were pragmatic in nature, not sealed by marriage; children born of them were of mixed-caste parentage, a fact that contributed to the persistence of 'open' sections in society (Srinivasan 1985:1870). These open, mixed sections were situated in between the local categories of 'pure' castes, providing an interface and a limited potential for contact and exchange between caste bastions, which would otherwise be self-contained and 'closed'.[10]

Informants

In addition to Dhanammal, I was able to interview Tirumati Sitammal (Ta. Cītammāḷ), a devadāsī from Tirumaṇi village.[11] Old age and the presence of her close relatives, in particular her son and daughter-in-law, during the interview restrained Sitammal from talking openly about the ritual, performance, and social aspects of her profession. My other principal informant was Tiru P.K. Bhupati (Ta. Pūpati) from Paṭūr village.[12] His mother, Kamalambal (Ta. Kamalampāḷ) or Kamalammā, was a devadāsī dedicated to Uñciyammāḷ, the village Goddess of Paṭūr. Like Sitammal, but unlike Dhanammal, Kamalammā was a full-fledged actress, in addition to being involved in the performance of songs and dance or *Sadirkkacheri* (Ta. *Catirkkaccēri*) on the occasion of religious festivals. Both women owned theatre companies operating on a commercial base and consisting of about six to seven actresses and the same number of male performers.[13] Tirumati Kamalamma died in 1972; Tirumati Sitammal died in 1998.

P.K. Bhupati, Kamalamma's son, is a retired *mṛdaṅga(m)* player. He performed in commercial *nāṭakam* or drama companies. These companies were the successors to the theatre companies run by the devadāsīs and their male relatives. Asked what happened to the exponents after the devadāsī tradition had disintegrated, Bhupati stated that

> . . . each of them went back to his or her original profession—weavers to weaving, those who had had a cycle repair shop to pumping up tyres. I didn't know any other job so I stayed on in the theatre. Those who had some money are now well off. But poor performers like me hung on trying to make a living. (de Bruin and Rajagopal 2000)

Informants said that the devadāsī custom occurred at all levels of society and that it pervaded all castes.[14] However, it seems to have been practised on a larger scale by persons at the middle and higher, economically viable, strata of the rural society, perhaps because the custom and its patronage required financial input in the form of training expenses and the upkeep of the devadāsī women. The upward mobility of persons, who traditionally were connected with the custom, may provide a possible explanation for the intensity of the stigma that came to be attached to the devadāsīs once the tradition had lost its social acceptance.

One of the most striking elements that surfaces in the biographies of Dhaṇammal and Kamalambal is the fact that devadāsīs like them were dedicated to village goddesses.[15] What does this finding mean for our perception of the devadāsī practice and our understanding of the significance of their ritual and dramatic performances within an agrarian village context? Much of the 'devadāsī debate', and the revival of the art of the devadāsīs as *Bharata Natyam*, have been informed by the praxis and lifestyle of devadāsīs attached to Agamic temples, while the occurrence of the devadāsī tradition in the rural areas of Tamil Nadu has been largely ignored. The following discussion attempts to redress this imbalance.

Village Goddesses

Village goddesses or *kirāmatēvatās* are one of the central foci of religious attention in villages in my fieldwork area. This area comprised the Vellore, Tiruvannamalai and Kanchipuram districts in north Tamil Nadu. In terms of cultural and ritual praxis this area links up with the southern districts of Andhra Pradesh rather than with the rest of Tamil Nadu.

Kirāmatēvatās go by names such as Poṉṉiyammaṉ, Puliyāttammaṉ, Uñciyammaṉ, Paintiyammaṉ, Ocurammaṉ, and Tulukkāṇattammaṉ ('Muslim-ammaṉ'). Informants perceived *kirāmatēvatās* as 'wild' forms of Pārvatī/Kālī. Furthermore, they emphasized the fact that village goddesses possessed a special connectivity with a particular location. Some equated the *kirāmatēvatās* with Piṭāriyammaṉ. Village goddesses were often said to be different to, for instance, Māriyammaṉ, Aṅkaḷammaṉ, and Draupadiyammaṉ. The latter goddesses were believed to be less bound to a specific location and to have a 'milder' character than the ferocious *kirāmatēvatās*. Though this local distinction between goddesses deserves further investigation, their cults of worship seem to share a number of characteristics (also Beck 1981: 86).

Rural Hindu goddess cults in south India appear to have preserved and to draw on Tantric, Buddhist, and Jain beliefs and practices (e.g. Gentes 1992: 309). These heterodox beliefs and practices co-existed for some time next to and in symbiosis with normative, smarta Brahminism and orthodox Vaishnavism before being 'marginalized' and 'demoted' to the fringes of the official Indian religious tradition.[16] Tantrism in particular reserves a central place for the Goddess as the active and pivotal force in the creation, destruction, and recreation of the cosmos (Mookerjee and Khanna 1977).

The Goddess is generally seen as the village's source and embodiment of potentially life-giving as well as destructive and therefore dangerously ambivalent power (*śakti*). Realization of this power so as to make it accessible, to contain it, and to utilize it for the general welfare of the village, is an important aspect of village religious cults. Realization of sacred power means that the Goddess has to be enticed out of her holistic self, given a name and a form (*nāmarūpa*) through songs and concrete representation, to be made 'present' in order for her devotees and the village to experience her directly and to tap the power she represents.

The accessibility of the Goddess is directly linked to her appearance, form, and the place where or the medium in which she is believed to reside. The Goddess may (re)present herself in different, temporary or more permanent forms involving different degrees of 'concreteness', embodiment, and presence: water, earth, a tree, a termite mound, a piece of stone, a *karakam* or pitcher, a *yantiram* (magic diagram inscribed on a copper plate), a stone head, a more or less refined statue, or the body of a human performer which serves as a vessel (*pāttiram*) containing her. In spite of the Goddess's local 'groundedness', to the extent that she is equated with the earth of the village (Bhūmidevī), she seems at the same time to be absent from the village proper, living at its liminal boundaries that she protects. She resides on the rim of or inside the spill-way of a water tank (Sarasvatī).[17] During festivals in her honour, she has to be 'collected' from the waters of an irrigation tank, river or well, watery resources which, like the earth, are essential to the agricultural prosperity of the village. The deity is contained within—or symbolically equated with—a pitcher (*karakam* or *kalacam*), and brought to the village where her presence, which is not without risks, is desired for the time of the festival only. At the end of the festival she is returned to the waters where she once again assumes an indeterminate, fluid form.

In contrast to more orthodox temples containing permanent representations of the deity, the shape and local rootedness of the Goddess are highly ambiguous if not paradoxical, combining form and formlessness, permanence and temporality, rigid, physical concreteness and flexible pervasiveness, fragmentation and fusion, geographical localization and omnipresence. In fact, it is within the ambiguity of seemingly paradoxical opposites that *śakti*, the Goddess's processional being, is located.

The presence of the Goddess offers access to sacred power, the vital source that generates life and death and that, consequently, is seen as essential within an agrarian context to stimulate fertility in its broadest sense as the basis for communal welfare and general well-being. The process of making the Goddess present involves all the castes of the village (*ūr*) as well as the former Harijans or outcastes living in a separate area outside the village proper. While ritual specialists, such as the devadāsīs, are needed to evoke, contain, and channel sacred power, devotees have direct access to the deity unmediated by brokers of ritual power.

Rural Devadāsīs and their Dramatic and Ritual Praxis

Rural devadāsīs appear to have been instrumental in activating, representing, and containing dangerous sacred power, which accompanies the increased presence of the Goddess. They did so through their handling of ritual and dramatic services and through their own 'presence' or 'being' in the form of their life-long state as women dedicated to and merged with the Goddess.[18] Our knowledge of the actual praxis of village devadāsīs is very limited. It is clear from the information provided by my informants that the praxis was flexible and allowed for local variations, which were accorded different social status by some of the interviewees.

As her most important tasks during the festivals in honour of Puliyattāmma<u>n</u> Dhanammal named (i) to walk in front of the deity when the latter was taken out in a festive procession through the streets of the village; (ii) to perform the practice of 'showing hands', which will be discussed below; and (iii) to sing songs. When asked, she said she had also performed *dīpārādhana* (Ta. *tīpārāta<u>n</u>ai*), the waving of lamps (*dīpa*) and of plates containing liquids coloured with turmeric (*ālam eṭuttal*) in front of the Goddess, but she did not mention this among her principal ritual tasks.[19]

Even though, as Veḷḷambi's village devadāsī, Dhanammal held

the local ritual and performance rights, she would hire devadāsīs from outside to sing and perform *Sadir*. She herself had never been trained in this form of dance, a privilege that, she said, was reserved only for the rich who could afford to pay the *naṭṭuvaṉar* (dance master). Dhanammal would accompany the hired devadāsīs, who would sing and dance. Because she had a good voice, she would participate in the singing of the prerequisite songs. These songs included items, such as a *eccarikkai* and *lāli*, which were performed when the Goddess had arrived in front of her temple and was lifted from her chariot at the conclusion of the procession. Saskia Kersenboom translates *eccari(k)kai* as 'caution' and *lāli* as 'lullaby'. She says the same items also occur in the repertoire of the *dāsīs* of Agamic temples.[20] P.K. Bhupati rendered the following versions of a *eccarikkai* and *lāli* as sung by his mother:

Eccarikkai
Kālī, Kaumarī,
Eminent Goddess whom I behold,
Nīlī, who lives at Kailāsa,
Protect the village of Nimali.[21]

And a *lāli* went as follows:

Beautiful one, Awesome one, Wielder
of the trident, wife of Śiva, holding a skull,
Luminous and subtle one,
Magic woman, be content![22]

In addition to *eccarikkais* and *lālis*, songs, such as *nāṭu, kirāmam,* and *maṅkalam*, were performed. The main objective of these songs appears to have been to praise the Goddess, to name, locate, and describe her in her different aspects, and to implore her to protect the village (*kirāmam*) and its wider context (*nāṭu*).[23] A *maṅkalam* invokes general auspiciousness and is usually sung at the end of any kind of performance.

Sadir and Naṭṭuvaṉars

While Dhanammal was not accomplished in *Sadir*, Kamalambal had been trained in the dance by a *naṭṭuvaṉar* of Venkachery village. I was able to interview Tiru C. Makarisvarar, a retired schoolteacher living in Venkachery whose father and grandfather, Chidambaram and Sundaram, were *naṭṭuvaṉars*. Makarisvarar did remember that his father used to teach dance to devadāsī girls. It stopped when he was about ten years old. He was not able to provide further information about the practice. Yet one interesting aspect surfaced during the interview, which seems to confirm the intimate connections between the rural devadāsī tradition and the village Goddess cults. Tiru Makarisvarar said that his predecessors were the hereditary priests of Ōcūrammaṉ, the village Goddess of Venkachery. The priests were locally known as *Ōcaṉ* or *Ōccaṉ vāttiyārs*. In addition to their ritual temple services, some members of the Ōcaṉ 'caste' were *naṭṭuvaṉars* who taught *Sadir* to rural devadāsīs.[24] Dhanammal, too, mentions the role of the *Ōcaṉ vāttiyār* of Veḷḷambi in the video interview. She said that he fulfilled important ritual tasks during the annual festivities for Puliyattāmmaṉ (de Bruin and Rajagopal 2000).

Bhupati provided the following information on *Sadir*, which he equated with the present-day *Bharata Natyam*:

When the Goddess had arrived in front of the temple there would be a Sadirkkacheri by women dancers. A man or a woman would play hand cymbals and recite rhythmical syllables. Another man would play the *mṛdaṅga(m)*. . . . In those days it used to be performed in many places. Even nowadays it is still found in some temples in the South. But no longer in our region. There's nobody left who knows how to perform it. *Tām ti ta tai, tadai tām ti ta tai* . . . these were the rhythmical syllables they would recite. And you had songs that went with them:

'What wrong is there
were you to embrace me
to please my desires?
Come Naṭarāja of Tillai, engrossed in puja
and satisfy my desires.'

This is how the songs would run, covering the whole gamut from straightforward desire to spiritual love. These were meaningful songs (de Bruin and Rajagopal 2000).[25]

The *naṭṭuvaṉar* would use *a taṭṭu pallakai* or wood block on which he would beat the rhythm. According to Bhupati, *naṭṭuvaṅkam* meant that 'the teacher would demonstrate the dance and the dancer would imitate him during the training. During the actual performance the woman would dance (in front) and the *naṭṭuvaṉar* would direct the performance (from behind)'. Asked why this practice had disappeared, he said that '. . . the hereditary performers abandoned the profession. Women chose to study and found paid jobs. They all dispersed' (de Bruin and Rajagopal 2000).

Showing Hands

Saskia Kersenboom mentions the 'show of hands' by devadāsīs attached to the Murukaṉ temple in Tiruttani. Her principal informant considered the custom outdated, saying, however, that it was performed by her predecessors (Kersenboom-Story 1987: 136). Bhupati, watching Dhanammal's interview on video, reacted by saying that his mother would not perform the practice of 'showing hands'.[26]

Kersenboom does not describe what the 'showing of hands' involved, or why it was performed. Dhanammal was unable to explain the meaning of the practice of 'showing hands' (to which she referred in colloquial Tamil as *kai kāmikkiṟatu*). However, she did demonstrate the practice during the videotaped interview (de Bruin and Rajagopal 2000). According to Dhanammal's demonstration, the devadāsī would walk in front of the deity. A light offering would be performed in the street in front of every house. At that time the devadāsī would show her hand. To do so she would face the processional icon of the Goddess. She would stand with an outstretched arm and flexed hand as if she would be showing the Goddess a mirror. Is the devadāsī trying to draw the Goddess's attention in order to make her realize who she is by confronting her with a symbolic mirror, or perhaps, with her own counter-image? Is it the devadāsī's intention to draw the Goddess out of her own, denser self so as to increase her self-awareness and her awareness of the world she has entered into?[27] Or is she perhaps trying to ward off ill effects from outside, which may disturb the thin balance between potentially auspicious or disastrous results accompanying the evocation of ambivalent, sacred power? Having acquired a more concrete, full, and articulated form at the point in the festival when she is taken in procession through the village, the Goddess is exposed to the public gaze. As a consequence, she becomes all the more vulnerable to the effects of the lived-in world. If not treated appropriately, disturbances of the Goddess's precarious state or 'mood' may reduce the efficacy of her presence and may even render her invited presence counterproductive.

Mirrors and mirroring, of which the practice of 'showing hands' could be a version, play a role in other south Indian rituals and performance genres, too. They have been given a number of different interpretations, which focus on issues of reflection, (self-) recognition and identification, as well as on ideas of drawing out and bringing together different aspects and layers of presence.[28] If not the devadāsī's flexed hand symbolizes a mirror, perhaps she herself provides the Goddess with the mirrored image of herself in an embodied, live form. Seen from the perspective of the deity, this would result in a greater degree of her presence and in her increased desire to act deliberately in this world. From the perspective of the devotees, the Goddess' increased presence ensures her greater accessibility. The willingness of the Goddess to act in or on the world is conditional upon the efficacy and success of the festival. In fact, to make the Goddess accessible and to persuade her to act positively appear to be important objectives of most other rural religious festivals. As we shall see below, the use of a mirror and the act of mirroring turn up once more during the grand festival of Puliyattāmma<u>n</u>. This time, however, it is the devadāsī who holds the mirror looking at her own image while walking 'in procession' through the streets.

After the devadāsī(s) had performed the ritual of 'showing her hand', the officiating priest would return the light-offering plate to the residents of the house. Thereafter, the devadāsī(s) would sing. Dhanammal rendered the following example of a song, which she would perform for the Goddess on such an occasion:

O Goddess, Protectress from suffering,
Celestial Beauty!
Eternal Nectar,
Only you are my refuge.
Now I have reached you, grant my wishes!
Destroyer of demons.
Majesty of the universe.
True heroine,
Wife of immaculate Śiva,
now that I have reached you, grant my wishes!

You who are ever young,
don't despise me!
It is your duty to give us rain
so that the land will prosper.
Mother, except for you, who else can we turn to?
O Goddess, Protectress from distress,
Celestial Beauty! (de Bruin and Rajagopal 2000)[29]

The performance of light-offerings in front of every house and the exchange of gifts—often special food items that are returned as *prasāda* (Ta. *piracātam*)—serve the purpose of re-establishing and rejuvenating the bond between the Goddess and the members of every household in the village. In a symbolic way, the exchange results in the Goddess or her 'grace', in the form of *prasāda*, being carried inside every house, where she becomes a member of the household (also Handelman 1995: 290-3).

Agriculture and Festivals

Festivals of village goddesses are closely connected to the agricultural cycle.[30] Puliyattāmmaṉ's principal occasions for festivals were the one-day festival of Kāṇum Pongal falling on the third day of the Tamil month Tai (mid-January to mid-February) and the grand festival (Brahmotsava) of ten or more days duration during the Tamil month of Āti (mid-July to mid-August). While Pongal celebrates the harvesting of the (rice) crops, the month of Āti sees the planting of the new seeds and the beginning of a new agricultural season. During the Goddess's grand festival, Dhanammal's services would include the acting out of a ritual event involving the dramatic character of Tīppāñcammaṉ (or Tīppāyntammaṉ), 'the Lady who transversed (or plunged into) fire', in addition to singing and dancing for which she would hire women performers. Dhanammal described the event as follows:

After her marriage on the (morning of the) ninth day, the Goddess would be taken in procession and I would accompany her. In the evening of that day I'd don the disguise of Tīppāñcammaṉ. The village devadāsī should take on that role.
They would give me a sari eight metres in length, a coconut, a hand mirror, and a *torā* or paper ornament resembling a fan. The coconut should be tied in the outer end of the sari around the performer's belly. I'd wear trousers

and over them the sari tied in Brahmin fashion around and in between the legs, and ankle bells. I would not wear real jewellery, but a headband and earrings made of palm-frond. A male performer disguised as Tāykkiḻavi or an aged 'Madame' would join me.[31] We would go through the whole village, passing from house to house. The deity would not be present. Everything would be over by four or five in the afternoon. Finally we would go to a special open place, where they would be kindling straw or hay into a fire. They would keep a male goat and a ritual gift of money ready for us. They'd break a coconut and burn camphor. I would sacrifice the goat or take it home after having cut its ear and letting it bleed a little whatever I thought best. Or I'd sacrifice a watermelon instead.
All of us, the 'Madame', I, the *mṛdanga(m)* player, the cymbal player, and the other women performers present, would circumambulate the fire while singing. We'd transverse the fire three times: two times in that direction and once in this direction. After that, we had to go straight home. This is what the Tīppāñcammaṉ disguise involved. That evening I would not walk in front of the deity. . . . On this occasion the Tāykkiḻavi would sing obscene songs with double meanings, like:
'The fruits of the cherry tree are ripe.
Shake it from above,
and I'll collect them below.'
She [i.e. the male performer acting the Tāykkiḻavi, HMB] would go through the streets teasing and intimidating the village people. Just for fun. . . . I would walk about holding the mirror and *torā* in my hands—nothing special . . . . The *torā* is a coloured cardboard ornament used to decorate the deity, which they'd give to us. While dancing, I'd look at my face in the mirror. The Tāykkiḻavi would make a great nuisance of herself beating up others with a broom and a winnowing basket she held in her hands. She would wear a black sari, a black blouse, and huge fake breasts. She would contribute hugely to the jest. She'd resemble the character of the Forest temptress, Kāṭṭupēraṇṭi or Kaṇṭapēraṇṭi, in the Kattaikkuttu play *Arjuna's Penance*. We ordinary women would accompany the Tāykkiḻavi (de Bruin and Rajagopal 2000).

Asked about the meaning of the event and how it related to the Goddess, Dhanammal commented:

Only previous generations might have known the answer to this question. . . . It's part of a big(ger) rite that took place on the ninth day of the festival. The holders of rights in the temple would carry earthenware pots filled with blood and pots filled with flowers tied around their waists. During the performance of Tīppāñcammaṉ nobody would dare to leave the house. Only people who had a particular responsibility would be outside—those who'd been initiated and wore a protective saffron wristband (*kāppu*). They included the persons carrying the blood pots and flower pots, the holder of the ritual sword and a person ringing the bell; about twenty people altogether.

The Goddess would be brought to a place referred to as the 'street's end' (*tettukkōṭi*). Priests, including the *Ōcaṉ vāttiyār*, would perform the necessary rituals. At midnight, the persons carrying the blood pots would leave for the village boundaries. . . . Before returning, they would smash the earthenware pots. These rituals were accompanied by a special custom: as long as the officiants had not come back safely, their wives would be waiting for them sitting on their knees, holding out the outer-ends of their saris as if asking for alms. The Goddess would demand all these rituals.

INTERPRETATION

The larger rite that Dhanammal describes appears to have had as its objective to mark the boundaries of the village, and to enclose and safeguard the village space, within which the Goddess was to assert her presence, against evil influences.[32] The performance by Tīppāñcammaṉ and Tāykkiḻavi is saturated with symbols of sexuality: the coconut—or foetus—carried on or in the belly by the female Tīppāñcammaṉ performer, the obscene songs performed by the Tāykkiḻavi, and finally the appearance of the Tāykkiḻavi wearing huge, fake breasts and indulging in a sexually provocative behaviour. The Tāykkiḻavi is an example of the 'black woman' or 'black Goddess', a character who appears in different south Indian rituals and performances. As far as I know this black, wild female character is always associated with explicit sexual behaviour, sexual abuse, anger, and (symbolic) sacrifice, and frequently she carries a winnowing basket used to beat people on the head with.[33]

The performance could be interpreted as the killing of a symbolic foetus—the coconut carried by Tīppāñcammaṉ[34]—or, following Brenda Beck, as the killing of an anonymous husband of the Goddess (Beck 1981: 83-96), or as a combination of both. Remember that this dramatic ritual takes place immediately after the marriage of the Goddess. Taking divine progress into account, she might well be pregnant from a partner unknown, absent, kept in the dark, or kept to be removed. The killing is marked by the breaking of a coconut and by a real or symbolic blood-sacrifice. In addition to marking the bloodshed, the symbolic abortion of the foetus and/or the killing of an unidentified husband would also serve the purpose of restoring the Goddess to her original, virgin, independent state again. Possibly it is the black character of the Tāykkiḻavi who carries out the foeticide. In actual practice, this task and its realization may well have been within the expertise of the Madame supervising the devadāsīs.

The polluting act of killing is followed by what is presumably a purification rite in the form of all the participants going through a fire. It is from this rite that Tīppāñcammaṉ, 'the Goddess who transversed or jumped into the fire', derives her name. In spite of the fact that she and her companions have transversed the purifying fire, Dhanammal termed herself 'unfit to walk in front of the Goddess that night'. From this we may conclude that the violence and pollution of the bloodshed, and possibly the widowhood of Tīppāñcammaṉ following the death of her husband, only gradually wear off.

During this performance the Goddess appears to split herself into different parts. The devadāsī and the female impersonator handle the violence of the killing and the impurity of death associated with the killing of the foetus and/or the killing of the husband. The devadāsī, in her role as Tīppāñcammaṉ, appears to coincide with or be a substitute for the newly-wed Goddess. The mirror, which she carries in her hand while looking at her own reflection, may be an instrument to stimulate her self awareness of her own, pregnant state. The Goddess in her more benevolent, unpolluted appearance is absent from the violent scene. Perhaps she has no knowledge of what happens to her, or of her own dark and violent side, which is the case with the Goddess Māriyammaṉ. Māriyammaṉ is beheaded by her own son, but she is said to have no memories of the violence meted out to her.[35] Procreative and destructive power and identity, purity and impurity, auspiciousness and inauspiciousness have here been feminised and divided over the different, but interconnected, bodies of the Goddess, the devadāsī, and the Madame performed by a male actor.

The Devadāsi and the Goddess

An initial analysis of the performance practices of the rural devadāsī tradition indicates that the devadāsīs were indeed living substitutes or fragments of the Goddess.[36] Dhanammal described herself as 'belonging to the Goddess' (*ammaṉukku uṭaiyavaḷ*), as 'an integral part of the Goddess' (*tevarukku uṭpaṭṭavaḷ*), 'serving the Goddess' (*ammaṉukku cēvai ceyya mātiri*), and 'being in bondage to the Goddess' (*ammaṉukku aṭimai*). These descriptions, the practice of showing hands in which the devadāsī and the Goddess mirror each other, the exchange of the *torā* ornaments between the Goddess and the devadāsī resulting in a kind of symbolic identification, and the performance of the Tīppāñcammaṉ rite, point to a constant, fluid process of fusion and fragmentation between the Goddess and the devadāsī. Validated by her dedication to the Goddess and her initiation into the devadāsī way of life, this process of fusion and fragmentation appears to determine the devadāsī's 'being' for the rest of her life. In a personal conversation Dhanammal matter-of-factly pointed out that the difference between dedicated women like herself and the performers of *Kaṭṭaikkūttu*, the locally popular, heroic theatre tradition which is the domain of male actors, lay in the fact that: 'We women were ourselves, while they played a role.' This remark seems to draw a fine line of difference between being a character or divine instrument for life through ritual dedication and initiation and performing a character for the time-bound duration of a ritual *Kaṭṭaikkūttu* performance.[37]

Written evidence of the shared being, rights, and tasks of the Goddess and the devadāsī are provided by the title deed naming both the Goddess Uñciyammāḷ and the devadāsī Kamalambal dedicated into her service as the recipients of a *kūttāṭi māṉyam* in Paṭūr village. Like the two Yoginis, who drink the blood of the Tantric Goddess, Chinnamasta, after she has severed her own head so as to prove her paradoxical power over life and death (Benard 1994: 1-21), the *kirāmatēvatā* and the devadāsīs share and exchange bodies, power, blood, and gender. Perhaps not accidentally, the story of the Goddess with the severed head has wide resonance and is recounted in different versions in India. Depending on the gendering of the context, these stories feature the Goddess as an active agent in the decapitation or, alternatively, as a victim of male aggression.

The idea of the devadāsī being a part of the Goddess co-exists with the idea of their potential complementarities. While fragmentation and equation may pre-empt or leave undetermined the formation of gender and identity, complementarity tends to play out gender and gender roles. Dhanammal was very clear about the fact that the sword placed against her left shoulder during the marriage ceremony symbolized a husband. Yet, her position as devadāsī of the village Goddess did not seem to exclude the possibility of her taking on a male identity in relation to the Goddess. Furthermore, within the context of the local kinship system and the ritual rights-cum-obligations governing extended Tamil families, Dhanammal fulfilled, and was seen by others as fulfilling, a male role. Dhanammal emphasized that her dedication to the Goddess had fundamentally changed her relationship with her younger half-brother, whom she brought up after the death of their mother. While they would normally have been each other's *cammantis*, they became *paṅkāḷis* as a result of Dhanammal having been dedicated to the Goddess. This reversal entitled her to the same ritual rights and property as her (half) brother, but also barred cross-cousin marriages between her own and her brother's children. Had they remained *cammantis*, this would have been a preferred marriage choice. However, Dhanammal said that contemporary society no longer respected her male prerogative:

> Because of my single state (*ta̱niya irukki̱n̠rata̱n̠ālē*), I became his, [that is, her brother's HMB] co-sharer (*paṅkāḷi*). Suppose that our father, mother or brother were to have died. Then both of us, after having been seated on the ridge of the village tank, would have been entitled to receive new clothes from our relatives (*cammantis*). But now they've abrogated that right, too, saying: 'Isn't she a mere woman? Where's the need for this?' When our mother died, both my brother and I received new clothes as part of the funeral rites. (de Bruin and Rajagopal 2000)

Dhanammal's ambiguous description within this particular context of her own condition as 'single' or 'alone' (*ta̱niya*) may be taken to refer to the fact that she has lost her patron (whom society considered to be her husband). However, it may also reflect her single status as devadāsī, who shares with the Goddess a marriage to an absentee-husband. A devadāsī's prerogative to male rights and rites in combination with her financial independence, seems to keep open the possibility of shifts in gender and gender roles, enabling her to fulfil when required the role of male consort and protector of the

Goddess and of her own family. From the point of view of the Goddess, outspoken martial behaviour and male guises fall well within her range of shifting shapes and identities.[38]

CONCLUSION

David Shulman and Don Handelman, on whose imaginative writings I am drawing here, have explored the creative genius embedded in the paradoxical conditions of the divine by assuming the perspective of God herself. While this approach seems equally (in)valid as that of taking the perspective of the devotee-scholar, it opens up new ways of perceiving and rethinking the issue of divine presence and sacred power. Shulman and Handelman conclude that the 'coming into the fullness of presence' or the 'being' of the deity results, in the case of the male Siva, in his loss of self (Handelman and Shulman 1997). Hence, Siva resists being drawn out of his holistic state by turning away, by renouncing the world. In the case of the Goddess Gangamma, however, the deity goes—increasingly willingly it seems—through a process of gradually becoming present, realizing herself in the course of the festival at Tirupati (Handelman 1995:283-337).

One wonders whether these contrasting reactions of the God and the Goddess reflect the two interactive paradigms of the male Brahminic renouncer and the earthy Tantric village Goddess. Following Tantric logic, the Goddess, of whom the devadāsī is a living embodiment, is the active power and source of fertility moving towards her human devotees, while the God is equated with the inactive element, aloof and difficult to reach for his *bhaktas* unless put under extreme pressure to make himself available. Translated into actual practice these paradigms appear to concern two different ways of conceptualizing and handling sacred power and representing it through performance. Agrarian village rituals display a preference for the deliberate evocation and representation of sacred power in temporary forms and at well-defined moments only. They are carried out by non-Brahmin specialists, who represent a number of different castes within the village and who may use their bodies to mediate power. They often involve blood sacrifices and are aimed at stimulating maximum fertility, prosperity, and the general welfare of the village through the physical representation of the Goddess in her manifold forms and moods. The lustful Goddess, the ultimate source of fertility, descends into the village to be propitiated, worshipped, and sexually enticed and abused through songs by all her (male) dependants, who often see themselves as close kin of the deity. Normative Hinduism or Brahminism, on the other hand, appears to favour a more permanent representation, which ensures a more constant access to the deity. However, this greater accessibility involves greater dangers in terms of containing sacred power. In terms of worship, the fixing of the deity in a physical, anthropomorphic form and its incarceration in a shrine require, therefore, a constant monitoring and brokering of this power through elaborate ritual attention paid by a single group of ritual specialists, the Brahmins. It also requires the sublimation or transformation of the dangerous aspects into a more containable form by attempting to delete its organic aspect involving dangerous sexuality, violence, and death. It is the latter view, which classical Indologists have considered the ultimate valid and authoritative one. The Brahminic view of sacred power has been strengthened by the impact of modernization. Modernization, as has been argued by different scholars, is often seen to tie in easily with processes of Brahminization.[39] As a result, the conceptualization of sacred power as an organic force represented by the sexually active Goddess and her devadāsīs has been marginalized in favour of a more male-oriented, ritualistic, and ascetic Brahministic view. Non-Brahmin village rituals and 'folk' performances directed at the invocation and representation of sacred power, as a live, embodied, and sexually loaded presence, acquired a negative connotation under the impact of modernization-cum-Brahminization. They came to be seen as anti-modern and irrational, the domain of the illiterate and uneducated and as the subjects of potential transformation into the direction of the more prestigious Brahmin paradigm.[40]

The stigma of the devadāsīs, which also attached itself to other professional exponents of the rural stage irrespective of their gender or performance style, appears to be the result of this process of marginalization, suppression, and transformation. I believe that the devadāsī debate is situated within this inner conflict of Hindu tradition, and that it should be reviewed within the terms of its two interconnected and interactive poles. This inner conflict cannot be resolved, but it does readjust and rejuvenate itself continuously through subtle shifts in the social and ritual appreciation of the status and praxis of its human agents and institutions. The devadāsī debate has not yet ended. The fact that the devadāsīs are well remembered but not much talked about by my older rural informants, including Brahmins, is indicative of their struggle with this inner conflict. Perhaps the debate has only now begun, for the disappearance of the devadāsīs and other professional performers from the rural stage has left an uncanny void. This void is the result of the impossibility to activate and propitiate the ambivalent and dangerous village Goddess effectively because of a lack of ritual specialists.[41]

NOTES

1. This is a reworked version of a paper presented at the 16th European Modern South Asian Studies Conference, held in Edinburgh from 5 to 9 September 2000. The paper is based on extensive fieldwork carried out as part of a research programme on the 'Performing Arts of Asia: Tradition and Innovation', sponsored by the International Institute for Asian Studies, Leiden, the Netherlands.
2. A description of this world can be found in the Tamil novel *Tācikaḷ Mōcavalai allatu Maṭiperra Mainar* published in 1936 and written by Muvalur A. Ramamirtattammal, a devadāsī who revolted against the Devadāsī custom. For a discussion of this unique novel see also Anandhi 1991, pp. 739-46.
3. Vellambi (Ta. Veḷḷampi) is a village near Kalavai in the Vellore district of north Tamil Nadu.
4. Prior to the interview recorded on video (see de Bruin and Rajagopal 2000), I interviewed Dhanammal in the house of her younger brother Chandiran in Kalavai in 1991 (see de Bruin 1999, pp. 100-1) and again extensively in 1999. Both interviews were recorded on tape.
5. The (civil) status of the devadāsīs caused problems to the British administrators whose bureaucratic system did not contain a category that could accommodate them: 'It was a standing puzzle to the census enumerators whether such women should be entered as married in the column referring to civil condition' (Thurston and Rangachari 1909, vol. 2, p. 127). Srinivasan and Kersenboom have discussed the different conceptualizations of the devadāsīs during the colonial time. These

centred on the perceived incompatibility of the devadāsī as 'wife of God'—a status which, in imitation of the Christian paradigm, was equated by the colonial administrators with celibacy—and the devadāsī's involvement, in actual practice, in economic and sexual activities, including childbearing (Srinivasan 1985, p. 1869; Kersenboom 1990, pp. 45-6).

6. The sexual content of the rural devadāsī tradition, and, by extension, of the village Goddess cults with which it was intertwined, included, among other things, verbal pornographic imagery of and obscene songs about the Goddess, sexually provocative behaviour, revilement of the Goddess, her temple, and the villagers (Elmore 1913 [1984], pp. 24-5, p. 141; Gentes 1992, p. 302 and *passim*; Handelman 1995, pp. 283-337; Tarabout 1993, p. 95). The *ecutal pāṭṭus* or songs of abuse, sung at the end of the festival of Māriyammaṉ when the Goddess was summoned to leave the village and not to return within the space of a year, tell about the Goddess's promiscuity and her sexual relationships with male members of all the castes constituting the village (personal communication P. Rajagopal).
7. Erving Goffman defines stigmatization as the 'disqualification from full social acceptance' (Goffman 1963 [1990], p. 9).
8. The anti-nautch campaign, which eventually culminated in the *Madras Devadāsīs Prevention of Dedication Act* of 1947, became inextricably linked up with the communal politics of the Dravidian movement. The revival movement, aimed at resurrecting the art in its 'pure form' as *Bharata Natyam*, was sustained by the Brahmin-dominated Theosophical movement and the Congress. For an elucidating discussion of the emergence of these two parallel, but equally vociferous, reform and revival movements and their effects on the social, religious, and domestic status of the devadāsīs, see Srinivasan 1985, pp. 1869-76. On the influence of local politics on the devadāsī debate, see furthermore Anandhi 1991, pp. 739-46 and Assayag 1992, pp. 153-67 and *passim*.
9. Yet repression appears difficult. Reports continue to appear in the popular press signalling the persistence of the devadāsī custom, or practices of prostitution equated with it, in Tamil Nadu (Ranganathan 1999), Andhra Pradesh (Akbar 1998), Karnataka (Singh 2000; Kirloskar 1997; Indian Express New Service 1999), Goa (D'Mello 1996) and Orissa (Kalidas 1999).
10. The perceived incompatibility of the status of the devadāsī as 'wife of God' and as a professional woman performer involved in economic and sexual activities, referred to in note 5 above, appeared to be less relevant to my contemporary rural informants. Instead, they struggled

with the problem of their community's mixed-caste descent, which had to be 'solved' or 'hidden' in order to be able to enjoy full social acceptance in present-day society.

11. The interview took place in Cheyyar in the house of Sitammal's son on 12 February 1991. Tirumani lies on the road from Cheyyar to Arani.
12. Paṭūr village, near Wallajabad, lies in the Kanchipuram District of Tamil Nadu. The names of other informants will be mentioned wherever I base my description or interpretation on their accounts. During the interviews with Dhanammal and Bhupati, the names of a number of potential informants surfaced. Quite a few of them declined to talk about their (devadāsī) background or were prepared to do so only on the promise that their, or their family's, involvement in the tradition would not become public knowledge.
13. These companies enjoyed local fame and patronage from the 1920s to 1950s. Their repertoires included all-night, Puranic plays, performed in a genre referred to as *devadāsī* (Ta. Tēvaraṭiyāḷ) *Nāṭakam*. Rural spectators and performers belonging to the older generation indicate that the *Nāṭakam* presented a novel performance style, which, in contrast to the *Sadirkkacheris* and other popular theatre performances, such as *Kaṭṭaikkūttu* or *Terukkūttu*, had a commercial base. To witness a *Nāṭakam* performance, tickets had to be obtained. At a time when social disapproval of the devadāsī tradition had become widespread and an issue of political debate, the devadāsī *Nāṭakam* offered rural devadāsīs new performance opportunities. Their involvement in *Nāṭakam* performances appears to have commanded a slightly higher social prestige than their fulfilment of obligatory ritual and dramatic tasks during the procession of the deity and their performances of *Sadirkkacheris*. Furthermore, *Nāṭakam* performances were economically more rewarding. The commercial base of the *Nāṭakam* ensured its detachment from the social, ritual, and economic interrelationships that contributed to the 'power of performance' of more 'traditional' performing genres (e.g. de Bruin 1999, pp. 100-1 and de Bruin 2000, pp. 1-7).
14. Interview with D.K. Aiyyar and Mani Aiyyar, Dūsi *agraharam*, on 28 October 1998. The informants said that the devadāsī custom was practised by a range of castes, including members of the Vaṇṇār (Washermen) community (the caste of the interviewer) as well as members of their own (Brahmin) caste.
15. The dedication of girls and women to Yellamma in Saundatti, Karnataka, has been elaborately discussed in the academic literature (e.g. Assayag 1992; Bradford 1983) and the popular press (e.g. Kirloskar 1997), but

a similar phenomenon has, with the exception of Ranganathan 1999, not been reported for Tamil Nadu.

16. Even today there is a small Jaina presence in Kanchipuram and its surrounding villages. Furthermore, Kanchipuram, as the seat of the Tantric Goddess Kāmākshi and the Sankaracharya *math*, serves as an appropriate example of the ambiguous, little explored relationships and complex tensions between the *kirāmatēvatā* tradition(s), Tantrism, and the Brahman-dominated smarta orthodoxy of Sankara.
17. Her presence is marked by a rough stone decorated with yellow turmeric and red *kuṅkum* powder. In addition to her 'out of bounds' abode, the Goddess may have a 'proper' temple situated within the village or near one of its boundaries. These different representations or abodes of the Goddess reflect the diffuse interactivity and transitions between the village religious worship and modes of more 'orthodox' Hindu worship.
18. The term *nityasumaṅgalī* conferred upon devadāsīs as the result of their marriage to an immortal male godhead requires redefinition in the light of the finding that village devadāsīs were dedicated (married?) to the Goddess whose relationship with an unidentified, absentee-husband is unclear. The initiation of this discussion is beyond the scope of the present essay.
19. Both rituals are supposed to have a cooling effect and to remove the effects of the evil eye (*kaṇ dṛṣṭi* or *ālam*). Tirumati S. Usharani, a contemporary *Nāṭakam* actress, confirmed the continuing importance of performing *dīparādhana* and the removal of *ālam*. She said that, when playing on the occasion of a religious village festival, she and her women colleagues were sometimes asked to appear fully dressed and made-up before the processional icon of the Goddess at the conclusion of the performance. At such a time they were requested to perform *dīparādhana* and/or the removal of *ālam*, as substitutes for the village devadāsīs whose services are no longer available (interview with S. Usharani and P.K. Prakasam, 27 September 1998; see also Kersenboom-Story 1987, p. 55).
20. Kersenboom mentions that these were folk songs employed to convey the message of bhakti. They were adapted into the devadāsī repertoire by composers of temple music (Kersenboom-Story 1987 [1998], pp. 61-2, p. 139 and pp. 159-160, where she provides examples of a *lali* and *eccarik(k)kai*).
21. An alternative translation of the last line reads 'Beware of the Immaculate Goddess (Nimali)'.
22. '*Lāli*. . .', which I have freely translated here as 'Be content!', forms the last, drawn-out word of the song from which it derives its name.

23. In this respect they can be compared to the practice of *varṇittal* or 'praising (colouring) the Goddess through songs', which is practised by the hereditary representatives of other castes (de Bruin 1999, pp. 68-9, 71-5, 83 and 96-7).
24. The practice is confirmed by Thurston and Rangachari. They provide the following description under the entry Occhan (*Ōcaṉ*): 'The Occhans are a class of temple priests, who usually officiate as pujaris at Pidari and other Amman (Grama Devata) temples. They are for the most part Saivites, but some belong to the Vadagalai or Tengalai Vaishnava sects. Some of the pujaris wear the sacred thread when within the temple. Their insignia are the *udukkai*, or hourglass shaped drum, and the *silambu*, or hollow brass ring filled with bits of brass, which rattle when shaken. In the Chingleput district (in which Venkachery is situated, HMB), some Occhans act as dancing-masters to devadāsīs, and are sometimes called Nattuvan' (Thurston and Rangachari 1909 (1987), vol. 5, pp. 419-20).
25. This statement nicely summarizes the gist of a heated popular and academic discussion regarding the interpretation of *śṛṅgāra rasa* in the devadāsī tradition (e.g. Kersenboom 1995, pp. 112-15, n. 63).
26. There was a hint of condescension in Bhupati's remark regarding the participation of devadāsīs in the procession of the deity and their carrying out of ritual tasks, like 'showing hands', in front of every house. A similar feeling appears to be involved in the rejection by hereditary Vaṇṇār performers of their participation in the mobile *Terukkūttus*, which forms part of the procession of the Goddess Mariyamman (de Bruin 1999, pp. 70-1).
27. With regard to the presence of the Goddess Gangamma during her annual festival or *Jātra* in Tirupati, Don Handelman remarks that 'she must be persuaded continuously to emerge from within herself, seduced into her self so that she remains among people during the *Jatra*.' (Handelman 1995, p. 292).
28. E.g. Freeman 1993, p. 125; Handelman 1995, p. 292, fn. 8; Nambiar 1993, pp. 145-57; Shulman 2006, pp. 17-20.
29. The last stanza of this song pointedly illustrates the limitations and worries of the human devadāsī. Unlike her divine counterpart who, in line with Tantric conventions, is described as ever young, the singer expresses her fear of becoming old and losing her beauty (and perhaps her patronage).
30. A cursory mapping of villages in my fieldwork area where village devadāsīs are known to have lived and worked indicates that almost all these villages are situated along waterways that provide the irrigation

water for local agricultural activities. Released from its main reservoirs, such as the Arcot *aṇaikkaṭṭu*, the irrigation water follows these waterways, passing through intermediate reservoirs *en route* to the sea. Beginning at the highest point where water is released from the Arcot/Putuppati *aṇaikkaṭṭu*, devadāsīs were found to have lived in low lying villages of Cakramallur, Perunkattur, Iluppai, Vembakkam, Mamandur, Dusi, Mannur, Kilnaykam Palaiyam, Punaitankal, Kundaiyartandalam, Ilaiyanar Velur, and Patur. After Patur the water flows into the combined Palar, Cheyyar and Vekavati rivers at their confluence at Tirumukkutal near Chingleput. Other villages with a devadāsī presence were situated at waterways that split off at different points from the Arcot (Palar river) and Arani (Cheyyar river) *aṇaikkaṭṭus*. Informants said that members of the Vēḷāḷar, Kaikkōlar, and Vaṉṉiyar castes, in particular, were involved in the devadāsī tradition, as (female) performers and as (male) patrons, resulting in 'intermediate' communities of mixed-caste descent sometimes referred to as Kūttāṭijāti or 'caste' of Kūttāṭis (de Bruin 1999, pp. 99-100). While members of both the Vēḷāḷar and Kaikkōlar castes in my fieldwork area attach the honorific title 'Mūtaliyar' to their names, Vaṉṉiyars (or Paḷḷis) carry the title 'Nāyakar' or 'Gounder'. Vēḷāḷars and Vaṉṉiyars are landowners involved in agriculture, while the Kaikkōlars or Ceṅkuntar Mūtaliyars are hereditary weavers. Spatial arrangements appear to have facilitated close contacts between members of these communities and the devadāsī community. For instance, the street where the devadāsīs used to live in Mannur village is situated immediately adjacent to the Vēḷāḷar Mūtaliyar street of Kilnaykam Palaiyam, the neighbouring village.

31. According to the Tamil lexicon *tāykkiḻavi* means the 'mother or the foster-mother of a dancing girl' (*Tamil Lexicon*, 1924-36 [rept. 1982], p. 1839). The character of the Tāykkiḻavi as the head of a brothel or the chaperone of a devadāsī appears regularly in modern Tamil novels and in the popular Tamil film.
32. According to Dhanammal the custom was more or less similar to the village custom called *pali oṭṭuṟatu*. During this ritual the officiants run to the boundaries of the village, screaming loudly. There they throw rice stained with the blood of the sacrificial animal into the air, presumably to feed the ghosts and keep them away from the village. See also Handelman's description of 'fixing the circle' in the context of the festival for Gangamma in Tirupati (Handelman 1995, p. 291). In my fieldwork area village informants told me that they should not leave their village during the time of its festival, as it would bring them misfortune.
33. Other examples of 'wild, black women' characters are the female

sweeper, who is one of the guises of the Goddess Gangamma at Tirupati (Handelman 1995, p. 297) and the black character who appears during the *Paṭukaḷam* (battlefield) or the off-stage performance by *Kaṭṭaikkūttu* actors of the final battle between Duryodhana and Bhīma. This angry, black, female character is seated on a ladder, carried by several men. She holds a winnowing basket in her hands with which she beats the noisy young male on-lookers surrounding her on the head. She is usually identified as Gāndhārī who mourns the death of her sons, Duryodhana in particular. Handelman interprets the symbolism of the clapping on the head with the winnowing basket by Gangamma as a (disguised) blessing to her devotees by the Goddess (Handelman 1995, pp. 297-8). In the case of Gāndhārī (and also in the case of the Tāykkiḻavi), the interaction between the angry, black, female character and the mob of young males appears to carry sexual connotations.

The *Kaṭṭaikkūttu* performance *Arjuna's tapas* features a black forest temptress, Kaṭṭupēraṇṭi or Kaṇṭupēraṇṭi, in addition to a black Pārvatī in the guise of a low-caste hunter (Hiltebeitel 1988, pp. 283-6). Both characters display their sexuality openly. Similarly, the wronged Śurpanakha in *Kūṭiyāṭṭam* performances is shown as a wild, black, angry character, who, according to the actor impersonating her, is worshipped by local women (personal communication Shri G. Venu, South Indian Theatre Festival, Kanchipuram, 6 March 2000).

34. The marriage ceremonies of members of some castes at the lower and middle levels in my fieldwork area include a ritual during which a coconut is tied in the outer-end of the sari of the bride, after which the couple retires temporarily. After their return to the marriage *pantal* it is said that a child has been born to the couple, of course to the amusement of the audience witnessing the marriage ceremonies.
35. On the story of Māriyammaṉ/Reṇuka, see also Masilamani-Meyer 1996, pp. 165-83; on the Tantric connections of the story of Reṇuka and the phenomenon of beheading, see Benard 1994, pp. 6-12 and 92-100.
36. Also Elmore 1913 (1984), p. 25 with reference to the Matangi, who is said to be Mathamma or the Goddess Ellamma incarnate.
37. Though both the devadāsī and *Kaṭṭaikkūttu* performers are instrumental in embodying and mediating sacred power, local perceptions about being and becoming the divine, and, consequently, about possession-like states, show a wide range of interpretations. The assessments of mediation and possession may differ depending on whether the informant sees it from a performer's or spectator's perspective (e.g. de Bruin 2006, pp. 124-30; Schömbucher 1993, pp. 239-67).

38. Other examples of the Goddess in a male role can be found in Handelman 1995 where the two Gangammas of Tirupati disguise themselves as a foreign prince and his minister in order to kill the Palegadu (Handelman 1995, pp. 300-2 and *passim*); on the paradigm of *mahiṣāsuramardinī* the 'male-like' warrior-Goddess killing the demon Mahisha in the performing arts of south India, see de Bruin 1999, pp. 90-1; on the status of the Tantric Goddess as a binary godhead, incorporating both the masculine and feminine, see for instance Brooks 1990, p. 88.
39. Heesterman 1985, p.16; Singer 1972; Singer 1971, pp. 160-95.
40. Singer, in a follow-up study of his earlier work on tradition and modernity in the city of Madras (Singer 1972), describes how modernization has engendered a reinterpretation of traditional norms and beliefs in an attempt to preserve or enhance the ritual status of the actors involved as they modernize (Singer 1971, p. 165 and *passim*). A similar process appears to be at work in the 'rejection' of village rituals and modes of worship, including the devadāsī custom, all of which are perceived as being no longer compatible with modern society. Consequently, these practices are being denied social recognition and appreciation, though not necessarily sacral efficacy.
41. One potential way of coping with this void, indeed, is the Brahminization of the Goddess. This process has been set in motion at a number of village temples, including the temple of Puliyattāmaṉ at Veḷḷambi. These temples and their rituals are being revamped into a more Brahminic mode: the deity is housed in a permanent structure, which is consecrated following Brahminic ritual. The Sankaracharya *math* of Kanchipuram financially contributes to the renovation of village temples and advises on the right way of carrying out the temple rituals (personal communication from Mr. Mohanam [Kanchipuram], who told us that the Ankalamman temple in his ancestral village Pannappakkam had been recently renovated with the financial help and advice of the Sankaracharya *math*).

REFERENCES

Akbar, Syed, 'Devadāsīs: Slave to Tradition', in *Indian Express*, 7 December 1998.

Anandhi, S., 'Representing Devadāsīs: "Dasigal Mosavalai" as a Radical Text', *Economic and Political Weekly* 26, 11-12, March 1991, pp. 739-46.

Assayag, Jackie, *La Colère de la Déesse Décapitée: Traditions, Cultes et Pouvoir dans le Sud de l'Inde,* Paris: CNRS edn., 1992.

Beck, Brenda E.F., 'The Goddess and the Demon: A Local South Indian Festival and its Wider Context', in *Purushartha 5: Autour de la Déesse Hindoue*, Madeleine Biardeau (ed.), 1981, pp. 83-136.

Benard, Elisabeth Anne, *Chinnamasta: The Awful Buddhist and Hindu Tantric Goddess,* Delhi: Motilal Banarsidass, 1994.

Bradford, Nicholas J., 'Transgenderism and the Cult of Yellamma: Heat, Sex and Sickness in South Indian Ritual', in *Journal of Anthropological Research,* 39, 3, 1983, pp. 307-22.

Bruin, Hanne M. de, *Kattaikkuttu: The Flexibility of a South Indian Theatre Tradition* (vol. 7 Gonda Indological Studies), Groningen: Egbert Forsten, 1999.

———, 'The Hybrid-popular Theatre Movement and the Tamil Natakam Theatre', in *Kolam*, vols. 5 & 6, Singapore: South Asian Studies Programme, National University of Singapore, and the Institute of Indology and Tamil Studies, University of Cologne, July 2000. http://www.fas.nus.edu.sg/journal/kolam/vols/kolam5&6/4BfolkCultur/natakam/natakam/htm

———, 'Donning the *Vesam* in *Kattaikkuttu.*', in *Masked Ritual and Performance in South India: Dance, Healing, and Possession*, David Shulman and Deborah Thiagarajan (eds.), Ann Arbor: Center for South and Southeast Asian Studies, The University of Michigan, 2006, pp. 107-34.

Bruin, Hanne M. de and P. Rajagopal, 'In Their Own Words: The Unheard History of the Rural Tamil Stage as Told by Four of Its professional Exponents' (video interviews with P.K. Bhupati, M. Dhanammal, M. Shanmugavalli and P. Rajagopal), Leiden: International Institute for Asian Studies, 2000.

D'Mello, Pamela, 'Goa Kalavants: Coming out of the Devadāsī Mould', 15 July 1996. http://hindunet.org/srhhome/1996 7/msg00093.html

Elmore, W.T., *Dravidian Gods in Modern Hinduism,* New Delhi: Asian Educational Services, 1913 (1984).

Freeman, Richardson J., 'Performing Possession: Ritual and Consciousness in the Teyyam Complex of Northern Kerala', in Brückner et al. (eds.), 1993, pp. 109-38.

Gentes, M.J., 'Scandalizing the Goddess at Kodungallur', *Asian Folklore Studies,* 51, 1992, pp. 295-322.

Goffman, Erving, *Stigma: Notes on the Management of Spoiled Identity,* Penguin Books, 1963 (1990).

Handelman, Don, 'The Guises of the Goddess and the Transformation of the Male: Gangamma's Visit to Tirupati and the Continuum of

Gender', in *Syllables of Sky: Studies in South Indian Civilization in Honour of Velacheru Narayana Rao,* David Shulman (ed.), New Delhi: Oxford University Press, 1995, pp. 283-337.

Handelman, Don and David Shulman, *God Inside Out: Siva's Game of Dice,* New York: Oxford University Press, 1997.

Heesterman, J.C., *The Inner Conflict of Tradition: Essays in Indian Ritual, Kingship, and Society,* Chicago: The University of Chicago Press, 1985.

Hiltebeitel, Alf, *The Cult of Draupadi: Mythologies: From Gingee to Kuruksetra,* vol. 1, Chicago: The University of Chicago Press, 1988.

Indian Express News Service, 'Despite Rehabilitation, Devadāsī Culture Haunts Tondehal Village', in *Indian Express,* 23 January 1999.

Kalidas, S., 'The Lord's Damsels', in *India Today,* 11 January 1999.

Kersenboom, Saskia, 'Devadāsī Murai', in *Sangeet Natak* 96, April-June 1990, pp. 44-54.

———, *Word, Sound, Image: The Life of the Tamil Text,* Oxford: Berg Publishers, 1995.

Kersenboom-Story, Saskia C., *Nityasumaṅgalī: Devadāsī Tradition in South India,* Delhi: Motilal Barnasidass, 1987.

Kirloskar, Savita, 'Indian Cult Supplies Child Sex Trade', in *Reuter,* 22 January 1997, http://www.hindunet.org/srhhome/1997ḷ/0107.html

Masilamani-Meyer, Eveline, 'Renuka und die vertauschten Köpfe'. in *Nanavidhaikata: Festschrift für Herman Berger,* Dieter B. Kapp (ed.), Wiesbaden: Harrassowitz, 1996, pp. 165-83.

Mookerjee, Ajit and Madhu Khanna, *The Tantric Way: Art, Science, Ritual,* London: Thames and Hudson, 1977.

Nambiar, Balan, 'Tai Paradevata: Ritual Impersonation in the Teyyam Tradition of Kerala', in Brückner et al. (eds.), 1993, pp. 139-63.

Ramamirtattammal, Muvalar A., *Tasikal mocavalai allatu matiperra mainar,* Madras: Peral Press, 1936.

Ranganathan, Maya, 'Dedicated to "Deity", 6-year-old Mathamma's Life Will Not Be Hers To Lead', in *Indian Express,* 21 October 1999.

Schömbucher, Elisabeth, 'Gods, Ghosts and Demons: Possession in South Asia', in Brückner et al. (eds.), 1993, pp. 239-67.

Shulman, David and Deborah Thiagarajan (eds.), *Masked Ritual and Performance in South India: Dance, Healing, and Possession,* Ann Arbor: Center for South and Southeast Asian Studies, The University of Michigan, 2006.

Singer, Milton, 'Beyond Tradition and Modernity in Madras', in *Comparative Studies in Society and History,* vol. 13, no. 2, April 1971, pp. 160-95.

———, *When a Great Tradition Modernizes: An Anthropological Approach to Indian Civilization,* New York: Praeger, 1972.

Singh, Vinita G., 'NGO Lobbies for Welfare Scheme for Devadāsīs', in *The Economic Times* (Bangalore edition), 25 April 2000.

Srinivasan, Amrit, 'Reform and Revival: The Devadāsī and Her Dance', *Economic and Political Weekly* 20, 44, November 1985, pp. 1869-76.

Tamil Lexicon, 6 vols. and supplement, Madras: University of Madras, 1924-36 (ret. 1982).

Tarabout, Gilles, 'Ritual Rivalry in Kerala', in Brückner et al. (eds.), 1993, pp. 81-108.

Thurston, Edgar and K. Rangachari, *Castes and Tribes of Southern India*, 7 vols., New Delhi: Asian Educational Services, 1987 (1909).

3

How to Attain Heaven: The Vājapeya Sacrificial Ritual[1]

Karin Steiner

THE ŚRAUTA SYSTEM OF SACRIFICIAL RITUALS

One of the the most prominent features of ancient Indian, that is Vedic, religion and culture is the highly developed system of sacrificial rituals, the so-called Śrauta rituals, the rituals 'founded on *śruti*'. Śrauta rituals were 'cultural performances' in Milton Singer's sense (Singer 1972: 71 and passim). As such, one can see them as 'elementary constituents' encapsulating the Vedic culture. From 500 BC onwards the ancient religion together with its sacrificial cult started to be replaced by other concepts and forms of religion and cult. The tradition, however, never disappeared completely and there were renaissances again and again up to the present day. The basis for research in those rituals is the elaborate corpus of Vedic literature. The contents of these texts are of two kinds: 1. texts of speech and recitation within the ritual, and 2. meta-texts which consist of normative texts containing detailed instructions concerning the performance of the ritual (Śrautasūtras) on the one hand, and explanations of the meaning of the ritual elements on the other (*Brāhmaṇa* portions of the *Yajurveda-Saṁhitās* and *Brāhmaṇas* proper). Even modern performances of such rituals are based on these ancient texts.

A great part of Śrauta rituals is devoted to the procurement of well-being and fertility in this life and the hereafter. Śrauta rituals are sacrificial rituals characterized by the offering of various substances (milk, ghee, vegetabilia, animals, Soma) into the fire.

The performances required numerous further activities distributed among priests who officiated on behalf of a ritual patron (*yajamāna*), who had an active role in the performance as well. The patron is the ritual subject who receives the religious merit resulting from the sacrifice.[2] The most complex sacrificial rituals taught by the normative texts are the Soma sacrifices (*somayajña*). The central event of the Soma sacrifice is the preparation, offering and consumption of the sacral drink Soma. Around this nucleus are grouped numerous ritual actions lasting several days. The ritual under discussion, the Vājapeya,[3] is classified by the normative texts as a modification of the Soma sacrifice. This means the features characterizing the Vājapeya against other forms of Soma sacrifice are embedded into the paradigm given by the basic form of Soma sacrifice, the Agniṣṭoma. This fact is an important structural characteristic of the Vājapeya.

History of Research

The Vedistic secondary literature concerned with Śrauta ritual is copious: there are studies of single rituals, studies of details and isolated aspects of the rituals, or studies of the 'Vedic' or Śrauta ritual in general. Out of this bulk the studies of single rituals are of special interest here. The earliest works are from the pioneering phase of Vedistic studies: To mention a few of them[4]: Hillebrandt (1879) on the new and full moon sacrifice (*dārśapūrṇamāsa*); Schwab (1886) on the animal sacrifice (*paśubandha*); Weber (1893) on the royal consecration (*rājasūya*); Caland (1893) on the offerings to the fathers (*piṇḍapitṛyajña*). The most recent studies are, e.g. Krick ([PhD. diss. 1972] 1982) on the ritual of establishing the sacred fires (*agnyādheya*), Einoo (1988) on the tertial sacrifices (*cāturmāsya*), Kolhatkar (1998) on the alcohol sacrifice (*sautrāmaṇī*). Most of the investigations of single rituals are largely descriptive presentations of the ritual activities according to the Brāhmaṇas and Śrautasūtras, often connected with investigations of philological, cultural, historical and other details. They do not try to analyse or interpret the *rituals as rituals* in a broader context. Often not even the explanations and initial stages of interpretation given in the *Brāhmaṇas* are utilized and considered to a full extent.[5] All these studies have in common that there was hardly ever an adoption by non-specialists.[6] It is likely that this non-adoption is due to the ways the material is being presented: the theory-oriented discourse on sacrifice and ritual prevalent in the social and religious sciences has had hardly any effect on studies of Śrauta rituals to an extent, that not even the terminology current in present academic discourse has been introduced.[7]

Since the nineteenth century nearly all theorists of socio-religious studies and anthropology have been working on the fields of sacrifice or ritual in more or less detail.[8] The pioneers of 'modern' studies in sacrifice and ritual, however, were Henry Hubert and Marcel Mauss with their classical article 'Essai sur la nature et la fonction du sacrifice' published in 1899. In a time dominated by evolutionist approaches to this field Hubert and Mauss were the first social scientists who engaged in analysing specific sacrificial rituals regarding their processual structure, their symbolism, and functions, also taking into account the intentions of the performers. According to Hubert and Mauss the ritual process is basically a transfer, a transition of the sacrificial matter from profane to sacral sphere. By this transfer the religious condition of the sacrificer is changed. Hubert and Mauss are of special interest in the present context, because they were the first social scientists who utilized Śrauta rituals[9] extensively for establishing a general theory on sacrificial rituals. On the one hand, their theory is obsolete nowadays because it focuses too exclusively on the fact of the sacrificial matter being destroyed or killed and above all because it is based on the Durkheimian dichotomy of profane vs. sacral. On the other hand, it still provides a good starting point from which adequate theoretical implications of ritual and its interpretation can be derived.

The first[10] Indologist introducing a sociological perspective in the investigation of a specific Śrauta ritual was Jan Heesterman in his book about the *Rājasūya*: The ancient Indian royal consecration (1957). Heesterman was inspired by Hubert and Mauss and by another classic of Mauss, namely the 'Essai sur le don' (1924). Starting from the study of the *Rājasūya* Heesterman, in a series of articles and finally in a monograph (1993),[11] developed a model in which he tries to explain the 'classical' ritual system presented in the Śrauta texts as originating from 'preclassical' structures. These preclassical structures, according to Heesterman, are characterized by two rivalling sacrificial parties engaging in real lethal combats/

contests. The basic structural principle would be violent 'exchange' between these two parties, according to Heesterman. The martial symbolism, being very prominent in the Śrauta texts, is explained by Heesterman as euphemized remainder of those real sacrificial combats. His explanation of the origin of Vedic sacrifice was not accepted because of its lack of historicity (see, e.g. Minkowski 1996: 343): the preclassical structures postulated by Heesterman cannot be located historically or textually. The Ṛgveda, as the most ancient textual source, does not figure in his speculations. The ways he tried to trace the antagonistic structures of preclassical times were criticized as 'highly idiosyncratic'. So in spite of Heesterman's many correct, astute and subtle observations and brilliant interpretations of details, the approach to Śrauta ritual, which can be deduced from Heesterman's writings, is acceptable only with reservations.[12]

One must mention Frits Staal. He started with a 'thick description' of the Agnicayana performed in 1975 by Nambudiri Brahmins in Kerala which was published in 1983 in two big volumes titled *Agni*. Finally Staal came to radically rejecting all existing interpretative approaches to ritual because of the postulated 'meaninglessness of ritual' formulated most effectively in 'Rules without Meaning' (1989), which was widely received. His famous work *Agni* (alongside with the film produced by Robert Gardner) is probably the only description of a Śrauta ritual being adopted broadly by non-Vedistic as well as Vedistic researchers. The documentation and investigation of such performances for their own sake, perhaps from a point of view different from Staal's, is valuable and necessary. But as has become obvious through the documentation by Staal, such performances contribute only in a rather limited way to a better understanding of the ancient textual sources. Regarding the language of the mantras and the symbolism of the other elements the Śrauta rituals performed today are extremely anachronistic. They have survived as pure activity detatched from their socio-cultural context. This is the reason for Staal's perception of the ritual's meaninglessness and his postulate that ritual has nothing to do with religion and society (Staal 1996: 123 and passim). Staal utilized the results which he found in the special case of the Nambudiri-Agnicayana for establishing a new ritual theory which radically challenged all former approaches. This is Staal's merit. Especially

Staal's insistence that ritual acts are meaningless has caused much discussion[13] and was indeed seminal to the most important work on ritual theory published during the last years, namely Humphrey and Laidlaw's *The Archetypal Actions of Ritual: A Theory of Ritual Illustrated by the Jain Rite of Worship* (1994).

To sum it up: Despite there being attempts at mutual exchange an interface between the philology-centred Vedistic studies and the theory-oriented fields of socio-religious studies and anthropology has not been established so far.

What Kind of Evidence Do We Have? What Kind of Ritual is the Vājapeya?

As mentioned above, Śrauta rituals can be regarded as 'cultural performances' and as such they can be read as 'texts' (Geertz 1973: 10). But most of those rituals have survived only as 'text' in a traditional sense, as descriptions or prescription in a scripturally and/or orally fixed form. This is also true for the Vājapeya.[14] There is no living tradition, no performance which can be attended or observed. There are no informants who can be interviewed. Sometimes historical, social or even material facts simply are not known to the researcher because the texts are silent about them. The context of those performances, being a 'text' in themselves as well as existing only on a textual level, can be detected only in traces. A 'text in context' study (Singer 1972: 39-52) is possible only in a limited way. A 'thick description' as outlined by Geertz (Geertz 1973: 3-30) is impossible. Also, essential aspects of the performance, such as emotional or aesthetic effects and experiences and beliefs of the participants, which would be especially interesting in the context of a performative approach, cannot be traced. Of course, the ritual texts sometimes do mention such aspects. But we do not know to which extent these were part of the actual experience of the participants. Not only therefore the question arises whether it is legitimate to see in the light of performance the ritual under discussion. The problem is much more fundamental because it must be asked whether something which has survived only as being reduced to a 'text' in an everyday sense[15] can be seen as 'performance' at all. As Schieffelin (1998: 198f.) puts it,

> The character of performance as accomplishment, together with its interactive quality and element of risk, make it easy to differentiate it from the notion of 'text'. Although some scholars have written as though performance could be treated as a form of text, in my view performance can never be text, and its unique strategic properties are destroyed when it is considered as, or reduced to, text. . . . While texts and performances may be produced out of one another, this is very different from saying they are reducible to one another. 'Text' can never be duplicated in performance, and performance is not reducible to text.

We also must ask, what kind of ritual the Vājapeya or Śrauta ritual in general is. Śrauta rituals should rather be seen as an example of liturgy-centred ritual in opposition to performance-centred ritual.[16] According to Atkinson (1989: 15), liturgy-centred rituals can be described by the preordained progression of delineated steps to which ritual practitioners and congregants collectively conform, whereas performance-centred rituals are characterized by a repertoire of ritual actions available to performers acting independently during the performance. Examples of performance-centred rituals are shamanism and initiation ceremonies.

According to Humphrey and Laidlaw (1994: 8), 'The central concern of performance-centred rituals is the genuineness or truth of the supernatural quality of the event . . . they rest on a stimulation, a half-believed fiction that some unseen supernatural event really happens as they are performed.' In liturgical rituals, on the other hand, the correct performance of the preordained steps is emphasized and held to be automatically effective, which is true for Śrauta rituals. But we don't know 'whether [the performers of the liturgy-centred Śrauta rituals also] believed or were supposed to believe, or at least were supposed to act as if they believed' [in a supernatural event taking place during the performance]. (Smith 1982: 105; the additions in [ ] are mine). As Humphrey and Laidlaw pointed out (1994: 8), 'in anthropology such a great emphasis has been placed on the latter (i.e. performance-centred ritual) that it has become to seem as paradigmatic of ritual in general'. Mostly performance-centred rituals were the object of research from which results that many categories of the anthropological theory of ritual were derived from performance-centred rituals, whereas the analysis of liturgy-centred ritual was neglected. Is the application of an approach derived from performance-centred ritual to liturgy-centred ritual legitimate? It must be asked also whether 'performativity' is present in such rituals. Rostas (1998: 90) described 'performativity' as follows: 'Performativity is a measure of the effort (or energy) put into an action. Performativity entails action that is not prescribed, the deployment of consciously formulated strategies. It implies individuality and resourcefulness as put into the movement: it can be seen as creative. On the whole, it is the performativity that gives an enactment its zest, that makes ritual and/or performance interesting to watch.' Whether performativity in this sense was present in a Śrauta ritual is very doubtful or at least cannot be decided from the exclusively scriptural evidence. Another notion of 'performance' is formulated by Baumann (1986) who characterizes performance as a display of expressive competence or virtuosity by one or more performers addressed to an audience. Such performances aim to evoke an imaginative reality or an intensification of experience among the spectators and bring about an altered awareness of their situation and/or a sense of emotional relief. Especially the fact that performances can evoke an imaginative reality and bring about an altered awareness of the situation not only of the spectators but also of the protagonist of the performance seems applicable to any ritual, hence to Śrauta ritual.

The Vājapeya

My presentation of the Vājapeya ritual follows the *Baudhāyana-Śrautasūtra* (11), for interpretation I draw some important points from the *Taittirīya-Brāhmaṇa* (1.3.2-9), both texts belonging to the Taittirīya school of the Black Yajurveda. This is an attempt in analysing the texts in their performance despite the critical thoughts outlined above. I utilize the not very far-reaching explanations of the classical texts as well as van Gennep's classical model of passage rites as reformulated by Turner. Some stress is laid on Turner's category of liminality although this category was developed from analysing rituals that should be seen as performance-centred, not liturgy-centred. Nevertheless, liminality is the category in the light of which emotional and performative aspects of the Vājapeya can be grasped best.

Purpose of the Vājapeya is the attainment of a position or state called *sāmrājya* usually translated as 'universal sovereignty' by the ritual patron. What this state or position exactly means, whether it is connected with certain socio-political functions or not, we do not know exactly. But it is most likely that in the form of the ritual laid down by the texts the title *samrāj* implies a prestigious social position but not any political office.[17] So the Vājapeya is a ritual of status elevation.[18] It effects or should I say accompanies a change of state of the ritual subject. The ritual subject is separated from his fixed position in the everyday social structure to be transformed, and to asume a better position in social life again after the liminal phase of transition. Inseparable from the attainment of this prestigious position are two further ritual topics (a term introduced by Turner): on the one hand, the attainment or reaching (*āpti*) of the creator god Prajāpati, which here means the union of sacrificer and Prajāpati; and, on the other hand, a 'journey to heaven' (*svargo loka, asau loka*) of the sacrificer. It is on this last topic I am going to focus on.

The characteristic features of the Vājapeya, distinguishing it from other Soma sacrifices, are:

(a) besides the regular sacral drink of Soma the alcoholic drink Surā is being prepared, sacrificed and consumed;
(b) a chariot race of 17 chariots with the sacrificer as a participant;
(c) the climbing of a short wooden post, which has a wheel of a chariot fixed upon it;
(d) the climbing of a long post, the so-called sacrificial pole (*yūpa*) by the ritual patron and his wife.

These four sequences of actions are, as we shall see, connected with the ritual topic of ascending (*ārohaṇa*) to heaven and descending again (*pratyāvarohaṇa*).

Structure of the Plot: Structure and Process

The plot (a term used by Turner) of the Vājapeya is characterized by two opposed processes, namely, ascension and the following descent, which the ritual subject undertakes or undergoes. During ascension the ritual subject is immersed deeper and deeper into the liminal state, whereas the descent is characterized by gradually decreasing liminality. These processes develop while the structure of the plot unfolds.

The plot is characterized by three interlocked sets of three phases each. The latter do not correspond exactly to the well-known three phases of separation, liminality, and reincorporation as we shall see later. Also, the phases actually cannot be separated strictly because transitions from one phase to the other are fluid.

Necessarily, the picture is somewhat idealized and simplified because it is impossible to discuss all details of the rituals' bewildering complexity.

The basic structure of Soma ritual resembles fairly well the model of van Gennep (1986): there are three phases, the introductory phase characterized by separation, which introduces the middle phase of liminality, finally the concluding phase of integration. The structure is illustrated by the following diagram:

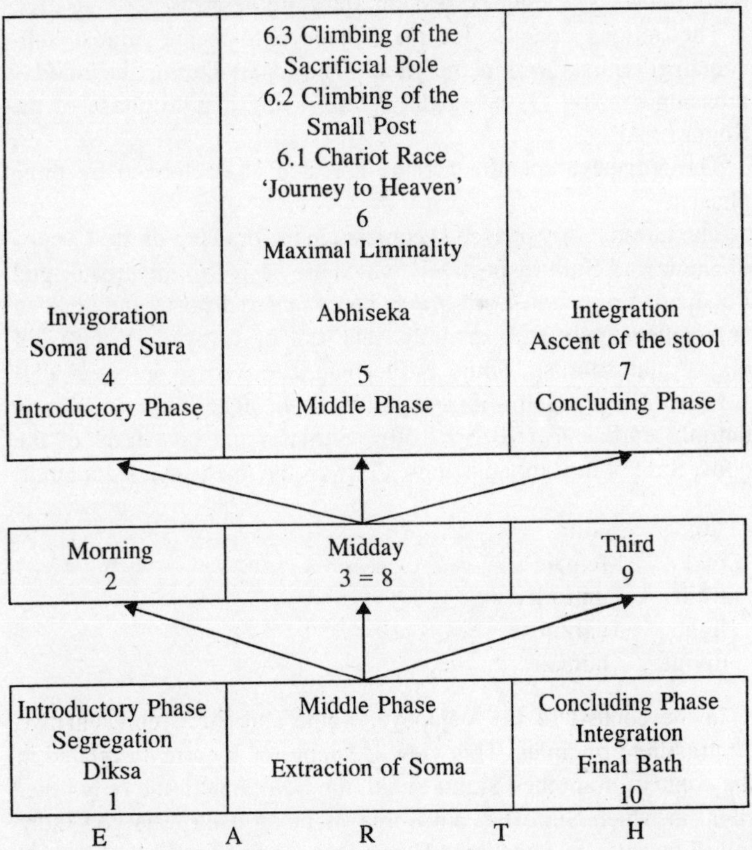

Dīkṣā (1),[19] which is, maybe, the most important rite during the introductory phase of Soma-ritual, means the transition of the ritual subject from secular to sacral behaviour. It is a rite of separation which brings about the detachment of the sacrificer from his everyday life and society. *Dīkṣā* is also an initiation of the sacrificer into the liminal and sacral cosmos of the ritual which is characterized by a temporary suspension of his established position within the social structure. The consecrated or initiated sacrificer (*dīkṣita*) becomes a Brahmin irrespective of his *varṇa.* This means he is sacralized. The sacrificer passes into the state of an embryo or temporary death to be born again from the ritual as is well known.

The middle phase, including the central event of Soma-sacrifice, the extraction of Soma, is divided into three sessions of preparation: morning-session, midday-session and third session.

The actions specific for the Vājapeya (4-7) are almost self-contained rituals within the ritual. They start during the midday pressing session (3) being the centre of the middle phase of the Soma ritual.

The Vājapeya-specific actions are also characterized by three phases:

The introductory phase (4) consists in the drawing of the 17 cups of Soma and Surā respectively which are sacred to the creator god Prajāpati. Soma and Surā are to be considered polar, they are an antagonistic pair with qualities that can be arrayed in terms of binary oppositions: 'Soma is the man, the woman is Surā' (TB 1.3.8.16-21) or 'Soma is prosperity, truth, light, Surā is misery, untruth, darkness' (ŚB 5.1.2.10). 'Soma is the best food of the gods, Surā of the human beings' (TB), as the *Brāhmaṇa* texts put it:

Soma	Surā
male	female
truth	untruth
light	darkness
divine	human

In the context of the Vājapeya, Soma and Surā represent two contrasting principles. This view is supported by a myth related in the context of another Śrauta ritual, the Sautrāmaṇī, the only other ritual in which Surā (but not Soma) is being used: The god Indra fell ill because he consumed Soma not sacrificed to him and could be cured only by Surā or Surā-ritual respectively. In the context of the myth Surā is the antidote to Soma and in the context of the Vājapeya the two contrasting principles have to be integrated. By this integration the sacrificer is healed and regenerated. This state of wholeness, integrity (*sarvatva*) is necessary for attaining heaven. The first interpretation, namely, regeneration through reintegration of the two contrasting principles, is related to the sacrificer himself. A second, coexisting interpretation pertains to the sacrificer's wife who accompanies him in his ascension to heaven, that is, climbing the sacrificial pole. It is evident that Soma has a strong relation to the sacrificer, while Surā is more related to his wife. 'The sacrificer sets himself free by the cups of Soma, his wife by the cups of Surā. By Surā he becomes united with his wife even in the other world' (TB).

So the introductory phase consisting of the drawing of the cups of Soma and Surā has the character of a rite of regeneration or healing, not of separation.

The middle phase is introduced by a consecration (*abhiṣeka*) (5) of the sacrificer. Although this consecration has some ritual elements in common with the *dīkṣā*, it has not the *dīkṣā's* character of a rite of separation. It includes, among other elements, the investiture of the sacrificer into the state of *samrāj,* which seems to be inconsistent at this stage of the ritual. For investiture implies integration which would be the end of the liminal state. It is clear from the context of the following actions that the liminal state does not end here but an even deeper immersion into it is enacted. The consecration proper consists in pouring a mixture of ghee and other ingredients over the sacrificer's head and face. The texts equalize the procedure of pouring with the process of eating (TS, BŚS). It is to be understood as the symbolic feeding of the sacrificer and aims at securing the power of disposal of the stocks of food (*annādya*) for him. So the *abhiṣeka* is to be understood as a rite of invigoration and preparation for the now following most critical, that is most liminal, part of the ritual.

Now follows the sacrificer's journey to heaven (6) which is enacted three times (6.1, 6.2, 6.3):

The chariot race (6.1) can be interpreted on two co-existing levels:

(a) In relation to the above-mentioned purpose of the Vājapeya being the attainment of *sāmrājya:* the race is a stylized battle for expansion of the ritual subject's sphere of influence (*loka*). This fact can be seen from the viewpoint of agency.

(b) In relation to the ritual topic of attaining heaven the race symbolizes a ride to the world of heaven. The post around which the chariots turn is equalized with heaven (TB 1.3.8.35-36). This latter interpretation is the more important one in the structure and conception of the Vājapeya. During the race the sacrificer leaves behind the other participants. This separation from his everyday companions can be interpreted as a deeper immersion into the liminal state as well. Moving into the world of heaven represents a time of high risk. The turning point, being the world of heaven, may turn out to be a point of no return, for 'those who are riding to the world of heaven may precipitate', as TB puts it. In the ritual the sacrificer returns unharmed after passing the turning point. The chariot race anticipates the actual ascension to heaven which is enacted by climbing the sacrificial pole and secures its safe end. It is an 'altitudinal' action by meaning which is physically projected into the longitudinal plane and aims at expanding ritual space and ritual subject. The chariot and horses are used here to reach heaven. By these the sacrificer wins an expanded sphere of influence (*loka*) and generative power (*vāja*) as prize. This enables him to manage the actual ascension to heaven by his own efforts.

Now the Brahman-priest climbs a small post, on which a wheel of a chariot is fixed (6.2). The climbing of this post is also an action symbolizing the ascension to heaven. The Brahman-priest here acts as a representative of the sacrificer. On the one hand, the small post must be understood as a reduced form of the sacrificial pole, and, on the other hand, it symbolizes the axis of the sacrificer's chariot and (*pars pro toto*) the chariot. The climbing of the post is an act of mediation: the two symbolic actions of the chariot race and the climbing of the sacrificial pole are united, while the latter is anticipated one more time. Longitudinal and altitudinal expansion of the ritual subject and his sphere of influence are enacted simultaneously.

In the centre of the ritual action is the sacrificial pole (*yūpa*). The normal function of this pole is that the sacrificial animals are tied to it. Concerning the main ritual topic of the Vājapeya the sacrificial pole is the dominant symbol. It is a polysemic symbol possessing many meanings at the same time. I can describe here only two of them.

(a) The sacrificial pole represents the sacrificer or his *ātman* respectively (self in the sense of 'trunk' or 'body'). More exactly speaking: it is the consecrated sacrificer (*dīkṣita*). Because with the pole the same rites are performed as with the sacrificer during *dīkṣā*: like the fitting out with a new garment and headgear as well as a girdle of grass, unction with water and ghee.

(b) The sacrificial pole represents the universe with triadic structure: earth (*pṛthivī*), intermediate space (*antarikṣa*) and sky (*div*). It is also the manifestation of the imagined connecting path between earth and sky/heaven: the cosmic pillar (*skambha*), which gives firm hold to the earth and supports the sky.

By climbing the sacrificial pole (6.3) the ascension to heaven and descent back to earth is enacted. Reaching the top of the pole is the point of maximal liminality of the ritual subject. The top of the pole is the place where the transformation, the change of state, the passage of the ritual subject takes place. It is the most dangerous place, the most dangerous period of time during the ritual. The risk of precipitating or not coming back (TB 1.3.8.40-47) is visible and tangible here. Climbing the pole/ascending to heaven means consciously exposing oneself to the possibility of death, perhaps it suggests sacrificial death. For being in heaven/in the beyond means having died. The reintegration of the ritually dead sacrificer can be brought about only gradually. The contact with life, earth, and society must be restored step by step. This process is also enacted dramatically: On his way down representatives of the peasantry (*viś*) hit the sacrificer with small packages of soil and ashes. The procedure of climbing down is characterized by ambiguity: on the one hand, the sacrificer must be reintegrated. Otherwise, he could not receive the advantages of his transformed state. On the other hand, the sacrificer's transformed state, which is inseparably connected with the location where he acquired it, shall be preserved. He climbs down onto the skin of a he-goat with a piece of gold placed upon it. The skin symbolizes prosperity (*puṣṭi*), the gold means continuity of life or immortality (*amṛtatva*). He then climbs a stool (7) which is carried away from the sacrificial pole by some of the officiants. Ascending the stool is again equalized with ascension to heaven. This ascending underlines the establishment of the sacrificer in his new elevated position, and being carried away by the officiants stresses the fact of integration, as well as acceptance by society.

This last action concludes the specific features of the Vājapeya, the ritual within the ritual. The ritual process is resumed following the paradigm of Soma-sacrifice with the midday pressing (8) and the Third pressing (9), then follows the concluding phase (10) with the final reintegration of the sacrificer culminating in the final bath of the main participants of the ritual.

'Heaven' is promised regularly also in other Śrauta rituals. But in none of them the ritual topic of ascending to heaven and descending again is enacted in such a drama-like way as in the Vājapeya. The attainment of heaven by ascension is made sensorially perceptible and visible in the form of symbols and symbolic action and is thereby made accessible to the purposive action of the sacrificer and society. It is in this act of making apparent, which Turner (1969: 31) called the 'principle of revelation', in which the power of performance manifests itself. The physical enactment of the ascension to heaven brings about an altered awareness of the ritual subject's situation. By the performance his status elevation is enacted and also legitimated, his agency (*sāmrājya*) expanded.

I hope to have shown that a performative approach to the Vājapeya or Śrauta ritual in general is not only legitimate but also throws new light on the interpretation of the ritual. I also hope to create an interface between philology-centred Vedistic studies, socio-religious studies and anthropology by applying suitable theoretical concepts to specific rituals.

NOTES

1. I am grateful to Ulrich Oberdiek for the many fruitful discussions about the 'anthropological aspects' of this paper.

2. The indigenous term for those rituals is *yajña* derived from the Sanskrit root *yaj-* which in the oldest Vedic texts means 'to worship [through sacrifices]'. In later texts *yaj-* is best translated as 'to sacrifice', hence *yajña* as 'sacrifice'. But it is clear that a Śrauta *yajña* includes many other ritual activities additional to sacrificing. Especially the Vājapeya is characterized by substantial acts which are not connected with 'sacrifice'.
3. The word Vājapeya is translated generally as 'drink (*peya*) of strength (*vāja*)'. An alternative translation proposed by Weber (1892) is 'Schutz oder Weihe der Kraft [protection or consecration of strength]' as *peya* can be derived from the root *pā*[1] 'drink' or *pā*[2] 'protect'.
4. The author is aware of the fact that a summary of this vast field necessarily will be selective and subjective.
5. Exceptions are the works by Heesterman (1957) and Krick (1982). Special cases are presented by Bodewitz (1973, 1976 and 1990) and Houben (1991) who investigate specific rituals in the light of a specific ancient interpretation. The attitude of Western scholars towards the genre of Brāhmaṇa even nowadays is characterized in many cases by a kind of—often unreflected—fascinated aversion, which results in an attitude that the texts can no more be taken seriously: Staal (1996:118f.), for example, expressly refutes the interpretations of the Vedic ritualists. Or the texts are exploited only with regard to very special mono-causal explanations.
6. Even researchers concerned with later or contemporary ritual practice which is replete with Vedic elements often pay only lip-service to the so-called 'Vedic sacrifice', repeating often quoted clichés, without ever having read a description of any ritual.
7. The state of affairs is similar regarding studies in (ṛg-)vedic religion. See Oberlies (1998: XII).
8. It is impossible to consider and discuss all the diverging approaches presented by numerous scholars and scientists, nor is it possible to give a summary of the discourse about ritual. A detailed and critical survey about the so-called theories of sacrifice is given by Drexler (1993); for a short summary see, e.g. Böhm (1998); detailed on ritual theories: Bell (1992); short summaries see, e.g. in Lang (1998), and Gladigow (1998); methodological criticism, e.g. in Bell (1987), Humphrey/Laidlaw (1994: 64-87) and Staal (1996: 115-31 and passim).
9. Their main sources were the *Paśubandha* according to Schwab (1886), but the *Dārśapūrṇamāsa* according to Hillebrandt (1879) as well. They were influenced by Sylvain Levi's classic 'La doctrine du sacrifice dans les Brahmanas' (1898).

10. Keith (1925) is the first Indologist who relatively broadly discusses the then current theories for interpretation of sacrificial rituals, though he does not apply them to specific rituals.
11. Heesterman in the first chapter of his monograph also discusses the theories of Meuli (1946), Jensen (1951), Girard (1972), Burkert (1972, 1987) and others who contributed to the discussion about 'sacrifice'.
12. Hertha Krick in her investigation of the *Agnyādheya* ritual follows Heesterman's conception of classical/preclassical, but does not give up the connection with philological and historical facts, in which lies the great value of Krick's work.
13. See, e.g. Grapard (1991), Mack (1991), Strenski (1991), Scharfe (1990), Witzel (1992). See also Staal's debate with his critics (Staal 1991 and 1993).
14. As far as the author knows, the Vājapeya was performed for the last time in 1955 at Poona. It was a revivalistic performance organized mainly out of scholarly and academic interest by members of the Bhandarkar Oriental Research Institute as well as Western Indologists. The performance was documented in a film produced by the Indologist Hans van Buitenen. The performance committee also published the brochure 'The Śrauta Ritual and the Vājapeya Sacrifice', Poona 1955. I have to thank Prof. J.C. Heesterman, who supplied me with a copy of this rare publication.
15. Of course, it may be asked, also, whether it is appropriate to apply anthropologist approaches to exclusively scriptural evidence at all.
16. This distinction goes back to Atkinson (1989) but has not been applied to Vedic material so far.
17. It seems possible to connect the meaning, or content of *sāmrājya* with the agency concept: the ritual aims at underlining or strengthening the ritual patron's agency.
18. I owe this term to Turner (1969: 160).
19. The numbers refer to the figure on page 93.

REFERENCES

Atkinson, Jane Monnig, *The Art and Politics of Wana Shamanship*, Berkeley: University of California Press, 1989.

Bauman, Richard, *Story, Performance, Event,* Cambridge: Cambridge University Press, 1986.

Bell, Catherine, *Ritual Theory, Ritual Practice*, New York: Oxford University Press, 1992.

———, Discourse and Dichotomy: The Structure of Ritual 'Theory', in *Religion* 17 (1987), 95-118.

Bodewitz, H.W., *Jaiminīya Brāhmaṇa I, 1-65. Translation and Commentary with a study of Agnihotra and Prāṇāgnihotra*, Leiden: Brill, 1973.

———, *The Daily Evening and Morning Offering (Agnihotra) According to the Brāhmaṇas,* Leiden: Brill, 1976.

———, *The Jyotiṣṭoma Ritual: Jaiminīya-Brāhmaṇa I, 66-364*, introd., transl. and commentary, Leiden: Brill, 1990.

Böhm, Thomas, 'Opfer', in *Handbuch religionswissenschaftlicher Grundbegriffe* IV (1998) 268-83.

Burkert, Walter, *Homo Neccans,* Berlin: de gruyter, 1972.

———, *The Problem of Ritual Killing*, in *Violent Origins*, Stanford: Stanford University Press, 1987.

Caland, Wilhelm, *Altindischer Ahnenkult*, Leiden: Brill, 1893.

Drexler, Josef, *Die Illusion des Opfers: ein wissenschaftlicher Überblick über die wichtigsten Opfertheorien ausgehend vom deleuzianischen Polyperspektivismusmodell*, München: Akademischer Verlag, 1993 (Münchner ethnologische Abhandlungen 12).

Einoo, Shingo, *Die Cāturmāsya oder die altindischen Tertialopfer dargestellt nach den Vorschriften der Brāhmaṇas und der Śrautasūtras*, Tokyo: Universität Tokyo, 1988.

Gennep, Arnold van, *Übergangsriten*, Frankfurt: Campus, 1986 (Translation of: *Les rites de passage*: *Etude systématique des rites*, Paris: 1909).

Geertz, Clifford, *The Interpretation of Cultures,* New York: Basic Books, 1973.

Girard, R.: *La violence et le sacrré.* Paris: Grasset, 1972.

Gladigow, Burkhard, 'Ritual, Komplexes', in *Handbuch religionswissenschaftlicher Grundbegriffe* IV (1998), 458-60.

Grapard, Allan G., 'Rule-governed Activity vs. Rule-creating Activity', in *Religion* 21 (1991) 207-12.

Heesterman, Jan, *The Broken World of Sacrifice*, Chicago: University of Chicago Press, 1993.

———, *The Ancient Indian Royal Consecration*, S'Gravenhage: Mutton & Co., 1957.

Hillebrandt, Alfred, *Das altindische Neu- und Vollmondsopfer*, Jena: Gustav Fischer, 1879.

Houben, Jan *Pravargya Brāhmaṇa of the Taittirīya Āraṇyaka*, Delhi: Motilal Banarsidass, 1991.

Hubert, Henry and Marcel Mauss, 'Essai sur la nature et la fonction du sacrifice', in *L'année sociologique* 2.1899. (English translation: *Sacrifice, its nature and function.* London: Cohen & West, 1964).

Humphrey, Caroline and James Laidlaw, *'The Archetypal Actions of Ritual. A Theory of Ritual Illustrated by the Jain Rite of Worship*, Oxford: Clarendon, 1994.

Jensen, A.E.: *Mythos und Kult bei den Naturvölkern,* Wiesbaden: Steiner 1951.

Keith, Arthur Berriedale, *The Religion and Philosophy of the Vedas and Upanishads,* Cambridge: 1925.

Kolhatkar, Madhavi Bhaskar, *Surā*: *The Liquor and the Vedic Sacrifice.* New Delhi: D.K. Printworld, 1998.

Krick, Hertha, *Das Ritual der Feuergründung,* Wien: Verlag der Österreichischen Akademie der Wissenschaften, 1982.

Lang, Bernhard, 'Ritual/Ritus', in *Handbuch religionswissenschaftlicher Grundbegriffe* IV (1998) 442-58.

Levi, Sylvain, *La doctrine du sacrifice dans les Brahmanas*, Paris: Bibliothèque de L'Ecole des Hautes Etudes, Sciences religieuses, 1973 (1898).

Mack, Burton L., *Staal's Gauntlet and the Queen*, in *Religion* 21 (1991) 213-18.

Maitrāyaṇī-Saṃhitā. Herausgegeben von Leopold von Schröder, Nachdruck: Wiesbaden: Steiner 1970.

Mauss, Marcel, Essai sur le don, in *L'année Sociologique* (*N.S.*) 1, 1923-1924, 30-186.

Meuli, Karl, 'Griechische Opferbräuche', in *Phyllobolia für Peter von der Mühl,* Basel: 1946.

Minkowski, Christopher, review of Heesterman (1993), in *JAOS* 116 (1996) 341-4.

Oberlies, Thomas, *Die Religion des Ṛgveda: Das Religiöse System des Ṛgveda*, Wien: University Vienna Press, Publications of the DeNobili Research Library 26, 1998.

Rostas, Susanna, 'From Ritualization to Performativity', in *Ritual, Performance, Media,* London Routledge 1998 (ASA Monographs 35).

Scharfe, Hartmut, 'The Great Rituals–Were They Really Meaningless?', in *Sanskrit and Related Studies,* Poona: Shri Garibdas Oriental Series, 1990.

Schwab, Julius, *Das altindische Thieropfer*, Erlangen: Verlag von Andreas Deichert, 1886.

Schieffelin, Edward L.: 'Problematizing Performance', in *Ritual, Performance, Media,* London: Routledge, 1998.

Singer, Milton, *When a Great Tradition Modernizes,* New York: Praeger, 1972.

Smith, Pierre, 'Aspects of the Organization of Rites', in *Between Belief and Transgression*, Chicago: University of Chicago Press, 1982.

Staal, Frits (ed.), *Agni: The Vedic Ritual of the Fire Altar,* Berkeley: Asian Humanities Press, 1983.

———, 'Within Ritual, About Ritual and Beyond', in *Religion* 21 (1991) 227-34.

———, *Ritual and Mantras: Rules Without Meaning* (reprint of 1989), Delhi: Motilal Banarsidass, 1996.

———, 'From Meanings to Trees', in *Journal of Ritual Studies* 7, 2 (1993) 11-32.

Strenski, Ivan, 'What is rite?', In *Religion* 21 (1991) 219-25.

The Śatapatha Brāhmaṇa, ed. Albrecht Weber. Reprint. Varanasi: Chaukhamba Samskrit Sansthan, 1964.

The Śatapatha Brāhmaṇa, transl. Julius Eggeling. Reprint. Delhi: Motilal Banarsidass, 1996.

Taittirīyabrāhmaṇam, E. Mahadevaśāstriṇā sampāditā. Reprint. Delhi: Motilal Banarsidass, 1985.

Turner, Victor, *The Ritual Process: Structure and Anti-Structure*. Chicago: Aldine, 1969.

Weber, Albrecht, *Über den Vājapeya*, Sitzungsberichte der Königlich Preussischen Akademie der Wissenschaften, Philologisch-historische Classe 39 (1892), 765-813.

———, *Über die Königsweihe, den Rājasūya*, Berlin 1893 (Aus den Abhandlungen der Königlich Preussischen Akademie der Wissenschaften zu Berlin 1893).

Witzel, Michael, 'Meaningful Ritual: Vedic, Medieval and Contemporary Concepts in the Nepalese Agnihotra Ritual, in *Ritual, State and History in South Asia: Essays in Honour of J.C. Heesterman,* Leiden: Brill, 1992.

4

Cākyār Initiation in the *Kūṭiyāṭṭam* Theatre of Kerala: The *Araṅṅēṟṟam* Performance[1]

Bożena Śliwczyńska

The *Kūṭiyāṭṭam* theatre of Kerala (south India) is the only surviving form of the Pan-Indian tradition of Sanskrit theatre. Up until the middle of the twentieth century it was exclusively confined to the temple precincts, being a part of regular temple (daily or annual) rituals. To perform *Kūṭiyāṭṭam* in the temple is a hereditary right and religious duty of two communities: Cākyārs, actors, and Nampyārs, musicians. The female folk of the latter, bearing a cognomen Naṅṅyār, are actresses and support musicians. Both, the Cākyārs and Nampyārs (plus Naṅṅyārs), belong to quite a vast group of the temple servants—Ampalavāsis. The Cākyārs' social rank is fairly high as it is only inferior to that of Nampūtiri Brahmins of Kerala. They undergo a ceremony of *upanāyana* and wear a sacred thread, still they are not allowed to study the Vedas and conduct temple rituals except for one—a stage performance. The place of Cākyārs' dharmic activities is a *kūttampalam*, or temple theatre, usually situated to the right of the flagstaff of the temple. The Cākyārs follow a matrilineal system, thus only a boy whose mother comes from the Cākyār family (she is called Illōṭamma) can become an actor.[2] He belongs to his mother's family, so his maternal uncle becomes his main teacher (not his father, even if he happens to be a Cākyār). The Cākyār boy starts his systematic learning and training quite early, usually at the age of five or so under the guidance of his maternal uncle. The boy follows his uncle-guru's tradition of staging Sanskrit dramas. It takes many years for the Cākyār boy to be prepared for his first public performance (*araṅṅēṟṟam*). His teacher decides about the moment when a debut of his pupil can take place. However, it is customary to have the *araṅṅēṟṟam* performance before reaching maturity (sixteenth birthday at the latest). A family astrologer is asked to fix the exact day and time of the performance.

Before the stage debut the boy used to undergo a *naṭābhiṣeka* ceremony, or consecration of an actor. He was purified by the chief priest of the temple. The sacred water brought from the sanctum sanctorum was poured on him, rice and flower petals were thrown on him and special mantras were recited. After the ceremony the Cākyār boy was ready for the performance. It seems that the *naṭābhiṣeka* ritual was quite an elaborate one.[3] At present it is not held in any ceremonial manner but rather symbolically. The young boy follows just regular preliminary rites all actors perform before every stage presentation. Thus he has a 'full shave' of the body and a purifying bath[4], pays homage to the temple deity, and so on.[5] The *naṭābhiṣeka* ceremony as such is not within living memory of the Cākyārs, even of the eldest generation.

The initial performance of every Cākyār always presents the same fragment of Bhāsa's *Bālacarita*, the only drama of his referring to Kṛṣṇa mythology.[6] The verse enacted during the performance is the first stanza of the play, the line of Sūtradhāra. It is an auspicious invocation to Lord Viṣṇu in his different manifestations—Nārāyaṇa, Viṣṇu, Rāma, Dāmodara-Kṛṣṇa. Enacting this particular stanza is part of an intricate performance unit. The verse presentation is preceded and succeeded by many *nṛtta* and *nṛtya* (dance) sequences of ritualistic character.

The *araṅṅēṟṟam* performance is held in a family temple of the young actor-to-be and it takes two days to complete it. The first day is dedicated to a *puṟappāṭu* part and the second to a *nirvahaṇa* one. The *puṟappāṭu* and *nirvahaṇa* are technical terms for two fixed initial parts of any regular *Kūṭiyāṭṭam* performance (of many days). In this case they constitute a performance unit of two days.

Thus after paying homage to the temple deity in the *garbhagṛha* the young artist prays on the stage with a red ribbon-like piece of cloth (*cuvapputuṇi*) in his hand. Then he goes to the green room and sits in front of an oil lamp, which is lit with the fire brought from the sanctum sanctorum. He sprinkles himself with water[7] and holding the red ribbon-cloth in both hands he prays (invoking his family deities and gurus). He ties the *cuvapputuṇi*, the very first piece of his costume, around his forehead. This is an important moment for the actor as it marks transition from one reality to another;[8] it is also meant to be very auspicious.[9] Next, the boy applies drops of clarified butter (*ghī*) on his forehead, nose and chin in order to smear them on his face. He repeats this thrice and only then he starts his make-up[10] followed by dressing up the costume. The guru blesses his disciple. The boy is ready for his stage debut. His guru stays near the stage to observe and support him, if he is in need. The first performance always creates a certain degree of stress and the guru's presence is of great help.

The Sūtradhāra's *puṟappāṭu*[11] making the first day of the *araṅṅēṟṟam* performance starts in the morning and lasts about two hours. It begins with sounding the *miḻāvu* drum (*miḻāvu occappeṭuttal*) for some minutes. Then a short *pūjā* ceremony conducted by the chief priest of the temple takes place on the stage, it is dedicated to Gaṇapati (Gaṇeśa). This is followed by a part named *gōṣṭhi* with the fixed musical pattern of two *miḻāvu* drums (played by Nampyārs) accompanied by a Naṅṅyār (sometimes two) playing on the small hand-cymbals (*tālam*). During the *gōṣṭhi* the Naṅṅyār sings an invocatory song called *akkitta* (*agaṇitaphaṇiphaṇa . . .*),[12] invoking Gaṇapati, Śiva and Sarasvatī. The *gōṣṭhi* part is pretty long [25 min.].[13] It creates an auspicious atmosphere and prepares all participants for further events. The *miḻāvu occappeṭuttal* as well as the *gōṣṭhi* with their set patterns are the same for every *puṟappāṭu*. Then *araṅṅutaḷi*, or 'sprinkling [with water] the stage', follows. A benedictory verse (*nāndī śloka*) is recited by a Nampyār in front of the stage oil lamp.[14] He recites it holding a bit of grass or flower petals and water in his right hand. At the end of recitation he throws the flowers and sprinkles the water on the stage. Then he goes back to the *miḻāvu* and sounds it. Here the Nampyār plays a role of Nāndī Sūtradhāra. The verse does not belong to the text of the drama enacted. Each act of a drama staged in the *Kūṭiyāṭṭam* (there is a tradition of presenting only a single act as a performance-unit, not the whole drama) has its own *nāndī śloka* composed by the Cākyārs or Nampyārs. For the first act of the *Bālacarita* whose introductory verse constitutes the middle part of the Sūtradhāra's *puṟappāṭu* the *nāndī* (*araṅṅutaḷi*) verse is as follows:

pāntu vo nārasiṁhasya nakhalāṅgala koṭayaḥ
hiraṇyakaśipor vaksaḥkṣetrāsṛkkardamāruṇaḥ.[15]

After the *araṅṅutaḷi* the presentation proper starts and a curtain is held by two stage-hands. Soon behind the curtain a young actor appears sprinkling the stage, his feet and face with water. He makes a salutation to the *miḻāvu* drums (*miḻāvu abhivādya*) followed by ritually set series of steps and gestures, the whole part is called *maṟayilkriya*, or actions / rituals behind [the curtain]. At the very end of it the actor makes a tying movement with his hands (*muṭippu*) which marks the completion of the scene as well as the end of 'the process of moving from the world of his everyday life into the world of the character he is to portray' (Sowle 1982: 244). He again sprinkles water, then he faces the curtain with flowers in his folded hands. The curtain is removed and he greets the audience (*puṣpa namaskāra*). Then he starts performing a *tēvaram*, or worship. It is an elaborate part describing happiness of the great day and offering to Śrī Nārāyaṇa. *I feel very happy. Why? Because I got up at the sunrise. I took my bath, I prayed, I had my food. I walked to the theatre and went on the stage. I looked around and saw many Brahmins! How are they? Their both-side lineage is perfectly pure. They perform only right and pious deeds, they are well-versed in the Vedas and in the Śāstras. I see these Brahmins with great joy.* The actor renders all these with *abhinaya*.[16] Then he plucks the flowers, walks around the stage, throws up the flowers, salutes and again walks around in a special manner (as is prescribed in the *āṭṭaprakāra*, or acting manual). Facing the stage lamp, the actor—Sūtradhāra—again looks around noticing the Brahmins gathered and enacts *'O Brahmins, may the Protector of Three Worlds, Śrī Nārāyaṇa, protect you! Śrī Nārāyaṇa!'* The ritual dance-steps (*nṛtta* and *nṛtya*) end the *tēvaram* part of the *puṟappāṭu* [30 min.].[17]

After completing the *tēvaram* sequence the actor stops the *miḻāvu* drums to recite the very first verse and line of Sūtradhāra from the *Bālacarita*:

śaṅkhakṣīravapuḥ purā kṛtayuge nāmnā tu Nārāyaṇas-
tretāyāṁ tripadārpitatribhuvano Viṣṇuḥ suvarṇaprabhaḥ.
dūrvāśyāmanibhaḥ sa rāvaṇavadhe Rāmo yuge dvāpare
nityaṁ yo'ñjanasannibhaḥ kaliyuge vaḥ pātu Dāmodaraḥ.[18] (*indala svara*)

Then he enacts it with *abhinaya* and again recites it concluding with the additional line—*sa Dāmodaraḥ nityaṁ vaḥ pātu.* The *muṭippu* tying gesture marks the end of the presentation of the Sūtradhāra's stanza [17 min.].

The next part of the *pu<u>r</u>appāṭu* contains a series of final ritual dance-steps and movements (*nitya kriyas*) accompanied by five invocatory songs, or a*kkittas* [25 min.]. The first three (in fact, 2nd, 3rd and 4th *akkittas* of the whole *pu<u>r</u>appāṭu* performance) are dedicated to Śiva and Pārvatī.[19] They are followed by a fragment called *Keśādipāda*, that is a detailed description ('from head to foot') of the beauty of the ideal hero and heroine, here of Śiva and Pārvatī. Then another Śiva-praising *akkitta* (*māraśarīra* . . . , three verses) comes and finally the last song—*dikpālakavandana*—praising the guardians of the quarters of the sky, and of the stage as well.[20] The *nitya kriyās* finish with a short sequence of swift dance-steps invoking all inhabitants of the Trailokya. Lastly come the *puṣpa namaskāra*, or flower salutation, and the actor's humble prostration towards the *garbhagṛha* with the idol of the temple presiding god.

Then the actor leaves the stage and preceded by the Nampyār carrying the oil lamp and followed by the Naṅṅyār goes to the sanctum sanctorum. He rings the bell in front of it, he prays and gets the *prasāda* from the chief temple priest. He also makes an offering. After that together with his 'court' (spectators may accompany him as well) he circumambulates the temple. He returns to the stage for a moment to close the first-day performance (the *muṭippu* gesture), to pay homage to the stage and to thank the audience. The ringing of the bell marks the very end of the Sūtradhāra's *pu<u>r</u>appāṭu* [2 hours].[21]

The next day is the *nirvahaṇa*, in technical sense it is a flashback. It recalls a story of the past up to the moment the action of a drama (-to-be-presented) starts. Its structure is quite intricate. First there is an *anukrama* portion, or a set of questions consecutively going back into the remote past. Then a *samkṣepa* sequence follows to answer the last *anukrama* question and to come back to the initial one. And finally the *nirvahaṇa* proper begins describing the story directly referring to the drama text. In the *nirvahaṇa* performance the actor acts as a narrator as well as different characters of the story. He never recites the verses. The story is presented in a quite peculiar way. The fragment of it is enacted with *abhinaya* by the

Cākyār and then concluded with the verse relating to it. The verse is recited by the Naṅṅyār. The moment she completes recitation the actor begins enacting the next stanza.

In the debut performance the *nirvahaṇa* presents the story of the Narasiṁha-*avatāra* of Lord Viṣṇu. The nowadays' practice is to enact only two verses describing this episode. Previously ten stanzas (or twelve) were presented.[22] The *nirvahaṇa ślokas* concerning the Narasiṁha-*avatāra* story do not belong to Bhāsa's *Bālacarita*. They can be understood as the Cākyārs' own composition or compilation.

Thus the second-day performance begins with sounding *mil̠āvu* (*mil̠āvu occappeṭuttal*) and a very short *gōṣṭhi* (without the initial *akkitta* song). There is no curtain. The actor enters the stage hiding his face behind an *uttarīya* (a shawl-like garment usually worn cornerwise on the chest) and stands in front of the lamp. He looks at the audience (*sabhānirīkṣaṇa*) and makes 'the lotus salutation' (*kamalaparivartana*).[23] He sits on the stool and starts performing the *anukrama*.[24] *So what is now? Long time ago Śrī Nārāyaṇa, incarnated as Narasiṁha, tore open the chest of Hiraṇyakaśipu and killed him. How did it happen? Before that, how did Śrī Nārāyaṇa incarnate as Narasiṁha? Before that, how did Hiraṇyakaśipu smash the pillar? Before that, how did Hiraṇyakaśipu try to kill his son Prahlāda? Before that, how was Prahlāda born? And before that, how did Śrī Nārāyaṇa take the form of Varāha, kill Hiraṇyākṣa with his tusks and save the Earth? Before that, how did Hiraṇyakaśipu do penance, obtain the boon and torment the Three Worlds? Before that, how were Hiraṇyakaśipu and Hiraṇyākṣa born? How did it all happen?* [20 min.]

The *anukrama* is finished with this question. The actor again makes the lotus salutation and begins the *saṁkṣepa* with an elaborate reply to the last question. *Long time ago Jaya and Vijaya, the doorkeepers of Śrī Nārāyaṇa's abode, refused admission to the sages (Śaunaka and others) who had come to see the Lord. They became angry and cursed the two. That moment Śrī Nārāyaṇa appeared and asked Jaya and Vijaya: 'Do you like to have seven births as my devotees and then attain salvation or to have only three births as my enemies and get salvation?' Both answered: 'O Lord, we would like three births as your enemies and then to attain salvation.' Śrī Nārāyaṇa replied: 'Let it be like that.' He blessed them and disappeared. Jaya and Vijaya were born as demons*

Hiraṇyakaśipu and Hiraṇyākṣa, the sons of Diti. The actor makes another lotus salutation and continues. *Then Hiraṇyākṣa rolled up the Earth in his ear and dragged it to the nether regions (Pātāla) to stay there. Śrī Nārāyaṇa as Varāha killed Hiraṇyākṣa and he brought back the Earth, and protected it for ever.*

The *saṁkṣepa* is over with the last lotus salutation [10 min.] and the final part of the *nirvahaṇa* starts. The actor sits on a stool in the demon pose and enacts how Hiraṇyakaśipu deliberated on his next action. Finally, he decides to go to a lonely place to do penance. He gets up from the stool and walks, jumping (demon's movement) around the stage. It indicates that *Hiraṇyakaśipu reached the Gokarṇa āśrama, took bath, purified himself, did not take any food and began his great penance and meditation on Brahmā.* After enacting this the actor stops the *miḻāvu* and the Naṅṅyār recites the first verse of the *nirvahaṇa*:

diteḥ putro mahāvīryo hiraṇyakaśipuḥ purā.
tapastepe nirāhāro bahuvarṣa sahastrikam.[25] (*antari svara*)

The actor starts enacting the second stanza. He stands on the stool as he plays Brahmā (he puts the *uttarīya* on his left forearm to mark it) in the heaven. *Brahmā is very pleased with Hiraṇyakaśipu's penance. He approaches him and tells him: 'O Hiraṇyakaśipu, I am very much satisfied with your penance. You may ask for any desire you have in your mind.'* The Naṅṅyār recites:

tapasā tasya santuṣṭo Brahmā tam prāha dānavam.
varam varaya bhadram te yatte manasi vartate.[26] (*antari svara*)

The actor again enacts (briefly) Brahmā's contentment. Then he finishes the performance making a tying movement. He makes a final salutation and leaves the stage. Usually the short *araṅṅēṟṟam nirvahaṇa* lasts 45 minutes to one hour. The *nirvahaṇa* can be performed any time of the day, but it should be over just before the last night ceremony in the temple.

Thus the initial—*araṅṅēṟṟam*—performance is completed. From now onwards, the Cākyār boy can regularly present *Kūṭiyāṭṭam* in the *kūttampalam.* He is consecrated to fulfil his religious duty of performing a visual sacrifice (*cākṣuṣa-yajña*). During his life-long acting career he will repeat all rituals and actions preceding his stage debut as they are indispensable before every performance.

To begin the stage activity with the *puṟappāṭu* and *nirvahaṇa* is of symbolic significance. These two, with their structure of the fixed patterns of ritual steps and gestures, are the regular introductory parts of any *Kūṭiyāṭṭam* performance. Thus after presenting his first *puṟappāṭu* and *nirvahaṇa* the young actor is to enact any drama next. What more, this is the Sūtradhāra's *puṟappāṭu*. And Sūtradhāra is a figure of a peculiar, if not of an ambiguous, character. He lives within the drama as well as out of it, he links two worlds, two realities. As a stage manager he initiates a performance (following all preliminaries involved) and introduces a drama he is very much a part of. To enact Sūtradhāra makes an important initial step for the Cākyār. It is meant to be an auspicious start. Since the very beginning the young actor becomes the essence of *nāṭya*.

The *puṟappāṭu* can be treated as an epitome of the art of *Kūṭiyāṭṭam*. One can find in this performance all fundamental constituents for enacting: dance and ritual dance patterns (*nitya kriyas*) to be repeated in many stage presentations, hand gestures and eye movements, so essential for acting (*abhinaya*), recitation with its various modes, a technique of narration. Therefore from the very beginning the actor deals with the whole spectrum of the *Kūṭiyāṭṭam* stage devices. Learning the *puṟappāṭu* is learning *Kūṭiyāṭṭam* as such. There is an important element of preparatory nature, both for the performers and the audience, in the *puṟappāṭu* since 'it provides the opportunity to establish him [the actor], as character and as performer, as a devotional object for the spectator' (Sowle 1982: 252). Devotion is the experience shared by all participants. No wonder that traditionally the *puṟappāṭu* should always be prior to the other parts of the complex *Kūṭiyāṭṭam* performance.

According to the tradition the *araṅṅēṟṟam* performance of the Cākyār always comes before his *upanāyana*, or an initiation ceremony of 'the twice borns' (including a sacred thread investment). Thus first he becomes a member of the acting community, only then of the community of the *dvijas*. Time distance between these two ceremonies can be even of a few years.[27] The *upanayana* is a family event held in the house of a boy.

Though the *araṅṅēṟṟam* performance makes the boy an actor and the *upanayana* a member of the society, there is still one more formality for him to be done. It is a debut Kūttu, or a solo performance. The Cākyār *Kūttu* is the domain of only one character, Vidūṣaka—the Jester. It is the performance by which he can display his wit as well as criticize everyone and everything. He makes a parody of the four *puruṣārthas*, or four aims of human existence. According to the Vidūṣaka they are deception (*vañcana*), enjoyment (*vinoda*), feasting (*aśana*), and flattering service of a king (*rājasevā*). To illustrate his very own interpretation of the four *puruṣārthas* he can use stories and stanzas from different sources. The main medium of the Cākyār *Kūttu* is speech. The Vidūṣaka is first and foremost an extraordinary story-teller and a great exponent of narrative *prabandhas*. It requires considerable knowledge of literary tradition and fluent imagery to perform the *Kūttu*. The invocation verse [to Gaṇeśvara] of the *aśana* (eating) portion is always enacted during the debut *Kūttu*:

yasyāsau prātarāśāya dhaneśo' pi na śaknuyāt
aparicchedyarūpaṁ taṁ gaṇeśvaramupāsmahe.[28]

Then a story chosen in accordance with the family tradition follows. Duration of the performance depends on skills of the young actor; however it is an event of one day only.

In fact, we may say, the initiation process of the Cākyār is only completed when his first *Kūttu* is finished.[29] It took many years from the first lesson when the boy paid homage to his guru offering him a betel leaf, or a customary token *dakṣiṇā*. Gradually he was introduced into new spheres of knowledge and art. Now the Cākyār boy is ready to undertake all stage commitments of his hereditary profession, both the *Kūṭiyāṭṭam* and Cākyār *Kūttu*.

The process described above concerns the members of the traditional Cākyār community. The twentieth century brought changes of different kinds that altered the *Kūṭiyāṭṭam* tradition. They could not be prevented the moment *Kūṭiyāṭṭam* left the temple premises.[30] Nowadays due to altering reality less and less Cākyār boys decide to continue the very demanding family profession. However, even those who choose to follow non-acting career have the *araṅṅēṟṟam* performance with the Sūtradhāra's *puṟappāṭu* and *nirvahaṇa*. It is essential for their 'Cākyārhood', even if the performance is their first and last.[31] And what else, the members of other social groups[32] are allowed to train and perform *Kūṭiyāṭṭam*, and the foreigners[33] as well. Thus it goes without saying that this fact changes a way of teaching and learning (the *gurukula* system is fading) and the whole initiation process culminating in the *araṅṅēṟṟam* performance. In changing circumstances the *araṅṅeṟṟam* performance (still with the same verse of the *Bālacarita*) can be held in a more 'secular' venue, lacking temple-based rituals.[34] This should remain the subject for further research.

NOTES

1. In this paper I focus on a lengthy and detailed description of the traditional initial (*araṅṅēṟṟam*) performance of the Cākyār. The *araṅṅēṟṟam* performance gives a perfect insight into the art of *Kūṭiyāṭṭam.* I refer to my observations and information collected during my research visits to Kerala since 1998 onwards.
2. It is said that some Cākyārs of the past were originally Nampūtiris who due to pollution caused by misdeeds or illicit contacts with lower social strata were excommunicated and lost their high Brahmin status. Though the Nampūtiris, contrary to the Cākyārs, follow a patriarchal system, they were accepted into the Cākyār families and became their regular members to fulfil family religious duty of performing *Kūṭiyāṭṭam* in the temple (Kuṭṭanceri Cākyārs of Nelluvayi).
3. There were works describing the ceremony, unfortunately we have only tiny bits of them: *Naṭābhiṣekavidhi*, *Naṭābhiṣeka*, *Nartana-raṅganavīkṛti.* Referring to the first two, N.P. Unni writes about the golden idol of Śrī Rāma placed on the actor's head, sanctifying the stage stool with Śrirāmamantra, etc. However, this particular *naṭābhiṣeka* ceremony concerns the consecration of an actor playing the role of Rāma. It was performed in the moment when, according to the drama text, Rāma was enthroned as the King of Ayodhya. It is called (*ceriya abhiṣeka*) and it used to be a stage ceremony while enacting the 7th act of the *Pratimānāṭaka* or staging together three dramas constituting the *Mahārāmāyaṇa* drama: *Abhiṣekanāṭaka*, *Āścaryacūḍāmaṇi* and *Pratimānāṭaka.* It is the rule of the past. Unni's statements are not clear enough and can lead to misunderstanding. Sullivan follows Unni and writes about installing the Rāma's idol, etc., during the initiation of an actor. Comp. N.P. Unni, 'Consecration of the Actor in Kerala', *Journal of Kerala Studies*, vol. IV, pts. II and III, June-September 1977, pp. 309-10. N.P. Unni and Bruce M. Sullivan, *The Sun God's Daughter and King Samvarana:Tapatī-Saṁvaraṇa and the Kūṭiyāṭṭam Drama Tradition*, Delhi: Nag Publishers, 1995, p. 46.

4. The temple premises are also purified before the ceremony and the performance.
5. For the sequences of preliminary rituals compare L.S. Rajagopalan, *Kūḍiyāṭṭam: Preliminaries and Performance*, Chennai, The Kuppuswami Sastri Research Institute, 2000, pp. 29-36. The *kalaśam āṭuka*, or pouring the pot of consecrated water, mentioned there (p. 29) is no longer in practice, though it belongs to prescribed rituals.
6. It is not easy to judge why the first stanza of the *Bālacarita* has been chosen for the initiation performance. For the Cākyārs it is just the tradition they follow from generation to generation. However, it could be linked with the development of the bhakti movement. The *Bālacarita* glorifying Lord Kṛṣṇa finds its place in the bhakti emotionalism. As we can see, in the Sūtradhāra's *puṟappāṭu* as well as in the *nirvahaṇa* Lord Nārāyana (Viṣṇu, Kṛṣṇa) is invoked and celebrated. The *puṟappāṭu* part with all its ritual dance sequences and praising songs displays the sentiment of devotion, or bhakti-rasa, and the *nirvahaṇa* narrating the Nārasiṁha-*avatāra* story culminates it.
7. It is obvious that water always symbolized purification. The purificatory rite is repeated before and during the performance a couple of times.
8. Farley Richmond describes it as a rite of separation. Farley Richmond, 'The Rites of Passage and Kūṭiyāṭṭam', *Sangeet Natak Akademi Journal*, no. 50, 1978, p. 29.
9. The *Bālacarita* Sūtradhāra's *purappāṭu* was performed as an annual ritual in the Tirumūḻikuḷam temple (Mūḻikuḷam). The tying of the *cuvapputuṇi* was held there very ceremonially and the worshippers could observe it. It was very auspicious to see that particular moment since it meant that one would see it next year as well.
10. The Sūtradhāra's make-up can be of two kinds. A face is smeared only with clarified butter or a face is painted rose-red colour and a black encircling line frames the face (sometimes, it is a regular *cuṭṭi*, or white three-dimensional frame traditionally made of rice paste, now of white paper). In both cases the black collyrium is put around the eyes and red powder is applied to the lips to make them 'more visible', on the forehead a *svastika* mark (*kuri*) is drawn.
11. In technical sense a *purappāṭu* is the first appearance of Sūtradhāra or any important character of the play on the stage; it is a very formal piece of the *Kūṭiyāṭṭam* performance. In case of the *araṅṅēṟṟam* performance we have the Sthāpanā Sūtradhāra's *puṟappāṭu*, or the formal entry of the Sūtradhāra of the prologue (*sthāpanā*). Traditionally it should always precede presentation of the first act of a drama. Nowadays it becomes a very rare event.
12. There are 14 stanzas whose sequences may differ according to the

Naṅṅyār family tradition. The text of this *akkitta* and of the others sung during the *puṟappāṭu* performance can be found in: Nirmala Paniker, *Nangiar Koothu: The Classical Dance-Theatre of the Nangiar-s*, Irinjalakuda: Natana Kairali, 1992, pp. 84-6.

13. The length of time of successive parts of the *araṅṅēṟṟam* performance refers to the performance-demonstration that took place in the Paluṅkil Temple in Killimaṅgalam on 23 January 2000. It may slightly differ according to the performances; it is just to show an approximate time as well as proportions. In the performance mentioned above Kalāmaṇḍalam Rāma Cākyār played the Sūtradhāra's part.
14. On both sides of the lamp eight auspicious articles (*aṣṭamāṅgalya*) are placed on plantain (banana) leaves: a huge container of unhusked rice, then polished white rice, popped unhusked rice, betel leaves, areca nut, plantain fruit, ripe coconuts, and flowers. The stage can be also decorated with stripes of palm leaves, plantain trees with fruit and bunches of green coconuts. Customarily all these items belong to the Cākyār when the performance is over.
15. '*May Nārasiṁha's plough-sharp nails protect you,*
[the nails that] made Hiraṇyakaśipu's chest dirty with blood.'
16. Enacting with hand-gestures, eye-movements and facial expressions.
17. The fragment of the *āṭṭaprakāra* concerning the *tēvaram* portion was recited to me by Śrī Ammannūr Parameśvara Cākyār (Iriññālakkuṛṭa, February 2000). I thank L.S. Rajagopalan who helped me translating it from Malayalam as well as the *āṭṭaprakāra* describing how to enact the *nirvahaṇa*.
18. '*May the Lord with a body white as milk and shell named Nārāyaṇa long time ago in the Golden Era,*
May Viṣṇu with a complexion shining bright who measured the Three Worlds with three steps in the Silver Era,
May the Lord dark green as durva grass, the Tormentor of Rāvaṇa in the Copper Era,
May Dāmodara black like collyrium in the Iron Era,
[May he] always protect you.'
19. 2nd (*kṣirasāgara* . . . , four verses), 3rd (*ambike girije* . . ., one verse), 4th (*adrimavidruma* . . . , four verses). See Nirmala Paniker, op. cit., pp. 85-6.
20. *Viśvajanādhipa* . . . , twelve verses; the gods praised: Indra, Agni, Yama, Nirṛti, Varuṇa, Vāyu, Vaiśravana (Kubera), Śrī Parameśvara (Śiva), Brahmā, Viṣṇu, Lakṣmī-Bhagavatī, Garuḍa; the two latter are not always invoked.
21. My thanks are due to Heike Moser whose *āṭṭaprākara* for (Ceṭī) *puṟappāṭu* I could use to clarify some technical points.

The actresses (Naṅṅyārs) present the *puṟappāṭu* for their *araṅṅēṟram* as well. Traditionally, it is the *puṟappāṭu* of Ceṭī, or Maid from the second act of the *Subhadrādhanañjaya* by Kulaśekharavarma. Its structure is almost the same (small variations due to the female part) as of the Sūtradhāra's one.

22. It seems that in the twentieth-century only Cākyārs attached to the Mūḻikuḷam temple performed the long *nirvahaṇa* (Mūḻikuḷam Koccukuṭṭan Cākyār, now in Mārgi, Tiruvanantapuram).
23. This is an elaborate salutation in the shape of a revolving lotus flower. It is only presented in the *nirvahaṇa.*
24. The stage presentation of the *nirvahaṇa* described here is in accordance with the acting manuals I collected at Kerala Kalāmaṇḍalam (Ceṟuturuti), Ammannūr Cākyār Maṭham and Natana Kairali (Iriññālakkuṭa).
25. '*Once upon a time Hiraṇyakaśipu—the son of Diti and the great hero – performed a severe and mighty penance, not taking food for many years.*'
26. '*Brahmā pleased with his penance addressed the demon: "You can ask for any boon you wish".*'
27. For example, Śrī Ammannūr Parameśvara Cākyār had his *araṅṅēṟṟam* at the age of 12 and his *upanāyana* at the age of 15; his son, Kalāmaṇḍalam Rāma Cākyār (belonging to the Paiṇkulam Cākyārs), had the *araṅṅēṟṟam* at the age of 11 and the *upanāyana* only a couple of months later.
28. '*The Lord of Treasure [Kubera] was verily unable to provide the [sufficient] morning meal for him; that Gaṇeśvara—the infinite and formless—we praise.*'
29. There is quite a time span between the *araṅṅēṟṟam* performance and the *Kūttu* debut, usually of some years. For example, Mūḻikuḷam Koccukuṭṭan Cākyār had his *araṅṅēṟṟam* at the age of 15, the *upanāyana* at 16 and first *Kūttu* at the age of 18.
30. The first Cākyār who performed outside the temple was Paiṅkulam Rāma Cākyār. In 1949 or 1951 (the year is still a subject of controversy) he gave a solo performance (*Kūttu*); in 1956 he presented *Kūṭiyāṭṭam* with his troupe in Calicut.
31. However, some of them undertake family duty, performing in the hereditary temples besides their other professional activities.
32. The first were A.M. Śivan Nampūtiri, a Brahmin, (1965) and P.N. Girijā, from the Mūssat community, (1971), both students of Paiṅkulam Rāma Cākyār at Keraḷa Kalāmaṇḍalam.
33. Among the first foreigners accepted for the *Kūṭiyāṭṭam* training was Christopher Byrski, a Polish Indologist, who was a student of Māni Mādhava Cākyār (1965). Later on Anna Lopatowska, a Polish actress,

became the first foreign woman allowed to learn *Kūṭiyāṭṭam*; she was a student of Māni Mādhava Cākyār, Kalāmaṇḍalam Śivan Nampūtiri and Kalāmaṇḍalam Girijā (1982). None of them had the *araṅṅēṟṟam* performance.

34. The first place with regularly admitted non-Cākyār (as well as non-Naṅṅyār and non-Nampyār) students is the Keraḷa Kalāmaṇḍalam in Ceṟuturuti where the *araṅṅēṟṟam* performances take place in the Kalāmaṇḍalam *kūttampalam*.

REFERENCES

Paniker, Nirmala, *Nangiar Koothu: The Classical Dance-Theatre of the Nangiar-s*, Irinjalakuda: Natana Kairali, 1992.

Rajagopalan, L.S., *Kūḍiyāṭṭam: Preliminaries and Performance*, Chennai: The Kuppuswami Sastri Research Institute, 2000.

Richmond, Farley, 'The Rites of Passage and *Kūṭiyāṭṭam*', *Sangeet Natak Akademi Journal*, no. 50, 1978, pp. 27-36.

Sowle, John Steven, 'The Traditions, Training, and Performance of Kūṭiyāṭṭam: Sanskrit Drama in South India', unpublished Ph.D. dissertation, University of California, Berkeley, 1982.

Unni, N.P., 'Consecration of the Actor in Kerala', *Journal of Kerala Studies*, vol. IV, pts. II and III, June-September 1977, pp. 305-12.

Unni, N.P. and Bruce M. Sullivan, *The Son God's Daughter and King Saṁvaraṇa: Tapatī-Saṁvaraṇa and the Kūṭiyāṭṭam Drama Tradition*, Delhi: Nag Publishers, 1995.

PART II

The Audience: The Interplay between Performer and Audience

5

Empowering Performance: the Choreographic Techniques of Uday Shankar

Joan L. Erdman

INTRODUCTION

In 1932 and 1933 Uday Shankar and his Hindu dancers and musicians appeared at the International Dance Festival in the United States, and were reviewed in the *Theatre Arts Monthly*,[1] which found them a 'striking feature' of the festival.

> The audience who greeted them expected to find in the highly stylized movement and gesture of this Oriental dance, and the unfamiliar tonalities of Hindu music, a form more satisfying to the curiosity than to the understanding or to aesthetic appreciation. But as so often happens in things that are completely right and true, Shan-Kar's dance did not seem strange at all, only replete with an unknown beauty. The idea of the dance, and its pattern, the movement of the dancer, the costumes, the music, were of a single purpose, easy to enjoy (no author given).

This glowing review, like many other accounts of the Shankar company of the 1930s, recognizes Uday Shankar's successful choreographic techniques, which empower his performances. Unlike what we now refer to as classical Indian dance, which can appear complex and impenetrable, not to mention, for Western audiences and many in India, 'in a foreign language', Shankar's choreography made his programmes accessible to the public. Choreography itself is alien to traditional Indian classical dance, in which, as Kapila Vatsyayan notes:

> The primacy of literature is recognised, the word is illustrated through a

Announcement of Sol Hurok's International Dance Festival, 1932-3, New York (Archives of Bibliotheque de l'opera, Paris).

known pose—a known gesture; traditional mythology forms the content: the objective is to evoke a cohesive harmonious state of being—a mood. In technique each of the styles stresses the significant power: these are strung together in a metrical cycle to emphasize and reinforce a point of timelessness in space. The human form achieves geometrical shapes in time rather than space, for the intricacy of the portions of dance (*nṛtta*) lies in the very fine and deliberate manipulation of rhythm to achieve a series

> of poses. [. . .] Since the dancer is not an individual expressing personal feelings or reactions, movement is stylized in a given framework where geometrical design with a repeated motif is important. [. . .] Choreographical design is limited. (Vatsyayan 1968: 86-7)

But when Uday Shankar started to create dances he was unaware of India's classical dance styles.[2] So he viewed his own tradition analytically and critically, 'outside the prescribed walls of the word-movement relationship and the metrical cycle-movement relationship' (Vatsyayan 1968: 87). His earliest dance creations were based on different assumptions, and he saw movement

> without mimetic significance only: he was looking at dance as a form capable of expression with aid of 'gesture language'. The whole body could be used as all manner of complex relationships between different geometrical motifs, such as the rectangular of Kathakali, the figure of eight, Manipuri, and the triangle of Bharatanatyam, could be established (ibid: 87).

Shankar's dances differed from India's classical styles which were being re-established during the 1930s dance renaissance in India. As a modern dancer, he was focused on 'movement in space rather than circumscribed time' (Vatsyayan 1968: 87). But his presentations were always based on Indian gesture and movement.

Uday Shankar's dance and music performances offered carefully timed and toned access to India's cultural heritage, presented as 'authentic' to audiences already accustomed to European versions of 'oriental dance'.[3] Being an Indian, Shankar was a novelty in the music halls and small venues where he began in Europe, since performing artists from India had previously been only examples of racial difference and oddity. But this handsome young man, direct from partnering prima ballerina Anna Pavlova in her Oriental Impressions 'Radha-Krishna', son of a prime minister of an Indian State, and with a stage presence noted by all who saw him, had international aspirations beyond those of bayaderes and dancing girls of the opera, beyond court dancers and devadasis of India's inherited dance communities. He was a man, not playing to the male gaze, not seductively sensuous or serpentine to masculine tastes, not sexually available to the male voyeur. He was, however, exceptionally attractive to women, fluid in his movements, and, though I won't discuss it in this context, sexually active. After

Uday Shankar as Gandharva, photographed by Lipnitzki, Paris (Vishnudass Shirali Collection).

seeing the provocative, veiled, bare-midriffed, bare-footed (we have forgotten how shocking this was) artistes, who brought oriental themes to European and American stages (Ruth St. Denis, Mata Hari, Loie Fuller, Nyota Inyoka, Tortola Valencia and many others), audiences found Shankar's performances at first peculiar, suited only to music halls where many curiosities were available, and then, with his company after 1931, delightful, engaging and spiritual. The key to this transformation in reception was Shankar's choreography, presented with masterful showmanship, and movements presumably Indian.

Shankar's showmanship and creative genius produced stunning effects for Western audiences, which were equally powerful in his home country.

> He created a sensation in Paris with his first stage performance which introduced the Shankar *genre* of creative Indian dance. It also generated a significant awakening throughout India on his first tour later in 1933. It was also the same awakening through America in 1932. (Shirali 1978: 25)

All of this was created by Uday Shankar out of a somewhat improbable *bricolage* of experience, knowledge and advice, which in the genius of his imaginings became a modern style for Indian dance. It is notable that as a child Uday was a poor student, skipping classes in both his childhood venues of the princely state of Jhalawar in Rajputana and his mother's natal village Nasrathpur, near Varanasi. He preferred to climb trees, watch the Chamars dance, and ride his bicycle full-speed in the lanes of his town. But he was attracted to three things: magical illusions, mechanical ingenuity (he once took apart an automobile and reassembled it) and visual

Sketch by Uday Shankar from a 1962 programme brochure for his new ballet, *Rhythm of Life* (Benade Collection, Chicago).

arts (a teacher finally caught his attention with books of European art). His father, Shyam Shankar Chaudhry, a distinguished Sanskrit scholar, and advisor to the Maharaj Rana of Jhalawar, despaired of his son's future, and eventually enrolled him in the J.J. School of Arts in Bombay, to study painting. In 1920 Shyam Shankar brought twenty-year-old Uday to London to help with charity productions for Indian soldiers injured in the Great War, and to study at the Royal College of Arts. Together they produced a Tagore musical (*The Great Moghul's Chamber of Dreams*) at Covent Garden in May 1923, and other shows. Shankar arranged magical effects, produced an ambience of dreamland, and danced, relying on what he had learned in Jhalawar and from Kukubai, a renowned Kathak dancer in the court of the Jhalawar Maharaj Rana who had been brought to London with his entourage. Intrigued by the staging of the shows, Uday Shankar was given charge of lighting and stage management.

When prima ballerina Anna Pavlova (who resided in London in Hampstead Heath) was looking for an Indian to help her create dances for her Oriental Impressions in 1923, she heard about this handsome young man. She asked him to tea at her Ivy House residence, and then invited him to join her in this venture. Though the artist (later Sir) William Rothenstein, then head of the Royal College of Arts, was reluctant to let a star pupil move from fine to performing arts, he bowed to Pavlova's enthusiasm, and Uday Shankar became a choreographer and dancer. Sources for Shankar's early choreographies were sculptures and paintings in the British Museum and Kensington Museum collections; his painter's understanding of the use of light and tableau transmigrated to his new medium.

Finding London producers uninterested in his dance after he left Pavlova in 1924, Shankar migrated, with two partners formerly in the ballet company, to Paris, and gradually developed his own dance style. According to Vatsyayan,

> . . . Uday Shankar's association with Pavlova led to two results: on the one hand he had made it possible to look at movement in Indian dance analytically and to use music to a dancer's purpose; on the other hand he had been made aware of an existing body of dance tradition which presented a challenge to the artist and the innovator. (Vatsyayan 1968: 88)

Uday Shankar as Krishna and ballerina
Anna Pavlova as Radha in his 1923 choreography.

After years of struggle in Paris, dancing in cabarets, and training a French partner whom he named Simkie, Shankar decided to form his own company. Hearing that there was in London a musician from Bombay's Gandharva Mahavidyalaya, Vishnudass Shirali, he invited him to Paris to be interviewed for the post of music director. Shirali accepted, and waited until Shankar returned from travel in India, with another music director, Timir Baran, who also joined the company. But it was Shirali who stayed with Shankar the longest, and worked with him on creating music for his ballets, his solos, and his Uday Shankar India Dance Centre at Almora in India's Himalayan foothills, which was founded in 1939.

Vishnudass Shirali was trained by Pandit Vishnu Digambar Paluskar, one of India's great music reformers in the early twentieth century. Shirali divides Shankar's contribution into three stages: the formative stage (1928-38), the fully matured stage (1939-44), and the diversified creative stage (1945-70) (Shirali 1978: 23). In order to discuss choreographic techniques of Shankar, this paper addresses mainly the formative stage of Shankar's choreography, and especially the development of choreographic techniques for his Uday Shankar Company of Hindu Dancers and Musicians starting in 1930 in Paris. I argue that there were three key characteristics of Uday Shankar's choreographic techniques which empowered his performances: being Indian (and using this identity), sophisticated technical values and use of illusion in staging, and authenticity (as a relative term) claimed and perceived. In addition, and related to the first characteristic, is the role played by European perceptions of India and Indians in the period between the great wars of the twentieth century.

Being Indian

In the West dance performances were not considered ritually powerful in the 1920s and 1930s. Oriental dance performers, ranging from seductive floozies to elegantly draped artistes in dramatic tableau, were presented in music halls and on concert dance stages as secular artistes, entertaining and beautiful, sensuous and sinuous (sometimes representing a challenge to Christian morality). Whatever they were, they were *not* Easterners, nor were they always entertaining; sometimes they were exotic, sometimes erotic, and at other times elegantly contorted. Their movements were designed to evoke the East, and sometimes provoke a spirituality of the senses, but it was an act, not 'the real thing'.

Ruth St. Denis, in a 1927 article entitled 'The Dance of the East' (written after her 1926-7 tour of the East, including India, China, Japan, Indonesia), sums up the limits of Westerners in Eastern dance.

Nyota Inyoko, 'Oriental dance', Paris.
Signed for Uday Shankar in the 1930s.

Mata Hari in Indian dress, some time after
her 1906 debut at the Musée Guimet, Paris.

> I would like to say, though, in reference to the study of Eastern dancing, that it has always been my principle to select and adapt only those ideas and that technique which seem applicable to our Western life. From a philosophical standpoint, I feel that we must do this with increasing care. There are, in Eastern cultures, certain ancient and dynamic truths, universal in their application, which point to that balance which only a greater attention on our part to things of the spirit can give. But in our attempt to arrive at these great truths we must not confuse our religious or artistic minds by blindly accepting all details of Eastern 'Mystery' and 'Atmosphere'.[4]

Western dramatic theory made the stage 'unreal' and its inhabitants, as actors or dancers, not what they pretended to be. The audience was expected to suspend disbelief long enough to enjoy the spectacle or entertainment, rather than witness or participate in an empowering event. Spiritual power was invoked but not intrinsic; such empowerment awaited a person and personality endowed with spirituality by birth: an authentic Easterner (one with the credentials and class status for the Western concert stage).

Even Uday Shankar, a young art student and co-producer with his father of Indian programmes, was unaware of what his Indian culture offered. In the 1920s, when Uday Shankar first came to Europe, and was sent to explore Indian art holdings at the British Museum by his mentor at the Royal College of Arts, William Rothenstein,

> . . . the industrialized West represented an apex of experience and artistic advancement to many Indian nationals. To learn from a Westerner that Indian culture had as much, if not more, to offer was a startling revelation. (Abrahams 1986: 37)

Rothenstein's long involvement with Indian art and culture had led to an understanding of its antiquity and wisdom, as well as its aesthetics. He knew that for Shankar, these aesthetic representations were the most direct way to convince his youthful student that he could find inspiration in his own culture's artworks. Rothenstein was, of course, concerned with Uday Shankar's development as a painter, but the lessons learned at the Royal College of Arts were reinforced when Pavlova suggested he explore and present dances of his own culture to Western audiences. For Shankar, painting and dance were facets of analogous cultural significance.

Rothenstein was only the first to point out to the young art student that India had its own artistic values. Later Pavlova told him, when Shankar asked to learn male ballet roles as he toured North America with her company in 1924, that he should go back to his own country and bring authentic Indian dance to the West.[5] And Swiss sculptress Alice Boner, who became his patron in the mid-1920s, recognized the importance of exploring arts and dance in India as a prelude to forming a company of Indian dancers and musicians to tour in the West. As an Indian, Shankar was charged with the responsibility of representing his culture (not yet a nation) for the Western public. His very being Indian, his personal interests and experiences, his aesthetic inclinations and the tenor of his times and context came together, and led to choreographic techniques which maximized this advantage and his success.

Shankar's initial European audiences for his own dances were Parisians, who had a facility for experiencing the 'other' with more than delight and curiosity. They welcomed access to the sensibilities of Eastern cultures at exhibitions and expositions and on their stages, which included, at the 1925 *Exhibition des Arts Décoratifs*, both Josephine Baker and Uday Shankar. For German audiences, Uday Shankar was the embodied representation of a high philosophical system reiterated in dance art as a living exemplar of the ideals of this ancient tradition.[6] Uday Shankar's performances in the 1920s and 1930s changed viewers' attitudes towards India and its arts from astonishment to adulation, from puzzlement to comprehension, and from considering this dance an art of dubious status to one of impressive achievement. What Diaghilev had done for Russian ballet, Shankar did for Indian dance.

Amala Devi,[7] writing about the discovery of the Indian dance in the Occident, said that it was from the appearance of Uday Shankar[8] that the public could finally discover the art of the dance of India. Speaking of Shankar's appearance at the *Exposition des Arts Décoratifs* in 1925, where Shankar gave his first recitals in Paris, she says:

> These spectacles left unforgettable memories in the lovers of the dance of this period, and it merits rewriting what was written then by the poet Rene Daumal: '. . . the beauty of these musicians and these dancers, their attitudes of soulful attention, of presence, of continual reality, the truth of

all this, the complete absence of decoration, or powder in the eyes, this splendid sound which is made together, this dance movement and the moving music which reiterates exactly the duration and significance of time eternal, all this marvel, I believe still to have dreamed, as a dream of a very old state of man very wise and very beautiful, of an age of gold.'[9]

The beliefs and prejudices of his times constitute a context essential to understanding the power of performances of the Uday Shankar Company of Hindu Musicians and Dancers. Power is always contextual, and it is not only time and place, but also perceptions, expectations, and attitudes which bring a context into existence. The power of his performances arose from dances, dancing and dancers arranged to communicate, educate, entertain, and evoke another way of being. Efficacy is based on the extent to which Shankar as a choreographer was successful in coordinating all of these aspects into a seamless whole, experienced by the audience members as a life-changing event. European audiences in the 1930s played a role in empowering Uday Shankar's performances, both through their construction of 'the Orient' as a site evoking an exotic erotic, and their perception of Uday Shankar as a 'divine dancer'[10] of Eastern sensibilities.

Staging the Dance Performances

What is choreography? For Shankar and other modern dancers it was not only making dances, but also producing them and presenting them in a programme. His choreography was an assemblage of concepts and techniques, including casting (and Uday was the singular star), visualization, technical values (including sound and lighting), timing (duration, sequence), citing, movement, patterns, blocking, programme sequence and composition, costumes and jewellery, and, first of all, a good idea or concept. Balance and harmony were important, as were beauty and ambience. In fact, his paintings had given him ideas for dance. In dance choreography is quotational: it illustrates visually what is the case as does a painting or sculpture. But it also effects the qualities of media: dances are moving images, paintings or sculptures in motion. Further, dancers are living beings, endowed with personalities (or obscuring them), and their presence presents possibilities available neither to still art nor to electronic or mechanical media.

Sketch by Uday Shankar for his *Rhythm of Life* ballet, from a 1962 programme brochure (Benade Collection, Chicago).

First a sketcher and painter, Uday Shankar 'loved movement'. Whatever I imagined in my own body movement I gave to the subjects in my own paintings. I gave them dramatic movement.'[11] He was inspired with themes and ideas from his 1930 India tour, and could visualize whole dances, as his music director Shirali notes:

He had, or must have foreseen what would be the final results with the dance and music rehearsals or had a concrete mental picture before his rehearsals had started. He was absolutely sure of the final results. His decade long stay in Europe and America in the twenties and the varied experiences he had in the entertainment world gave him a complete assurance and confidence of what the ultimate results were going to be. (Shirali 1978: 26)

The young choreographer was aware of the balances and subtleties of the erotic in his art. Pavlova's longtime dance partner Algeranoff describes the love idyll of Krishna and Radha, which Shankar choreographed for and danced with Pavlova:

Pavlova was all submission, and Shan-Kar, handsome, masculine and graceful, was indeed Krishna, the Eternal Lover. He carried a flute to show

Poster for performance by Uday Shankar's troupe,
Paris, by Alice Boner, 1931.

that he was appearing in the guise of a cowherd. The costumes were made of genuine Indian fabrics, and we were all convinced that this new addition to the repertoire would be an overwhelming success. (Algeranoff 1957: 105)

Shankar also learned the business and technical aspects of dance productions. In 1924 Algeranoff had been given the task of educating the youthful Indian dancer in the customs and habits of Pavlova's company by Monsieur Dandre, the ballerina's husband and manager. When Shankar formed his first company in the1930s, his co-founder Alice Boner, a Swiss sculptor, managed the business requirements of his company. She contributed significant financial support, created

Uday Shankar (centre) with Rajendra Shankar, Kanaklata, Simkie, and Debendra Shankar in Sword Dance, *c.* 1933 (Alice Boner Collection, Zurich).

costumes and headdresses, produced publicity materials, and used her excellent social connections to generate performance venues and audiences.[12]

But most significant in Shankar's staging was his powerful showmanship, remarked upon in reviews both at the time and in memories of his performances. The *New York Times* dance critic, Anna Kisselgoff, writing in 1985 on the occasion of the Festival of India in the United States, recollects seeing Uday Shankar and his company in New York as a child:

> The 'theater' of Uday Shankar was what dazzled a child's eye—the dance-dramas enhanced by astute lighting and costumes as well as formally composed presentations that took advantage of the Western world's proscenium space. Above all, there was Uday Shankar's own spellbinding presence. There seems no better way to describe his eloquent masculinity than to say he looked beautiful. Or if you prefer, like Mr. Fernau Hall, you could call it sex appeal. (Kisselgoff 1985)

La Meri (Russell Meriwether Hughes) saw Uday Shankar for the first time, in the 1930s, in Paris, and later wrote that

When the quiet curtains opened, Shankar and his partner Simkie were seated upstage center in gold, and glittering with jewels, as Siva and his consort Parvati. Across the back of the stage his orchestra was seated, in pristine white dhotis and velvet jackets. Beside them stood their shining, exotic instruments: *veena*, *tampoura*, *sitar*, *sarode*, *esraj*, *flutes*, *sur-bahar*, *sarangi*, many drums of various shapes and sizes, and the fearsome *bhudaka* [large *sarangi*?]. The dances were varied, brilliant and totally expressive. 'The Snake-Charmer,' 'the Sword Dance,' and a succession of aspects of the God-Head ('Indra,' 'Kartikeyya,' 'Ganesh') followed each other with breathtaking beauty. (La Meri 1984: 12)

The created impression was astonishing and elegant, carefully structured to induce the audience into another world, that of India's ancient and exotic culture, rather than its economic or political problems and issues. For Europeans the arts were about beauty and light, high principles, grace and urbanity, ancient and mysterious cultures, with allegories from which Westerners could fathom profound and vanishing knowledge. Constructed realities, on stage, were central to Shankar's conveyance of his art's potential fulfilment of these criteria.

Uday Shankar with Simkie, Kanaklata and Rajendra Shankar. Music director Vishnudass Shirali is to Shankar's right, and brother Ravi Shankar behind Uday to his left. *c.* 1932, Paris (Amala Shankar Collection, Calcutta).

Writers in India also noted Shankar's positioning as the forerunner of a renaissance in Indian dance. Suresh Awasthi, in an article on 'Indian Ballet—a critical survey', calls Uday Shankar 'the pioneer of modern ballet' which he created on the basis of the indigenous dance-forms and his study of Indian sculpture and painting'.

> His ballets on modern themes like *Rhythm of Life* and *Labour and Machinery* are powerful interpretations of contemporary life through the medium of gesture, sound and music. Uday Shankar's ballets present a unique synthesis of several dance-forms and styles. He gave to the orchestral music a deep dramatic purpose and significance. He utilized Western presentational material and techniques and recreated traditional theatre costumes and masks making them theatrically more effective. (Awasthi 1963: 9)

While Shankar created short dances like Pavlova's *divertissements*, as a choreographer he took ballet as his major form, but his was not a toe-danced, tutu and character-costumed Western ballet emanating from the opera stages. Rather, he adapted choreographic elements of Western ballet to invoke an Indian form which integrated the staging of Kathakali dance-drama with Western realizations of dance on stage. One of his partners, Zohra Segal, defines the essential character of choreography for Shankar's ballets, specifying as central the harmony of relationships rather than repetition of movement or accumulation of melody.

> Unless a group or solo dancer forms the supplement to the other, it becomes repetitive and meaningless. One set of movements should form a complementary pattern to the other, highlighting and emphasizing the main motif in balancing form and not repeating it or imitating it in a weaker strain. Each set of movements should have their own pattern, their own voice and never be the weaker echo of the soloist. Unless this principle is followed, the work becomes a group dance and will never achieve the character of a ballet. (Segal 1963: 24)

For Shankar ballet was an international form, not a style of dancing, and its structure allowed him to create meaning through dance while preserving the Indian character of the motions. His experiences were cross-cultural, but his aesthetics and training emphasized the arts of India.

Programmes were carefully assembled to balance dance and music, duets and solos and ballets, energy and calmness, excitement and serenity. At the premiere of the new company on 3 March 1931

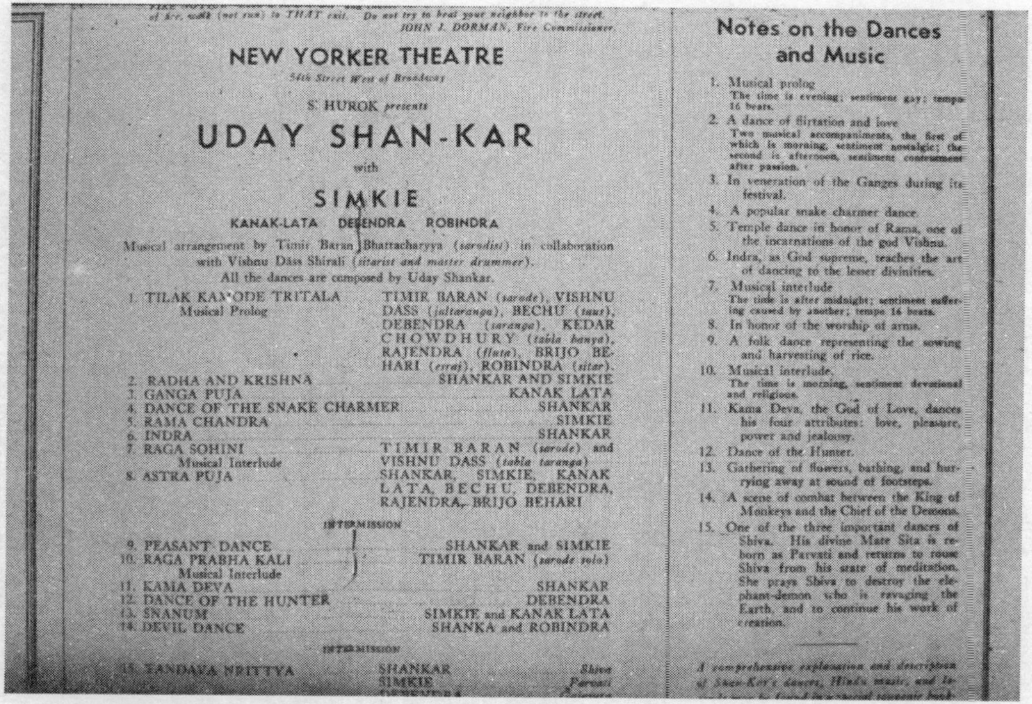
JOHN J. DORMAN, Fire Commissioner

NEW YORKER THEATRE
54th Street West of Broadway

S. HUROK presents

UDAY SHAN-KAR

with

SIMKIE

KANAK-LATA DEBENDRA ROBINDRA

Musical arrangement by Timir Baran Bhattacharyya (sarodist) in collaboration with Vishnu Dass Shirali (sitarist and master drummer).
All the dances are composed by Uday Shankar.

1. TILAK KAMODE TRITALA — TIMIR BARAN (sarode), VISHNU DASS (jaltaranga), BECHU (taus), DEBENDRA (saranga), KEDAR CHOWDHURY (tabla banya), RAJENDRA (flute), BRIJO BEHARI (esraj), ROBINDRA (sitar).
Musical Prolog
2. RADHA AND KRISHNA — SHANKAR AND SIMKIE
3. GANGA PUJA — KANAK LATA
4. DANCE OF THE SNAKE CHARMER — SHANKAR
5. RAMA CHANDRA — SIMKIE
6. INDRA — SHANKAR
7. RAGA SOHINI — TIMIR BARAN (sarode) and VISHNU DASS (tabla taranga)
Musical Interlude
8. ASTRA PUJA — SHANKAR, SIMKIE, KANAK LATA, BECHU, DEBENDRA, RAJENDRA, BRIJO BEHARI

INTERMISSION

9. PEASANT DANCE — SHANKAR and SIMKIE
10. RAGA PRABHA KALI — TIMIR BARAN (sarode solo)
Musical Interlude
11. KAMA DEVA — SHANKAR
12. DANCE OF THE HUNTER — DEBENDRA
13. SNANUM — SIMKIE and KANAK LATA
14. DEVIL DANCE — SHANKA and ROBINDRA

INTERMISSION

15. TANDAVA NRITTYA — SHANKAR Shiva, SIMKIE Parvati

Notes on the Dances and Music

1. Musical prolog
The time is evening; sentiment gay; tempo 16 beats.
2. A dance of flirtation and love
Two musical accompaniments, the first of which is morning, sentiment nostalgic; the second is afternoon, sentiment contentment after passion.
3. In veneration of the Ganges during its festival.
4. A popular snake charmer dance.
5. Temple dance in honor of Rama, one of the incarnations of the god Vishnu.
6. Indra, as God supreme, teaches the art of dancing to the lesser divinities.
7. Musical interlude
The time is after midnight; sentiment suffering caused by another; tempo 16 beats.
8. In honor of the worship of arms.
9. A folk dance representing the sowing and harvesting of rice.
10. Musical interlude.
The time is morning, sentiment devotional and religious.
11. Kama Deva, the God of Love, dances his four attributes: love, pleasure, power and jealousy.
12. Dance of the Hunter.
13. Gathering of flowers, bathing, and hurrying away at sound of footsteps.
14. A scene of combat between the King of Monkeys and the Chief of the Demons.
15. One of the three important dances of Shiva. His divine Mate Sita is reborn as Parvati and returns to rouse Shiva from his state of meditation. She prays Shiva to destroy the elephant-demon who is ravaging the Earth, and to continue his work of creation.

A comprehensive explanation and description of Shan-Kar's dances, Hindu music, and ...

Programme for the New Yorker Theatre, December 1932 and January 1933, with notes (Alice Boner Collection, Zurich).

at the Theatre des Champs Elysees in Paris, 'Uday Shan-Kar et Simkie avec Orchestre Hindoues' offered nine dances and seven classical Indian music works.[13] Eight dances were performed by Shankar and Simkie: *Indra*, *Gandharva*, *Danse Nuptiale*, *Danse du Printemps*, *Danse du Temple*, *Danse Paysanne*, *Radha et Krishna*, and *Danse du Sabre*. Of these three were solos for Shankar, two solos for Simkie, and three duets for this pair. The ninth item was a ballet *Tandava Nrittya* with Shankar as Shiva, Simkie as Parvati, Kanaklata as the maid-servant Joya, and Debendra as the villainous elephant-demon Gajasur.[14] *Tandava Nrittya*, his first new choreography after his travels in India, incorporated *Kathakali hasta mudras* (hand gestures) in his own unique style, imaginative and free-form interpretations, effective despite their inauthenticity to the classical structure (Abrahams 1986: 120). Other elements were borrowed from Kathakali, including an introductory half-curtain, wide-skirted costume, massive headdress, and an elaborate make-up for Gajasura. Both Alice Boner and Uday Shankar had been deeply affected by their encounter with Kathakali during their 1930 India tour, and the *Tandava Nrittya* ballet, Shankar's first narrative choreography for his new company, reflected his expanding knowledge of India's dance cultures.[15] As Shirali noted later,

Uday Shankar with Simkie and Debendra as Gajasura in *Tandava Nrittya* ballet, *c.* 1932 (Amala Shankar Collection, Kolkata).

> . . . It was amazing how he conceived the idea and was able to create the dance of *Tandava Nritya* [sic] without having any training in classical Indian dancing. By merely seeing, observing and imagining a static pose of *Tandava*, he created a cycle of reasonable imaginative movements and brought out the concept of Shiva's dance. (Shirali 1978: 24)

The great impresario Sol Hurok, though not particularly enamored of the 'ethnic' dance of Shankar, still recognized his potential for commercial success:

> Possessed of a fine scholarship, a magnificent three-fold talent as producer, choreographer, and dancer-musician, he also possessed to a remarkable degree a sense of theatre showmanship and an intuition that enabled him to grasp and quickly understand the space-time limitation of the non-oriental (commercial) theatre. (Hurok 1953: 54)

In Shankar's choreography, music was 'vision of sound, not necessarily a musical sound, but a totality of sound-effects of an entirely new dimension' (Shirali 1978: 25). Typical was the music for *Tandava Nrittya*:

> The idea had come to him from a number of sources. During his childhood in Jhalawar, Nasratpur, Ghazipur and Varanasi, he had occasions to witness *Nautanki* and other folk dances with their drums, *dholak, duff* and *chang*. He was also familiar with the general effect created by the sounds of *nagada*, bells, *jhaanj, manjira* and singing in the morning and evening *arati*s at the Kashi Viswanath Shrine and other temples and on different ghats on the Ganga in Varanasi; the music of *shehnai* accompanied by *chowgahada* and other drums. (Shirali 1978: 25)

When he had studied art in Bombay in 1918-20, he attended music classes and concerts at the music school Gandharva Maha Vidyalaya, hearing and viewing many instruments played by students:

> Finally, there was the effect created in his mind by the *Kathakali* drummers, the terrific consequent result created by *chenda* and *maddalam* players accompanied by other drums and cymbals, on his Kerala tour of 1930. All this had made a deep and lasting impression on his creative mind, which in turn was developed during his work in Paris, and on which he experimented. (Shirali 1978: 26)

He also used his creative powers and imagination to make dance movements based on temple sculptures or traditional paintings, starting from the pose, and conjuring the motion which might lead to it, and that which followed thereafter. These became the basis for the Shankarstyle movements and exercises.

In the mid-1930s, during two long stays at Dartington Hall at the invitation of patrons Leonard and Dorothy Elmhirst, Shankar met and observed Michael Chekhov, author of *To the Actor: On the Technique of Acting*,[16] who had opened a drama school there in 1936 at the Elmhirsts' invitation. Chekhov's teaching methods and technique influenced Shankar, especially later in developing curriculum and classes at his Almora Centre. Another influence was Guru Sankaran Namboodri, whose performance of Kathakali Shankar saw in Kerala, and whom he brought to Calcutta during a rehearsal period there.[17]

According to Ruth Abrahams,

> The basic element in Shankar's musical compositions was the envisioned sound image or, as Shirali had identified it, the 'musical visualization'. [from her Shirali interview, July 15, 1980]. Through the process of experimentation, Shankar would present his choreographic theme, then proceed to explain, through a variety of metaphorical descriptions and vocal examples, the effect he wanted to produce in the music.
> An example of this process is illustrated in the creation of the work, 'Karthikeya' [sic]. 'Karthikeya' was the first new work Shankar composed upon his return to Calcutta, in 1934. Its inspiration was drawn from Shankar's new relationship with Guru Shankaran Namboodiri . . . , the Kathakali master of Vallathol's school, the *Kerala Kalamandalum* [*sic*].[18] (Abrahams 1986: 141-2.)[19]

In creating his solo dance *Kartikeyya* and the ballet *Nritya Dwandva*, with the guidance of Guru Shankaran Namboodri in Calcutta in 1935,[20]

> The dance and music composition progressed simultaneously in order to get the maximum coordinated impact of the theme. (Shirali 1978: 28)

Total effect was the guiding principle of Shankar's choreographic imagination.

Another balance was the choice of company dancers. When, for a later American tour, he added Madhavan (replacing two of his brothers who had returned to India), and Zohra (who replaced Kanaklata), Shankar assured that there was no competition with his starring role from their performances. Madhavan had a completely different aspect than Shankar, according to dance critic John Martin.

> [Madhavan] is at the very opposite end of the scale from Shankar in almost every way, substituting for the subtlety, the serenity, the nobility of the older dancer a vital kind of nervous energy and an earthier temperature. (Martin 1937)

These few examples illustrate Shankar's mastery of staging techniques and the logistics of operating a dance company. But it was his presentations themselves that persuaded audiences and critics of his authenticity.

In the Name of the Authentic

For Shankar, combining his own life with dance and its access to the divine spirit became a creed, evident to those who saw his performances:

> 'Dance is my life. When I dance I am nearer to God; I am not myself'. (Kisselgoff 1985)

Many dancers had presented 'oriental dances' by the time Uday Shankar arrived on the scene in Europe. Shankar was, however, more authentic, in the sense that he was an Indian by birth, and his presentation of the Hindu divine seemed, to Europeans at the time, a representation of the 'real thing', a god dancing before their eyes. He was a singular illustration of the East's spirituality; his beauty and choreographic techniques were accepted as a mission to bring the Orient to a Western audience directly and in person, rather than through a mediator, like St. Denis. From the audience perspective, rampant orientalism, European translations of Indian texts, the widespread influence of Theosophical beliefs, and a fascination with dance as an aesthetic medium of personal representation, abstract but also concrete, were all contexts for Shankar's empowerment.

'Authenticity' is a contested term, and particularly in the creative arts. But the designation and perception of an artform as 'authentic' is a matter of historical record, distinctive in its temporal and spatial location.[21] Shankar employed creativity and imagination in his depictions, never presenting himself as a traditional or classical artiste. For example, 'Kartikeyya', only four minutes long, combined the theme of a warrior-god preparing to fight a demon with his own interpretion of Kathakali style, yet

The result was not a mere literal representation of the story with an expected focus on the battle (an ideal dramatic conflict), but rather a portrait of qualities of psychological preparation needed for impending confrontation. Based on just a few elemental *Kathakali* movements taught to Shankar by Namboodiri and the sculptural images carved into the walls at Ellora, 'Kartikeyya' possessed a profound spiritualism not previously found in Shankar's choreography. (Abrahams 1986:143)

Thus 'authenticity' was not only being Indian, but also conveying an Indianness based on this ancient culture's representations, its complex heritage and the delicately textured emotions of its dramatic arts.

The English writer Fernau Hall (in an article on the 1983 Uday Utsav celebrated in New Delhi which marked the sixtieth anniversary of Shankar's professional debut) cites one further context, noting that Shankar was a modern dancer, like his contemporaries, Mary Wigman and Martha Graham. Like most modern dancers, Shankar is credited by *New York Times* dance critic Anna Kisselgoff with creating his own dance technique:

. . . he was essentially a creative artist, not content with fixed forms. At the same time he drew consistently from India's mythological themes and from the classical dance imagery of the subcontinent. 'The task he set himself as an Indian modern dancer with roots both in India and the West was an excruciatingly difficult one.' (Kisselgoff 1985)[22]

She notes, citing Fernau Hall.

A review of the September 1923 Covent Garden (London) presentation of Pavlova's *Oriental Impressions*, which included the *Radha-Krishna* Pavlova/Shankar duet, suggests Westerners' difficulties in deciding what criteria to use in judging authenticity.

"These [dances] were given to music by Miss Commalata Bannerjee," *The Times* went on, "music in which long and wandering dance tunes with percussive accents and drones cleverly devised in Western orchestration produce effects which belong to the East. Again, we are not prepared to say how far either the stage designs or the music are actual reproductions and how far imaginative, but the second of the two, *Krishna and Radha*, certainly produced its own imaginative atmosphere". (in Algeranoff 1957: 107-08)

Zohra Segal, now a famed actress who was a member of Uday

Shankar's company from 1935 to 1942, sums up Shankar's dancing as 'the expression of all ecstasy, all excitement, all passion.'

> The tradition of a nation is steeped in its people and from time to time a genius is born who expresses its characteristic virtue in a new form. This, at first, is so alien to what has already existed, that the guardians of its [sic] tradition think it is a 'foreign element, borrowed style, an imitative art,' whereas in reality it is a fresh expression of art. Such a genius is Uday Shankar who danced without knowing any dancing and created a style all his own. His early creations were composed in solitude, without any previous training in dancing, out of the sheer necessity for expression. They were raw and naive but the spark was there. It was later when he studied under various Gurus who, in spite of their own traditional training, appreciated and recognised his genius, that Uday Shankar reached his true forte, the Indian Ballet. He was the first dancer to bring choreography to Indian dancing, to give it a third dimension, to introduce harmony in movement. (Segal 1963: 22)
>
> The West applauded Shankar's work as the best from the East as, in reality, it was. The East applauded or condemned it for being ultra-modern which it was in comparison to the existing traditional forms. (Segal 1963: 23)

To be Indian and not reiterate traditional arts, but take them to a new embodiment was Shankar's forte and a sign of his courage. A 1933 letter from Rabindranath Tagore to Uday Shankar tried to define Shankar's project and inspiration:

> Genius is defined in our language as the power that unfolds ever new possibilities in the revolution of beauty and truth. It is because we are sure of your genius that we hope your creations will not be a mere imitation of the past nor burdened with narrow conventions of provincialism. Greatness in all its different manifestations has discontent for its guide in the path to victory where there are triumphant arches but never to stop at, merely to pass through. . . . (Cited in Segal 1963: 23)

Shankar's choreographic techniques foregrounded his Indianness, offered technical sophistication, and a repertoire based on Indian life and stories of the gods. His authenticity must be assessed relative to his times and the Oriental dancers he followed to Western stages. His art was not a recovery of the ancient, but a movement towards the new, imbued with the philosophical and sacred teachings of his Indian culture. The initial success he had in India, followed by indigenous purist critique of his innovations,[23] or so-called deviation from 'classical dance', are emblematic of the occidentalism which swept India in its pathway to nationhood and world acceptance as an ancient civilization.

FINALE

When Chicago anthropologist Milton Singer suggested that the study of religious and cultural performance provided access to the 'elementary constituents of culture and the ultimate units of observation', he encompassed the spiritual and the mundane in a single category. In Uday Shankar's cultural performances, what constituted an 'art', a dance performance, for Western audiences, was transformed by its 'authentic' Eastern origins into a spiritual and empowering experience. Singer also produced an anthropological argument that has relevance both for researchers and for the public. Cultural performances give the public access to their own, or another culture's, values. In a like manner, Uday Shankar, using a keenly-honed sense of showmanship to entertain, and a public anticipation of Eastern spirituality to empower, offered audio and visual evidence to observers of his representations of India. His choreographic techniques convinced audiences that India's culture had an aesthetic beauty and Indians had an efficacy in their notions of value; his personal charisma and elegance brought heightened praise for India's arts.

Thus during the period between the twentieth century's world wars, Uday Shankar was the ultimate representative of India's dance culture in Europe, in the United States, and in India's major cities. In 1982, in response to a query in the *New York Times*, Oneita McCulloch wrote to me about her first experience of Uday Shankar:

> In 1937, my brother and I came into Calcutta. As we were registering at the Great Eastern, I asked the clerk 'Where can we see some Indian dancing?' He paused, then said, 'Sorry, Shankar is in Bombay.'
>
> After visiting the great cities of India and houseboating in Kashmir, we got to Bombay where I asked the clerk at the Taj Mahal Hotel the same question, 'Where can we see some Indian dancing?' He replied, 'Sorry, Madam, Shankar is in Paris.'

In due course, we reached Paris—one traveled by boat in those days. The concierge at the Raphael gave the address of a theater where Shankar was appearing. However, when the curtain went up, the performance was a French play. We consulted the ticket seller who directed us up an outside staircase to a little small theater, a sort of barnacle on the main house. Some charming Indian music and a few dancers—and then Shankar came on, a resplendent, playful half-god, taut, flowing, centered, radiant. You know the beautiful adornments culminating in a glorious headdress, a bursting seventh chakra—all one piece with that splendid body. His energy heightened with each appearance, flowing, quivering, vibrating. Then, a motionless classic attitude, Lasar! The atmosphere split. It changed my life. I never was the same. (personal communication, 29, May 1982)

Shankar's choreographic techniques translated himself, his staging and his message into a powerful synthesis of dancer, dancing and the dance, suggesting a model for performance analysis that includes who and what is presented, how it is projected, and what it all means. Personal charisma, precise and disciplined staging, and the subtlety of deep meanings are a powerful combination.

NOTES

1. 'The World and the Theatre', in *Theatre Arts Monthly* XVII, 2 (February 1933): 94. N.S.
2. 'Classical' is a term which was not used in regard to India's dance arts in the 1920s and early 1930s, until attempts were made to describe this sophisticated ancient kinetic medium in terms which conveyed to non-Indians, and to Indians who saw their dance arts as improper, that India's dance was and could be a highly admired evidence of their ancient culture. For a discussion of Uday Shankar's 'authenticity' see Erdman 1998.
3. For a discussion of Uday Shankar's performances and their relation to earlier versions of India's dance, see Erdman1987.
4. St. Denis 1927. The issue also includes articles on Ted Shawn, Michio Ito, Pavlova, Isadora Duncan, Ruth Page, Marie Taglioni, Michel Fokine, Ida Rubenstein and dances of the Pueblo Indians, all current performers.
5. In a presented paper, 'Uday Shankar: The European Years' (October 12, 1983), Ruth K. Abrahams (see her dissertation, 'The Life and Art of Uday Shankar', 1986) pointed out that while touring with Pavlova in 1924 in the United States, Shankar trained and rehearsed the company in the dances he choreographed, and also observed backstage, lighting,

designs of technical and mechanical aspects, and had an interest in 'systems of created illusion', as a magician. She notes that Shankar was presented by Ananda Coomaraswamy with a copy of his *Mirror of Gesture* (1917) during his U.S. tour with Pavlova. A famous Shiva image in the Madras Museum influenced Uday to 'invent on that Nataraj', imagining how the figure got to that pose and moved from it. When Uday Shankar met Alice Boner in Switzerland in 1926 during his tour, she, like Rothenstein and Pavlova, urged him to consider his own country's more authentic models. Yet even earlier reviews focused on Uday's Indianness; he was assumed to be doing Indian dance.

6. My thanks to Heike Moser for her summary translation of an article on Uday Shankar by Hermann and Marianne Aubel (1932).
7. An editor's note in *La Recherche en Danse*, numero 2 (1983), says that Amala Devi began her studies of dance in 1949 with Simkie, then with Shrimati Malashri Sen of Kalakshetra in Madras, and Shri Ganesan of the company of Guru Gopinath. In 1952 she was invited to join Ram Gopal's company, and she studied Bharata Natyam in the Pandanallur style with Ram Gopal, disciple of Pandanallur Meenakshi Sundaram Pillai. After nine years with Ram Gopal's company, she spent eight years in India where she collaborated in the direction of the Academy of Music and Dance, 'Bharat Sangeet Vidya Bhavan', founded in Bombay in 1964 by Master N. Moinuddin Dagar, returning in 1969 to Paris to teach Bharata Natyam at Ecole de Danse de L'Opera de Paris until 1972. Currently she teaches a course in Indian dance (Bharata Natyam) at University of Paris-Sorbonne (Paris IV).
8. Amala Devi states this occurred in 1919, but in that year Uday Shankar was still in India, leaving for London only in 1920. Perhaps she meant 1929.
9. Amala Devi 1983. Translation by Joan Erdman. Amala Devi, 'La découverte de la danse indienne en Occident', pp. 107-11, in *La Recherche en Danse*, Numero 2, 1983.
10. Uday Shankar was not the first or only artist perceived as a 'divine dancer' in the early twentieth century. As Suzanne Shelton Buckley so clearly points out in her book on Ruth St. Denis, this American dancer was also designated as a 'divine dancer', for her depictions of the sacred in her dances of the East, and for her dancing itself, which brought to the European stage a highly idealized display of Oriental insights.
11. Cited in Abrahams 1986: 38 note 1 from a 1973 interview with Mohan Khokar.
12. According to Ruth Abrahams,

    [Alice Boner] created costumes, subsidized orchestrations, booked performances throughout eastern and western Europe, wrote press releases and other publicity materials, including publicly published statements on Indian dance directly attributed to Shankar. Her guidance broadened Shankar's perception of the role of art and of the artist, and impressed upon him the need for integrity in the creative process. . . . (Abrahams 1986: 95)

However, it is also true that Shankar spent lavishly on his productions, and regarded it as the artist's prerogative to care more for the effect the performances created than for balancing cost and income, or 'the bottom line'.

13. The programme is reproduced in Khokar 1983, pp. 60-1.
14. Based on Khokar 1983 and lists in Abrahams 1986: 119.
15. Alice Boner wrote about these encounters in her diary, published as *Indien, mein Indien: Tagebuch einer Reise* (1984) after her death with the guidance of her sister Georgette Boner.
16. Chekhov, *To the Actor: On the Technique of Acting* (1953), with a preface by Yul Brynner, deals with the actor's body and psychology, imagination and the incorporation of images, improvisation and ensemble, atmosphere and individual feelings, the psychological gesture, character and characterization, creative individuality, composition of performance, different types of performances, etc.
17. Shankar performed in Calcutta in July 1933 (Madan's Theatre and University Institute), in March 1935 at the Old Empire Theatre, and stayed in Calcutta in that summer for rehearsals and then performances at the Madan Theatre and Chaya Theatre in August and September, before embarking on a tour to Rangoon, Singapore, and Kuala Lumpur in September and October of 1935. The revised choreography for *Kartikeyya* was most likely done during a rehearsal period in 1934, or in 1935, as suggested by Shirali. Abrahams says it was during his 1934 Calcutta stay, in a gap between touring in the United States, England and France, and an India tour beginning in February 1935.
18. Shankar met Shankaran Namboodiri when he first saw him perform in Trivandrum, Kerala, during a visit there in 1934 (Khokar 1983: 83). It appears that Shankaran Namboodiri was not at Kerala Kalamandalam when Shankar and Boner visited there earlier, as Alice Boner does not name him amongst those they knew there. Abrahams provides no evidence of her assertion that Shankar met Shankaran Namboodiri earlier at Kerala Kalamandalam.
19. Though Abrahams designates Shankaran Namboodiri as 'the *Kathakali* master of Vallathol's school, the Kerala Kalamandalum [*sic*]' (Abrahams 1986: 142) and as Kathakali's 'leading exponent', suggesting that Shankar studied with him at Vallathol's Kerala Kalamandalam

(Abrahams 1986: 103), it does not appear that Shankaran Namboodiri was at the Kalamandalam at that time, nor that he taught Shankar on his initial trip in 1930. See note above. Furthermore, Shankar had already performed a dance called 'Kartikeyya' in 1933, which is listed in Abrahams' Choreochronology (Abrahams 1986: 248), so his later work with Shankaran Namboodiri was a revision of an already existing piece.

20. This is the year given by Shirali (1978: 28), who kept a calendar of performances and a diary of events.
21. For a discussion of Uday Shankar's 'authenticity' see Erdman 1998.
22. Kisselgoff 1985 contains the quote from Fernau Hall, 'Honoring Uday Shankar', in *Dance Chronicle* 7, 3.
23. John Martin addressed some of this critique in a 1934 review, describing two articles by G.K. Seshagiri in the Indian journal *Sound and Shadow* and Shankar's reply in *The Bombay Chronicle.* Seshagiri objects to the popularity of Shankar's performances, his breaches of 'the canons of the Indian classic dance', and says some of Shankar's dances are just 'glorified forms of street dances'. Shankar points out that traditions are always changing, and 'All that we could properly do was to adopt the best from the past and mould it to the requirements of our present-day life.' He accepts Seshagiri's characterization of some of his dances as a compliment. The article is reprinted in Khokar 1983: 78.

REFERENCES

Abrahams, Ruth K., 'The Life and Art of Uday Shankar', Ph.D. Dissertation, New York University, 1986.

Algeranoff, H., *My Years With Pavlova*, Melbourne, London, Toronto: William Heinemann Ltd, 1957.

Aubel, Hermann and Marianne, *Die Bedeutung der alten indischen Tanzkultur. Betrachtungen und Bilder zum Auftreten der Hindu-Tanzgruppe Uday Shan-Kar*, Verlag der Arbeitsgemeinschaft für Natur und Völkerkunde, 1932.

Awasthi, Suresh, 'Indian Ballet—A Critical Survey', in *Natya* (dance, drama and ballet issue), New Delhi, 7, 4 (December 1963): 8-11.

Boner, Alice, *Indien, mein Indien. Tagebuch einer Reise*, Zürich and Stuttgart: Werner Classen Verlag, 1984.

Chekhov, Michael, *To the Actor: On the Technique of Acting*, New York: Harper & Bros, 1953.

Devi, Amala, 'La découverte de la danse indienne en Occident', pp. 107-11, in *La Recherche en Danse*, Numero 2, 1983.

Erdman, Joan L., 'Performance as Translation: Uday Shankar in the West', *The Drama Review* 31, 1 (T113), Spring 1987, pp. 64-88.

Hurok, Sol, *Sol Hurok Presents: A Memoir of the Dance World*, New York: Hermitage House, 1953, p. 54, cited in Abrahams 1986: 126.

Khokar, Mohan, *His Dance, His Life: A Portrait of Uday Shankar*, New Delhi: Himalayan Books, 1983.

Kisselgoff, Anna, 'One of India's Early Ambassadors', in *The New York Times*, 6 October 1985.

La Meri, 'Uday Shankar', in *Arabesque* X, 11 (July-August 1984): 12-13, 20-1.

Martin, John, 'The Dance: Art of India. Shan-Kar Criticized as Departing From the Canons of the Indian Classic Dance', *The New York Times*, 4 February 1934.

Segal, Zohra, 'Shankar's Ballet', in *Natya* 7, 4 (December 1963): 22-4, 100.

Shirali, Vishnudass, 'Experiments in Music and Dance: My Years with Uday Shankar', in *Journal of the Sangeet Natak Akademi* 48 (April-June 1978): 23-9.

Vatsyayan, Kapila, 'Is There an Indian Modern Dance?', in *Journal of the Sangeet Natak Akademi* 7 (January-March 1968): 85-91.

6

Between Performance and Competence: Exploring the Idea of Audience According to Indian Classical Views*

Mirella Lingorska

In the 30 years after its emergence in the 1970s the so-called 'performance perspective' opened up many fruitful approaches to the investigation of Indian drama. The increased attention to the stage happening, to the training and specific techniques of the actors, developed a sensitivity towards the tangibility and the direct appeal of the dramatic representation. The interpretation of the dramatic event as a total interdependent involvement of performers and audience in the construction of a unique time-space continuum with specific emotional charge suggested a parallel treatment of performativity in religious rituals and stage plays.

Since different kinds of social communicative phenomena are marked by distinct time and space coordinates, a prescribed course of acts and fixed roles of performers and audience (Brückner, Schömbucher 2003: 599), an intellectual challenge arises to 'approach the genres of theatre, dance, music, sports, and ritual as a single, coherent group, as performances' (Schechner, Appel 1991: 3). Seeking general principles—so-called 'universals of performance' (Turner 1991)—, anthropologists are inclined to stress the ritual potential of stage plays and, *vice versa*, to emphasize the

* I am indebted to Prof. Klaus Butzenberger for his commentary and helpful suggestions on a draft of this paper and to Anne Katrin Madlung and Diarmuid Ó Shéaghdha for their improving my English style. My colleague Dr. Galina Rousseva I thank for one useful hint on the performative practice of the *rasika sampradāya* in the *bhakti* movement.

dramatic acting and show aspects of cult scenarios. With regard to Indological subjects this uniform approach was partly supported by the strong exploration of dramaturgical elements in some religious communities[1] in contemporary India and partly by some views of authoritative ancient treatises on drama, for example the *Nāṭyaśāstra* (*NS*). However, a closer observation reveals that this inclination towards a common underlying structure exposes only certain features of the phenomena in view, representing them in the rather fundamental frame of research, which distinguishes the 'performance turn' in the humanities. The performance-focused view concentrates mainly on aspects of production and takes into consideration those parts of the teaching texts which concern staging, training of the actors, musical accompaniment, costumes and make-up. This approach easily creates the impression of different genres of the dramatic performance—be it a classical court-play, an enacted rite, a devotional celebration, or a possession cult (Richmond, Swann, Zarilli 1990 : 5)—sharing one and the same essential characteristic. Parallel to this more technical approach pragmatically different cultural enterprises are basically treated in sociological terms as means for dissolving social tensions, rearranging power resources, creating or recreating identity and integrity (Turner 1991). This emphasis on 'doing things' defines the performativistic reply to the constructivistic approach of the previous, more conventional, methodology, which dealt primarily with abstract ideas and notions about the world rather than with actions in the world. And still, a cautious examination would be worth considering as to how far the adaptation of this basically anthropological approach is useful with regard to the classical Indian drama. What we have today is the dramatic poetry as a text[2] since we do not know exactly how the plays were performed in the frame for which they were composed. It is also obvious that the present-day heir of the classical Sanskrit drama, *Kūṭiyaṭṭam*, presents considerable deviations in the mode of performance. Notwithstanding the effects of the fresh insight into the living dramaturgical practice and contemporary devotional or semi-devotional performances, a question may be asked about the scope and the applicability of the broad anthropological notion of performativity regarding such paradigmatic examples of the Sanskrit classical stage play as *nāṭaka* or *prakaraṇa*, which are treated in the *NS* as drama *par excellence*.

Yet another point is whether we would be able to view in a non-trivial way the best extant examples of classical *nāṭaka* and *prakaraṇa* as social dramas or redressive rituals from the Turnerian point of view. How much does the Sanskrit court play resemble this kind of universal rituals?

Undoubtedly, there are some constitutive elements which are shared by the stage play and the ritual performance. There is first of all the participation in a more or less vivid way in a world different from the everyday involvement of the participants, which includes a temporary change of roles and adopting of others' personalities, suspension of disbelief in certain causal relations, increased sensitivity to emotional appeals and physical stimuli. Nonetheless, the question still arises as to whether these similarities entitle us to consider the phenomena of ritual and various kinds of aesthetic performances as belonging to one and the same coherent generic group. In this article I will concentrate on the dramaturgical event, which is mainly discussed in the *NS* and which is rather remote from the purely folk traditions or purely temple or devotional performances. In this respect the role of the audience will be of utmost importance because it is obviously treated as a constituent and at the same time distinct part of the single performance. At least in the later texts of the theoretical tradition the boundary between the public and the performers of an aesthetic play is more noticeable than in any ritual or ritual-like performance.

An 'agent-centred view' (Baumann, Briggs 1990), focusing on the audience as the second constituent of a performance, reveals that it is exactly the epistemological shift of the interpretation angle which changes the expectations towards, and the practical benefits from, different kinds of performances. According to its knowledge about the intention behind the actual event the audience behaves and experiences it differently and even performances with 'blurred edges' tend in the final analysis to get the one or the other definition. Thus we expect to find in the extant descriptions of the classical audience some specific attitudes or behaviour patterns, which would allow us to distinguish a ritual context from an aesthetic one.

The dramaturgical teaching of the *NS*, which had won the recognition of some performatologists (i.e. Schechner 1991: 33) due to its contributions to the bodily representation of certain deep mental processes, has given rise to the notion of the qualified spectator embedded in a more or less social frame. Later commentators developed this notion into a full-fledged and highly esteemed theory of classical audience where desirable qualities and appropriate behaviour are described in a remarkably keen manner. The attention of the theoreticians shifted from the social parameters to psychologically defined characteristics of cognitive processes and emotional experiences. A closer look at the texts of this theoretical tradition would allow, if not a full insight into the way the Sanskrit drama was staged and appreciated in the classical period, at least a glimpse of the notion of an aesthetic stage play as it was promoted by some of the most inspired philosophers and literary critics of medieval India. As often happens in the history of ancient Indian literature, many of the original texts are now lost and can be traced only through scattered quotations or later exponents. For our present purpose we will rely on the Kashmiri commentator of the *NS*, Abhinavagupta, who in the eleventh century amalgamated some of the most important previous views into a very influential theory on aesthetic reception.[3]

In contradistinction to the view of the later commentators the *NS* mentions common unsophisticated people among the public of a stage play.

> Hence, because the objects of knowledge are so numerous, and the span of life is so brief, the inferior common persons in an assembly which consists of the superior, the middling and the inferior members, cannot be expected to appreciate the performance of the superior ones.[4]

> Young people are pleased in seeing [the representation of] love, the learned a reference to some [religious or philosophic] doctrine, the seekers of money [topics of] wealth, and the passionless topics of liberation.

> Heroic persons are always pleased with the Odious and the Terrible Sentiments, the personal combats and battles, and the old people with tales of virtue and Puraṇic legends. And the common women, children and the uncultured men (*mūrkha*) are always delighted with the Comic situations and [remarkable] Costumes and Make-up.[5]

Parallel to various psychological types, the *NS* enumerates members of different social classes and groups, each of them bearing a specific response to the dramatic representation.

> This [i.e. *nāṭya*, M.L.] teaches duty to those who go against duty, love to those who are eager for its fulfilment, and it chastises those who are ill-

bred or unruly, promotes self-restraint in those who are disciplined, gives courage to cowards, energy to heroic persons, enlightens men of poor intellect and gives wisdom to the learned.[6]

In a more specific passage the *NS* makes a difference between the common public and the experts as it exposes among the spectators (*prekṣaka*) the circle of arbiters (*prāśnika*) and exalts their theoretical knowledge.

In order to assess the virtues and blemishes of a dramatic performance arbiters should be employed possessing the following qualifications:

Those who are possessed of [good] character, high birth, quiet behaviour and learning, are desirous of fame, virtue, are impartial, advanced in age, proficient in drama in all its six limbs, alert, honest, unaffected by passion, expert in playing the four kinds of musical instruments, very virtuous, acquainted with the costumes and make-up, the rules of dialects, the four kinds of histrionic representation i.e. speech, emotion, gesture and dress, grammar, prosody, and various [other] śāstras, are experts in different arts and crafts, and have fine sense of the sentiments and the psychological states, should be made spectators[7] in witnessing a drama.[8]

The later view of the ideal spectator deviates from the apparent democratic idea of the *NS*. At first we come across a very fundamental characteristic of the classical audience: its sound and thorough knowledge of the contents and the technical intricacies of the stage performance, which facilitates not only the appreciation but also the evaluation of the play. The typical distinction between the hermetic information of the experts of rituals[9] and the unarticulated sensitivity of the neophytes does not hold in the case of the aesthetic drama. The competence of the public is an essential prerequisite for the enjoyment of the play.

The evaluation through the competent audience is particularly important if the winner of a contest has to be chosen or the merits of a piece has to be pointed out in order to honour and reward the actors. The ascetic Kauśikī praises the performance of Mālavikā in Kālidāsa's *Mālavikāgnimitram* in the terms of the well-established theory of the representation of aesthetic emotions (*rasa*), and it is her knowledge of the *Nāṭyaśāstra*, for which she is vested by the king with the responsibility of being an arbiter in the controversy between the drama instructors Gaṇadāsa and Haradatta:

The proper sense was outlined with gestures in accordance with the words, The posture of the feet was following the time, there was congruity towards the *rasa*-s,

The hands performed in gentle manner, one feeling replaced the other in the continuance of variations according to the context, and yet the structure of the *rāga* stayed the same.[10]

Such estimation derives its legitimacy from the rules of the *śāstra* and uses its technical vocabulary to such a high degree that sometimes it is not intelligible on its own. In a famous novel of the eighth century, prince Samarabhaṭa evaluates the presentation of the play *Ratnāvalī* by a women ensemble in the following enigmatic expression:[11]

This performance rests on the seven, its essence are the six, it is embodied, it covers the three authorities, and is superb owing to the excess of *sattva*, it should be accomplished by the three, which are presented both in separate and united manner, its actions are delicate and energetic, it is entertaining through affecting emotions and has various styles; it is accomplished with feelings, which are to be taken up and be quitted or held in-between. No *laya*-time is dropped by the musician who is presenting a variety of deep and sweet tones connected with manifold variations of the powerful melodies. The recitation is blameless in all vernaculars, most charming, uninterrupted, endowed with words of precise phonetic articulation whose meaning was clearly expressed with an intonation full of *rasa*-s. The singing of the singers is excellent, with accomplished homogeneity, endowed with sounds full of *rasa*, its dynamical structure well balanced with regard to the crescendo and decrescendo, combined with the slow, middle, and fast time-intervals. The mimesis attended fame through the achievement of the double success based on the whole complex of composition, informative costumes, plot sections and distinct characters. This is the way how the harem women of King Nahuṣa were taught by Bharata's sons—I think that even they did not access such complete excellency in the drama. Interwoven with well-arranged *sandhi*-s, furnished with real, 'golden', actors, perceived by skilful experts the brilliant *Ratnāvalī* shines in an excessive way.[12]

As the competence of the experts was rooted in the theoretical rules of the *śāstra*-s, it was finally their judgement which fixed the value of a play.[13] In the process of time a respectful address to the esteemed audience developed to a standard formula in the prologue of the play. We come across it in Kālidāsa's plays as well as in later authors like Bhavabhūti.[14] It is usually the *sūtradhāra* who addresses the audience in a very respectful way. Thus in *Śākuntalam* he confesses to his wife:

Director: Truth to tell, my dear,
Till the critics applaud
I despise my skill as a director.[15]

Or even more pathetic in Viśākhadatta's *Mudrārākṣasam*:

Director: And indeed it gives me the greatest pleasure to perform before so discriminating a public, for
Even a fool can farm
When he alights on fertile ground.
Rich crops have no need
Of merit of the sower.[16]

In Bhavabhūti's *Mālatīmādhavam* it is the assistant of the *sūtradhāra* who is expressing the obliging desire of the public to see something special:

Assistant: Sir, the assembly of the wise and learned is asking to be entertained with a new comedy *prakaraṇa*, and we are at a loss for a work which meets their requirements.[17]

The later, more elitist, concept of an art connoisseur reflects presumably the change of view on drama as poetry. The experts of poetry are enjoying an elevated status because of their highly cultivated taste. In a typically circular manner it is presupposed that their specific sensibility evolves from the constant occupation with poetry. In their mind, which is bright like a mirror as a result of poetic exercise and practice, they bear the ability to identify with the objects of description.[18] Thus a *sahṛdaya*'s heart stays in accord with the emotions of a poem. The connoisseur creates the context of the described situation by supplying through his imagination what happened before, after that, etc.

Visual subjects are turning more and more into elaborated *śravya-kāvya*. It was Ānandavardhana who incorporated the unique ability of a stage play to present emotional, directly perceptible, phenomena in the apparatus of recited poetry. Thus the central aesthetic phenomenon of a play is found with dramatic vividness in poems as well.[19] The *rasa*-s emerge when the content of a poem brings about a kind of perception, which resembles a direct perception.[20]

Hence, another defining feature of the ritual—its immediate presence, its physical process from stage to stage—turns out irrelevant with regard to the aesthetic appreciation as the latter evolves from a mental vision.

In the case of a poem, an empathy (*tanmayībhāva*) to the hero is born in the heart of the listener according to the emotional determinants, consequents, etc. Owing to this consent of the heart (*hṛdayasaṁvāda*) the consciousness behaves as totally immersed in the emotional core of the poem. But this absorbing state of consciousness, which is comparable to a direct perception, does not arise in everyone through merely hearing a poem. In the case of a stage play, however, the pragmatic propensity of the spectators is suppressed under the influence of fascinating songs, music, etc.[21] There are connoisseurs who possess by nature hearts like spotless mirrors, whose mind is therefore not under the influence of desires, infatuation and anger, which are typical of everyday life. By merely hearing a play the totality of *rasa* is clearly perceived by them as being dramatically marked by an amazement, based on generalized relishment. But there are also others who are different; for them Bharata created first the rules for the actors, etc., in order to make available an amazement, which has the nature of a direct perception, and, second, the rules for the songs, etc., in order to break the knots of the heart, which is filled with its own anger and sorrow.[22] From this perspective a visual performance appears a less sophisticated art meant for simpler minds.[23] The theatrical conventions (*nāṭyadharmin*-s) covering peculiar dialects, dances, the stage, the back stage, divisions, etc., provide for a restriction on the scope of any practical implications.[24] The audience's feelings about the stage events are not of an ordinary nature and differ from reactions to similar circumstances if they were to happen outside the theatre. Personal affairs do not have any scope in the fictional frame of the stage play. The delight evolving from the delectation of the aesthetic emotions has nothing to do with the private joy of receiving a son, for example.[25] The happening on the stage should not be confused with real life, as in this case the spectator would be afflicted by his personal concerns, an identification would be precluded and neither delight nor education would arise.[26] This process of de-contextualization occurs in ritual setting, too, but there the objectives of the participants are explicitly personal. In the ritual context an experiencer is segregated as a social element in order to be reintegrated in the social frame with changed personal status. In the drama the experiencer is not segregated at all but just confronted with a development of situations, which do not bear any causal relevance to his personal circumstances. What the spectator gets from the play is not a changed attitude of the community towards him or her but an intellectual insight in the way the world goes on and an aesthetic delight of the representation of probable world's affairs.

In order to establish the emotional climax of the performance—the tasting of the aesthetic emotion—the dramatic text spreads out a progressive series of events (*arthaprakṛti*-s). These stages of action are, however, not strictly defined as are the stages of a ritual. They just build up the narrative structure and the fundamentals of the fictional world, which serves as a screen for the transcended self-reflection of the spectator. A sympathetic response can thus emerge when a certain correspondence exists between the represented events and the world's affairs (*lokasāmānya-vastuviśaya*). Since the drama is a representation of the world with its different divisions and inhabitants, less probable, unworldly, events of divine nature should be at least censored by traditional belief.[27] A true connoisseur has to merge his or her own self into the represented events without wholly suppressing his on her individual cognition or recognition of certain behaviour types but by taking the enacted world as contingently true.

Thus, swinging between a carefully cultivated knowledge vested in competent interpretation on the one side and the hypnotic illusion of the play on the other side, the spectator has the unique opportunity to perceive—without being directly involved—the fruits of other people's deeds and share other people's lives save for the logical consequences of their decisions. Under the perspective of the aesthetic perception this ought to be acknowledged as the essential wonder of dramatic experience: the direct tasting of an abstract, ideational content on the base of a mental unification (*sādhāraṇībhāva*) without any differentiation between own and other's or time and space. When a qualified connoisseur perceives the lines of the famous verse of the hunted deer in *Śākuntalam*:

Gracefully arching his neck to throw a glance at our pursuing chariot,
Then drawing his hindquarters into his forepart in terror of our arrows,
Strewing his track with half-chewed grass from a mouth slackened in weariness,
In his bounds he travels the sky and hardly touches the earth.[28]

—a clear apprehension arises in his mind, which is not subjected to the distinction of time and space, where neither the deer nor the pursuer are perceived as qualified and real entities and no sensation related to oneself or someone else appears but the very fear—unrelated to time and space—which is just evolving before one's eyes and is directly penetrating the heart. In this presentation of fear the self is neither completely eclipsed nor specifically manifested.[29]

In this relation of mutual obstruction between reality and poetical fiction, where the poetry is restricting the world and the world is censoring the poetry, in this realm, where one is not delimited but included both in the real and the poetic sphere, where the distinctions of time, space and cognizing subject completely vanish, the state of universalization (*sādhāraṇībhāva*) is promoted in the best way.[30]

The meaning of *sādhāraṇīkaraṇa* as universalization emphasizes the universal dimension in which the aesthetic drama is transmitting its insight into the human nature. The transcendent effect of poetry is thus best described not by the notion of liminality but by the notion of lysis. The transcendental effect of the aesthetic experience does not involve a change of the identity or the personal circumstances of the members of the public and thus it is substantially different from the *transitio vitae* of the ritual shift (Michaels 1999: 29).

The self-reflection of the spectator is not an individual self-cognition but an epistemological prospect towards the essential *conditio humana*.[31]

This is the axiomatic limit, which restricts the number of the *rasa*-s or the underlying *sthāyībhāva*-s, the variety of the phenomenological world is contracted to a minimum of cognizable, concise patterns. The characters of the play also transcend their prefigured worldly patterns and rise to the level of types described in the usual meticulous manner like other elements of the play in the *śāstra*. Despite their depicting worldly interactions they too are condensed around standard situations and it is the poetic speech, rather than the dramatic actions, that drives the plot and furnishes the *rasa*-s.[32] At that level, when the personal, private context begins to fade, a certain compactness (*ekaghanatā*) of all participants emerges. It develops in accordance with endless previous impressions (*vāsanā*), thus variegating in a corresponding manner their consciousness and accomplishing the experience of the *rasa*-s.[33] The equation of the time and space coordinates and the collective attention directed to the same object provides presumably for the apparently liturgical atmosphere of the stage drama. This state of mind, which is free from any obstacles, is called amazement (*camatkāra*) or absorption (*nirveśa*), relishment (*rasanā*), savouring (*āsvādana*), enjoyment (*bhoga*), accomplishment (*samāpatti*), dissolution (*laya*) and rest (*viśrānti*).[34] In its climax the aesthetic rapture is approximate (*savidha*) to the tasting of the impersonal *brahman*. Nevertheless, it is still specific and has to be differentiated from the mystical ecstasy of a yogi because of the maintenance of the intellectual ability to reflect upon this experience as connected with certain sensual objects.[35] Besides, the yogic *pratyakṣa* is considered to be attained only through hard effort and particular concentration, while the experience of *rasa* is accomplished with delight and pours out over the *sahṛdaya* like the cow's milk for her calf.[36]

The outlined theory of the audience certainly possesses a restricted historical scope and reflects the distinctive public of the Sanskrit classical court play. In this sense it is not informative about other kinds of evaluation, i.e. in the frame of folk theatre or in devotional ceremonies. The exposition of Abhinavagupta, which is utilized here, includes some earlier, now lost, aesthetic theories and derives its material from the artificial stage production of individual professional authors and not from the epic or folk tradition. A Turnerian approach (which lays much stress on sociological embedment) might of course view these artefacts as redressive rituals or might emphasize their instructional impact and de- and re-constructive power towards familial and social configurations.[37] The point, however, is that the Indian classical tradition, without completely neglecting such implications, defines the essence of the performed or literary dramas in purely aesthetic terms, i.e. the achievement of universal human knowledge without any practical demand. The actual self-detachment and total impracticability of this aesthetic transcendence of the participant distinguishes the theatre setting from the ritual one, where the beneficiary is undergoing a change of his or her individual personality or at least social status.[38] In contradistinction to the ritual passage this experience—while sharing some common features with it—does not transform the real status of the participants. It has its purpose in itself (Zweckmäβigkeit ohne Zweck). In this sense this approach towards the stage play reveals it as a completely artlike art (Kaprow 1990; quoted from Baumann & Briggs 1990).

As already mentioned, it is primarily the text as *kāvya*—since *nāṭya* is *kāvya par excellence*—which has a prominent role in the Sanskrit stage play. In this respect we could look for a frame in which to apply the notion of performativity on the linguistic level of speech usage and its specific effects in drama. But a closer look at the metatexts, which rule and set up the scenic speech and action, reveals that this kind of fictional language is even more 'grammaticalized' than common language, as it is not 'naturally born' in an independent, universally shared, world outside the stage. The genuine emotive charge of the dramatic speech cannot be treated like a speech-act in terms of the classical speech-act theory as it is filtered by the literary or theatrical conventions in order to become an aesthetic, and not an ordinary, emotion. This conclusion is not a step backwards to the traditionalistic view of poetic language as secondary, derivative, and etiolated, rather it stresses the different, non-pragmatic, off-world communication evolving from dramatic speech.

In conclusion, it appears that the notion of performativity, which could be very useful for folk theatre or devotional celebrations,[39] tends to shrink to the conventional aspects of staging and enactment in the case of classical aesthetic plays.

Similar to the diffuse atmosphere of religious liturgical performances (Mayerhoff 1991: 247) contemporary experiments with various, more or less innovative, dramatic forms try to stir the boundaries between the dramatic plot and the 'ordinary mundane world' but the main interest of the classical aesthetic attitude seems to lie in the physical distinction of the two. Of course, there are no limits for interpreting or rather deconstructing ancient Sanskrit plays in different hermeneutical frames, and for such purposes the postulates of the autochthonous criticism are not binding at all.[40] In this case they would just blossom out into new flowers under the rays of different suns.[41]

NOTES

1. One characteristic example is the enactment of mythological subjects in some *bhakti* performances where the aesthetic emotion is experienced as an instrument for approaching god or the so-called paradigmatic individual. Cf. David Haberman, *Acting as a Way of Salvation*, New York: Oxford University Press, 1988. Cf. also Richard Schechner, 'Ramlila of Ramnagar: An Introduction', in *Performative Circumstances from the Avant Garde to Ramlila*, Calcutta: Seagull Books, 1983.
2. About ritual elements in the composition of a play as one part of the performance tradition on the one hand and about drama as a literary text on the other cf. Herman Tieken, 'The Pūrvaraṅga, the Prastāvanā, and the Sthāpaka', in *WZKS*, 45, 2001, pp. 91-124, reference to pp. 117-18.
3. The sketch of the classical views on audience presented in this paper is drawn mainly from Abhinavagupta's commentaries on the *NS*, the *Abhinavabhāratī* (= *Abh*), and on the *Dhvanyāloka*, the *Dhvanyālokalocana* (= *Dal*). I am quoting by page and line from the *Abh* after the Baroda edition of the *NS* 1956[2] (= *GOS*) and from the *Dal* after the 1965 Chowkhamba edition of the text with the Hindi commentary of Jagannātha Pāṭhaka. As the exposition of Abhinavagupta is extremely technical and syntactically complicated, I decided for a clearer transmission of his main points to paraphrase the relevant Sanskrit passages. For those who want to go into detail I always point to the translation of Gnoli or Masson and Patwardhan wherever there is a correspondence. Cf. Gnoli, R., *The Aesthetic Experience According to Abhinavagupta*. Varanasi 1968[2] (Chowkhamba Sanskrit Studies LXII); Masson, J.L., Patwardhan, M.V., *Aesthetic Rapture: The Rasādhyāya of the Nāṭyaśāstra*, vol. II: *Notes*, Poona, 1970. Very helpful is also the Hindi commentary of Viśveśvara Siddhānta Śiromaṇi to the edition of the *Abh*, Chaps. 1, 3, and 6 of Nāgendra, quoted below as Hindi-*Abh*.
4. The *Nāṭyaśāstra*. (A treatise on Ancient Indian Dramaturgy and Histrionics) ascribed to Bharata-Muni. Completely translated for the first time from the original Sanskrit with an Introduction, Various Notes and Index by Manomohan Ghosh, Calcutta: Granthalaya Private Limited, 1967[2], vol. I (translation) (Chaps. I-XXVII), p. 524, Chap. XXVII. 57.
5. Ibid., pp. 524, chap. XXVII. 60-1, cf. vol. I (translation), pp. 77-8, fn. 16.
6. Ibid., vol. I, pp. 14-15, Chap. I.108-9.
7. *prekṣaka* in Ghosh's main text F (cf. vol. I (text) Chap. XXVII, p. 227) but *prāśnika* among the variant Skt. readings and according to

Daśarūpaka. Cf. also N.P. Unni, *Nāṭyaśāstra.* Text with introduction, English translation and indices in four volumes, Delhi: Nag Publishers, 1998, vol. II, p. 739.

8. Ghosh, op.cit., vol. I (Translation) p. 523, Chap. XXVII. 50-3.
9. About the notion of the ritual experts (Ritualspezialisten) cf. Cancik, Gladigow, Kohl (eds.) in Handbuch religionswissenschaftlicher Begriffe, vol. IV, p. 447.
10. The Complete Works of Kālidāsa. The Text in Sanskrit and Prakrit. Ed. with an Introduction by V.P. Joshi. Leiden: E.J. Brill, 1976. p. 377.
11. I became aware of this passage through a hint from Prof. Gyula Wojtilla in a discussion of his German translation of the Kuṭṭanīmattam of Dāmodaragupta.
12. Dāmodaragupta, Kuṭṭanīmattam or Śambhali-matam. A Didactic Poem Composed about AD 755-86. Ed. with a New Commentary Rasa-Dipika by Tanasukharam Manasukharam Tripathi. Varanasi: Krishnadas Academy, 1991. Krishnadas Sanskrit Series 130, pp. 374, 940-7. The description of the performance becomes intelligible only if one is acquainted with the list of various elements constituting a stage play. So the seven are the musical tones; the six are presumably the fourfold performance (*abhinaya*) *āhārya, vācika, āṅgika,* and *sāttvika,*—plus the *rasa*-s and the *bhāva*-s; the three authorities refer to the sources of knowledge about the mimesis of the world: the people, the Veda, and spiritual introspection; *sattva* is the technical term for the mental foundation of involuntary physical reactions; the three are either the *yati*-s or the *laya*-s, i.e. the structuring pattern of the pauses or the pauses; the styles are the four performance styles according to local peculiarities; the *bhāva*-s are the eight or nine main feelings which cause the aesthetic emotions (i.e. the *rasa*-s); the double success refers to the human and to the divine kind of accomplishment of the stage production; the *avasthā*-s are the five stages in the development of the main characters and, correspondingly, the *sandhi*-s are the five joints of the composition where the stages of the character are going interwoven with events of the plot.

    This judgement of Samarabhaṭa is so extremely overloaded with obscure technical expressions that one can hardly suppress the feeling of the author mocking his character. On the other hand, the knowledge about the basic theory is presupposed in every special discourse, so that Samarabhaṭa might not need to speak in simpler words at all.
13. In this respect another point has been debated extensively concerning the obligation of the poets to the rules of the *śāstra.* As no great importance was attached to the presentation of fresh subjects, it was rather the skilful arrangement that played a more prominent role.

Moreover, the education and the training of a poet included most of the prerequisites, which distinguished a true connoisseur as well.

14. Significantly, this seeking of the audience's favour does not appear in the so-called Bhāsa-plays, which are held to be older than Kālidāsa. There can be yet another explanation even if not all of the plays are written by Bhāsa and are later than Kālidāsa. Their composition might be a special arrangement for the purposes of the later *Kūṭiyaṭṭam* when plays were acted in the temple not for a common audience but for the god. (I am exploring here an opinion of Anna Esposito stated in a personal conversation.)
15. Michael Coulson, Three Sanskrit plays *Śakuntalā* by Kālidāsa, *Rākṣasa's Ring* by Viśākhadatta, *Mālatī and Mādhava* by Bhavabhūti translated with an introduction by M. Coulson, Bungay, Suffolk: Penguin Books, 1981, p. 41.
16. Ibid., p. 178.
17. Ibid., p. 307.
18. *Dal*, I, p. 39, 10; p. 40, 1-2.
19. *Abh GOS*, I, p. 290, 25-6: *(na)nāṭya eva ca rasāḥ/Kāvye'pi nāṭyāyamāna eva rasāḥ/* Note, however, the objection of Masson and Patwardhan who prefer to read 'nāṭya eva ca rasāḥ' instead of 'na nāṭya eva. . .'. The next sentence, however, establishes the emergence of *rasa*-s in non-acted poetry as well. Cf. Hindi-*Abh*, p. 504.
20. *Abh GOS*, I, p. 290, 26.
21. *Abh GOS*, I, p. 36, 4-10. Cf. Gnoli, pp. 96-7. Cf. Hindi-*Abh*. p. 186.
22. *Abh GOS*, I, p. 291, 12-16; Cf. Gnoli, p. 69, fn 2. Cf. Masson and Patwardhan, II, p. 72, fn. 390. Cf. Hindi-*Abh*., p. 505.
23. Cf. Gnoli, p. 96, fn. 1.
24. *Abh GOS*, I, p. 281, 2-3. Cf. Gnoli, p. 65. Cf. Hindi-*Abh*., p. 475.
25. *Dal*, I, p. 80, 12-13.
26. *Abh GOS*, I., p. 27, 5-6. Cf. Gnoli, p. 64 fn. 1. Cf. Hindi-*Abh*., p. 146.
27. *Abh GOS*, I., p. 280, 14-16; Gnoli, p. 63 a. Cf. Hindi-*Abh*., p. 280.
28. Coulson, op. cit. p. 43.
29. *Abh GOS*, I, p. 279, 4-9. Cf. Gnoli, pp. 55-6. Cf. Hindi-*Abh*., p. 471.
30. *Abh GOS*, I, p. 279, 12-13; Gnoli, p. 58. Cf. Hindi-*Abh*., p. 471.
31. *Abh GOS*, I, p. 290, 20-21. Cf. Masson and Patwardhan, p. 69, fn. 388. Cf. Gnoli, p. xxxviii. Cf. Hindi-*Abh*., p. 503.
32. Cf. D.H.H. Ingalls on *Subhāṣitaratnakośa* (Ingalls 1965: 25-6). A peculiar feature of the Sanskrit court poetry is its fondness of types and not individuals, as Ingalls points out with respect to the anthology of Sanskrit court poetry *Subhāṣitaratnakośa*. It is not surprising that the drama which is mainly defined by its textual constituent, *vācya*, shares the basic characteristics of the general *kāvya*. Some

commentators on famous Sanskrit plays even identify certain compositional elements of the plot via statements (and not actions) of the dramatis personae. Cf. Kāṭayavema on *Śākuntalam* who is concerned to find some equivalent between the name of a *sandhyaṅga* and the corresponding statement of the character. Even the most appreciated *āṅgika-abhinaya* of present-day *Kūṭiyaṭṭam* presents in fact an increase in 'text' and not in action as it repeats through gestures the meanings and even the grammatical categories of the characters' words.

33. *Abh GOS*, I, p. 279, 13-15; Gnoli, p. 58. Cf. Hindi-*Abh*., p. 471. Note that authentic *rites de passage* cannot utilize previous experience because they transform the individual consciousness through unique experiences.
34. *Abh GOS*, I, p. 280, 10; Gnoli, p. 62. Cf. Hindi-*Abh*., p. 473.
35. *Abh GOS*, I, p. 290, 21-2. Cf. Hindi-*Abh*., p. 503.
36. *Dal*, I, p. 93, 1-2.
37. Edwin Gerow, 'Plot Structure and the Development of Rasa in the Śākuntala, pt. I in *Journal of the American Oriental Society* (*JAOS*) 99.4, 1979, pp. 559-79 and pt. II in *JAOS* 100.3, 1980, pp. 267-82. Reference to pt. I, pp. 564-6.
38. About a secondary ritualization of the classical play see some suggestions in Herman Tieken, op. cit., pp. 121-2. Even in this case it is not the dramatic structure itself which is treated like ritual frame. There are rather some purely ritual elements which precede or follow the actual body of the play and reflect the different 'usage' of the artefact in hieratical way.
39. Certainly a distinction should also be made between contemporary non-devotional plays with their strong psychological and social implications and the classical Sanskrit play. Yet another case would be the psychodrama. The analysis of the involvement in the 'magic of performance' would be also considerably different in the case of the actors, musicians, and singers versus the members of the audience of stage plays. Cf. Mayerhoff 1991: 246.
40. We should only consider the obvious accessibility of Sanskrit classical subjects for varying staging projects up to the twentieth century. Cf. Ananda Lal and Chidananda Dasgupta (eds.), *Rasa: The Indian Performing Arts in the Last Twenty-five Years*, vol. II, *Theatre and Cinema*. Calcutta: Anamika Kala Sangam, Research and Publications, 1995.
41. In this sense one may take a Prakrit verse by Ānandavardhana to reveal the essence of the artistic perception:
'In that moment the merits arise when a *sahṛdaya* perceives them. Grasped by the sun's rays the lotuses become lotuses.' *Dhvanyāloka* II.1. Cf. *Dal*, II, p. 178, 2-3.

REFERENCES

Abhinavagupta

[*Abh*]: *nāṭyaśāstram*. śrīmadabhinavaguptācāryaviracitavivṛtisametam = Nāṭyaśāstra of Bharatamuni with the Commentary Abhinavabhāratī by Abhinavaguptācārya. Chaps. 1-7, vol. I. Edited by M. Ramakrishna Kavi. Revised and critically edited with Preface and Appendices by K.S. Ramaswami Sastri, Śiromaṇi, General Editor: G.H. Bhat, Gaekwad's Oriental Series, no. XXXVI, Baroda: Oriental Institute, 1956[2].

[Hindi-*Abh*]: hindī abhinavabhāratī, abhinavagupta-viracita nāṭyaśāstravivṛti abhinavabhāratī ke 1, 2, aur 6 adhyāya kā pāṭhānusaṃdhāna, pāṭhasamīkṣā hindī-anuvāda evaṃ viśada vyākhyā sahita abhinavabhāratī-sañjīvanabhāṣya. pradhāna sampādaka: ḍā. Nagendra. sampādaka tathā bhāṣyakāra [. . .] ācārya Viśveśvara Siddhānta-śiromaṇi, dillī: hindī vibhāga, dillī viśvavidyālaya, 1960.

[Dal]: śrīmadānandavardhanācāryaviracitaḥ dhvanyālokaḥ śrīmad-abhinavagupta viracitalocanasahitaḥ saṭippaṇaprakāśahindī-vyākhyopetaś ca. The Dhvanyāloka of śrī ānandavardhanācārya with the Locana Sanskrit Commentary of śrī Abhinavagupta and the Prakāśa Hindī Translation of both the Texts and Exhaustive Notes by ācārya Jagannātha Pāṭhaka. Vidyabhawan sanskrit granthamala 97, Varanasi: Chowkhamba vidyabhawan, 1965.

Bauman, R. & Ch. L. Briggs, 'Poetics and Performance as Critical Perspectives on Language and Social Life' in *Annual Review of Anthropology*; vol. 19. Palo Alto: 1990, pp. 59-88.

[Ghosh]: *The Nāṭyaśāstra.* (A treatise on Ancient Indian Dramaturgy and Histrionics) ascribed to Bharata-Muni. Completely Translated for the First Time from the Original Sanskrit with an Introduction, Various Notes and Index by Manmohan Ghosh, Calcutta: Granthalaya Private Limited, 1967[2].

Brückner, H. and E. Schömbucher, 'Performance', in *The Oxford India Companion to Sociology and Social Anthropology*, ed. Veena Das, New Delhi: Oxford University Press, 2003, pp. 598-624.

Cancik, H., B. Gladigow and K.-H. Kohl, *Handbuch religionswissenschaftlicher Begriffe*. Bd. IV. Stuttgart: Kohlhammer, 1968.

Coulson, M., *Three Sanskrit plays Śakuntalā by Kālidāsa, Rākṣasa's Ring by Viśākhadatta, Mālatī and Mādhava by Bhavabhūtī.* Translated with an Introduction by M. Coulson, Bungay, Suffolk: Penguin Books, 1981.

Dāmodaragupta, Kuṭṭanīmatam or Śambhalimatam, *A Didactic Poem Composed about A.D. 755-786*, ed. with a New Commentary Rasa-Dipika by Tanasukharam Manasukharam Tripathi. Krishnadas Sanskrit Series 130, Varanasi: Krishnadas Academy, 1991.

Gerow, E., 'Plot Structure and the Development of Rasa in the Śakuntalā, pt. I in *Journal of the American Oriental Society* 99.4, Ann Arbor, 1979, pp. 559-79 and pt. II in *JAOS* 100.3, 1980, pp. 267-82.

Gnoli, R., *The Aesthetic Experience According to Abhinavagupta*, Chowkhamba Sanskrit Studies LXII, Varanasi: Chowkhamba Vidyabhawan, 1968.

Ingalls, D.H.H., *An Anthology of Sanskrit Court Poetry: Vidyākara's 'Subhāṣitaratnakośa'*. Translated by D.H.H. Ingalls, Harvard Oriental Series 44, Cambridge: Harvard University Press, 1965.

The Complete Works of Kālidāsa. The Text in Sanskrit and Prakrit, ed. with an Introd. by V.P. Joshi, Leiden: E.J. Brill, 1976.

Lal, A. and C. Dasgupta (eds.), *Rasa: The Indian Performing Arts in the Last Twenty-five Years*, vol. II, Theatre and Cinema, Calcutta: Anamika Kala Sangam, 1995.

Masson, J.L. and M.V. Patwardhan, *Aesthetic Rapture*. The Rasādhyāya of the Nāṭyaśāstra in two volumes, vol. II: Notes, Poona: Deccan College, 1970.

Mayerhoff, B., 'The Transformation of Consciousness in Ritual Performances', in *By Means of Performance: Intercultural Studies of Theatre and Ritual*, ed. R. Schechner and W. Appel, Cambridge: Cambridge University Press, 1991.

Michaels, A., '"Le rituel pour le rituel" oder wie sinnlos sind Rituale?' in *Rituale Heute: Theorien—Kontroversen—Entwürfe*, ed. C. Caduff and J. Pfaff-Czarnecka, Berlin: Reimer, 1999.

Richmond, F.P., D.L. Swann and P.B. Zarrilli (eds.), 'Introduction', in *Indian Theatre: Traditions of Performance*, Honolulu: University of Hawaii Press, 1990.

Schechner, R., 'Ramlila of Ramnagar: An Introduction' in *Performative Circumstances: From the Avant Garde to Ramlila*, Calcutta: Seagull Books, 1983.

Tieken, H., 'The Pūrvaraṅga, the Prastāvanā, and the Sthāpaka', in *WZKS*, 45, 2001, pp. 91-124.

Turner, V., 'Are There Universals of Performance in Myth, Ritual and Drama?' in *By Means of Peformance: Intercultural Studies of Theatre and Ritual*, ed. R. Schechner and W. Appel, Cambridge: Cambridge University Press, 1991.

Unni, N.P., *Nāṭyaśāstra*, Text with Introduction, English translation and Indices in four volumes, Delhi: Nag Publishers, 1998.

7

The Power of Listening: Giving Meaning to Divine Words in Possession Performances

Elisabeth Schömbucher

The best we can do, however, with paper and types, or even with voices, will convey but a faint shadow of the original.[1]

Introduction

The problems of representing cultural performances with 'paper and types' as posed by Allen in 1867, regarding the transcription of African-American music, are still not solved. When, according to Bendix, 'expressive culture' gets textualized, 'all the levels of perception and associated experience that had enthralled scholars in the first place, [. . .], are eliminated from consideration' (Bendix 2000: 2). It is generally agreed upon, that the meaning of cultural performances, especially oral performances, cannot be found in the text alone, but also in paralinguistic features such as loudness, speed, pitch, rhythm, in body gestures—and in listening. Until now, listening as a practice through which meaning is given to an orally performed text has been mostly neglected. In his *The Conditions of Listening*, Richard Burghart investigates how the speaker is transformed by listening (1996: 300). According to Burghart, the listener is not passive in an act of communication but active in the sense that the listener gives voice to the speaker, or, in other words, 'people who are listened to gain a voice' (ibid.). It is argued here that not only does the listener give voice to the speaker, but that he also gives meaning to an oral text. An oral text doesn't have a meaning in itself. It is the audience, and especially professional listeners, as will be shown, who give meaning to an oral text.

This article deals with a form of possession mediumship among a south Indian fishing caste. It focuses on speaking and listening. A performance of possession is seen as a product of speech or rather 'enacted speech'. But it is also a product of listening. A performance of possession could not happen without those who hear, see and experience possession from the audience's point of view. Performer and audience are equally agents in the process of interpreting and giving meaning to utterances during states of possession. The medium gains voice by careful listeners who through their interpretation give meaning to or make sense of what the deity says. Without 'professional listeners' the divine words would remain opaque to the audience. In other words, listening means also understanding, interpreting and interlingual translation (Jakobson 1993).

Persons possessed by different kinds of spirits, demons or deities are a common sight in India. The various dimensions of possession cults have been widely portrayed in anthropological literature.[2] The different forms of possessions have been interpreted as illness, as a healing ritual, or as a cultural performance in a wider sense (Claus 1984). Correspondingly, the possessed person has been portrayed as a victim or patient, as a ritual specialist or as a cultural performer (Schömbucher 1993). Whereas the early anthropological literature has considered the possessed person as the main focus of investigation, more recent approaches view possession as a cultural performance. A performative approach not only considers the possessed person and his or her mental state, but also the whole setting in which possession takes place, such as cultural concepts of the person, indigenous cosmologies, ritual preparations and arrangements, the utterances of the possessed person and the role of the audience. According to Bendix, however, the sight has been overemphasized in performance studies to the detriment of the ear, although, as she rightly states, sound (such as screaming, cries of pain) can arouse human emotion to a more intense level than can sight alone (Bendix 2000: 35).

When I first witnessed a possession séance among the Vāḍabalija, a south Indian fishing caste, I couldn't understand a word. I was frightened by the loud and forceful voice of the female medium, which sounded dangerous and fierce to me. Her rage became even more perceptible when she suddenly threw a burning cigar into the audience. With cold shivers running down my spine, I sat in the audience highly attentive, always prepared to hide or run away, in case it would get even more dangerous. Much later, after having witnessed numerous possession séances, I wasn't frightened any more. I had seen many outbursts of rage, but they were always controlled. In course of time, other questions became relevant: What exactly does a medium say when she is possessed by a deity? What does the audience hear? How do they listen? What is important for them? What else do they hear besides the words actually spoken? How does the audience recognize that the speech is divine? What makes words, spoken by a medium in trance, divine words? I will try to answer these questions at the end of this article.

POSSESSION AMONG THE VĀḌABALIJA

The Vāḍabalija are a caste of Telugu-speaking maritime fishermen on the coast of Andhra Pradesh. Many of them have migrated to different parts of Orissa and more recently to Tamil Nadu. They fish for the commercial market with fish being packed on ice and shipped to large cities like Kolkata and Chennai. A considerable amount of fish is dried by women, carried to Andhra Pradesh and sold there on the peasant market.

Different forms of possession occur frequently and on a regular basis in their villages. Men, women and children can be possessed by deceased relatives, who in the form of *bhūt* visit their relatives to show them their dissatisfaction with how they are treated. This form of possession is considered harmful. Efforts are taken to exorcise and pacify the possessing entities.[3] In contrast to this harmful form of possession, a few women can get possessed by deities and the deified dead who then speak through their medium to an audience. It is this form of possession mediumship or oracular possession that is dealt with here. Female media get 'selected' by a god or goddess when they are young, usually at puberty or around their marriage. The first manifestation of the god or goddess is a rather dramatic affair and leads to a period of uncertainty in which the identity of the deity has to be found out and the girl and her family have to get used to the burden of being the vessel for a deity. Once they are accustomed to their new role, the media can handle their possession states as a matter of routine. Among the Vāḍabalija who have settled in Puri (Orissa) either permanently or for a couple of months during the main fishing season in winter, four deities and the deified dead speak through their human vessels regularly every week. The local village goddesses Nūkālamma and Kotta Rājulu speak on Thursdays, and the Vaiṣṇava gods Veṅkaṭeśvara of Tirumala and Gōvinda of Tirupati speak on Saturdays, if required. Since all deities have their temples in Andhra Pradesh, they are invited to Puri for a short period of time, when people seek their advice. Especially Veṅkaṭeśvara is considered to be a god who fulfills all wishes. All the Vāḍabalija I know have been at least once on a pilgrimage to Tirupati/Tirumala. In contrast to this god, village goddesses, especially Nūkālamma, are much more fierce and demanding. They seem to be never sufficiently worshipped.

Each possession séance is an event which is ritually marked. After detailed preparations, such as cleaning the floor with cow dung and a bath of the medium, in order to bring both into a state of utmost ritual purity, the people in the audience who have gathered by now take their seats in front of the medium. A priest (*dāsuḍu*) is summoned, who invokes the deity into the body of the medium.[4] When his pleas finally succeed, the deity starts speaking to the audience through its medium. At the end of a séance, which lasts for approximately one hour, I usually asked the participants, what the deity said. While the medium claimed amnesia, I always got a very short and laconic answer by some members of the audience, consisting of about two sentences. 'You didn't worship me, therefore you have these problems now. You should make *pūjā* to me. That's what the goddess (or the god) said.' The discrepancy between the long verbal recitation and the very short synopsis of it caused me to emphasize my research on what is said how, and what is heard by the audience.

The Case Study

During my first field research among the Vāḍabalija from 1979 to 1981, when I studied the social organization of a maritime fishing community in India (Schömbucher 1986; 1988), one Saturday morning I was on the way to visit the house of a Vāḍabalija family at the other end of the village. When I passed the small footpaths through the dense agglomeration of palm leave huts with thatched roofs, I heard for the first time what was explained to me as *ammoru* ('the goddess'). I could see that a few women were crouching outside the low door, obviously because there was not enough space inside the small hut. I couldn't see anything of *ammoru*, I only heard the sound of the voice of a woman. It sounded as if somebody was crying, sobbing, moaning and sighing, all at the same time, but the voice was never faint, weak or feeble, never hesitating, never stumbling. On the contrary, the voice I heard was powerful, threatening, and somewhat dangerous. The woman recited fluently at a very high speed. The loud breathing in at the end of each line gave her recitation a certain rhyme pattern.

Instantaneously, I was thrilled by what I heard. The impression of 'otherness' and the desire to understand what it was that a goddess was talking about to a very attentive audience over long stretches of time, persisted even after having observed many possession séances.

When I began my second fieldwork among the Vāḍabalija, this time on possession mediumship in 1991, I was facing an unexpected problem. Although I had the confidence of the Vāḍabalija, it was nevertheless difficult to attend numerous possession séances. 'Why?', I was asked again and again, 'for what reason?' One doesn't attend possession séances without a reason. My explanation, that I wanted to write a book, didn't convince the Vāḍabalija. Finally, Rājamma, an elderly woman who was known to me for more than ten years, came up with a reason that immediately convinced everybody. In the eyes of the Vāḍabalija, I had been childless for many years, although I was married. They urged me to worship various village deities in the eighties and ask them for a child. When I returned in 1989 with a two-year-old daughter, everybody was sure that the gods had fulfilled my wish. However, in 1991 my daughter was already four years old and it seemed to be justified to ask the gods for a son this time.

The request for a son appeared meaningful to everybody and I was able to attend as many possession séances as I wanted. Not only Veṅkaṭeśvara and Gōvinda, but also the goddesses Nūkālamma and Kotta Rājulu referred to my wish for a son. Gōvinda and Veṅkaṭeśvara promised that 'a son would play in your arms within a year's time'. When I returned two years later with my then six-month-old son, the Vāḍabalija were confirmed in their conviction that Gōvinda and Veṅkaṭeśvara granted every wish. According to the 'rules', the child should obtain the god's name and it should be brought before the god together with the promised gifts. One of the child's names is in fact Gōvinda. A pilgrimage with a six-month-old baby to Tirupati, however, seemed to me too difficult to carry out. I talked with Rājamma and several other women about the strain especially for the baby and about my consideration of postponing the pilgrimage. After initial scepticism on their part, they accepted my reservations.

One Saturday morning in January 1993, several people, including Rājamma and me, were gathering in front of the medium's house and waited for the séance to begin. This is an occasion to talk about problems and questions that would be dealt with shortly in the divine discourse. Rājamma, who considered herself as my mother, told the others, that today she would 'ask' on behalf of her elder daughter. In the following section I will compare the text spoken by the medium with what has been heard and passed on to me by Rājamma who may be called a professional listener.

The Text Spoken by the Gods

Māmmalu and Sattiyamma, the two vessels for the gods, had taken their seats. After the priest had invoked Veṅkaṭeśvara and Gōvinda into their bodies, both media fell in trance and began their recitations with the usual praising of all the other gods and goddesses in a rather general way. This was followed by a short interval of about 90 seconds, during which Rājamma and the others got somehow insecure and wondered if and what the gods would say. Finally, Māmmalu, Gōvinda's medium, began again.

Gōvinda:

1. *ayyo!* You know, unknown people came, my Śrīnu
2. *ōle*, innocent children, to our innumerable feet [*Rājamma*: yes]
3. to the children who came, [my] innumerable justices
4. they are happy through me, my innocent younger brother
5. is there shadow in front of my eyes?[5]
6. why are you ridiculing me now, *ayyo*?

7. in the Oriya kingdom of my Lord?
8. they enter the large house [without asking]
9. for them, there is no shame
10. on the day, when I come, *ayyō*
11. the valuables will be available, *ayyo*[6]
12. today the innocent children came
13. you have to give them the desired justice
14. my innumerable justices will be distributed

A short interval follows, during which Rājamma and others commented on what was said. '. . . there was no boy. There is a girl, she said. . . . I don't know . . .' After about one minute, Sattiyamma, Veṅkaṭeśvara's medium, began with her recitation.

Veṅkaṭeśvara:

15. Gōvindā, Gōvindā[7] [short interval of 10 sec.]
16. *ayyo*, my elder brother Gōvindā
17. elder brother, praise to you
18. elder brother, I, *annagāni, ōri*
19. the child will go forward, *ōri*
20. it will not go backward
21. *ōri*, almighty elder brother
22. in the previous days
23. *amma*, caste without caste
24. *ayyo*, to the children, *gani anna*
25. whoever it is, *ayyo*, you have to look after them
26. *ōri*, almighty elder brother
27. *ayyo*, with desire to you, elder brother
28. with your advice, elder brother, *ōri*
29. elder brother, your name is the *nāmā*[8]
30. *anna*, I brought
31. *anna*, my five justices
32. *anna*, you please distribute them, *ōri*
33. *anna*, a [my] child, *anna*
34. *ayyo*, during the pregnancy
35. *ayyo*, in this way, *ōrē*
36. *ōri*, she thought, *ōrē*
37. *ōri*, in the same way
38. *ō*, my silver chairs

39. *ōri*, should be respected [After a short interval, Gōvinda begins again to speak.]

Gōvinda:

40. *ayyo*! My innocent younger brother, you
41. *olē*, my innocent younger brother, you
42. *ōri*, in the kingdom of our Lord, *ōri, ayyo*
43. so much justice we showed
44. in this Oriya kingdom, in their kingdom
45. whether we are valued or not, my innocent Śrīnu
46. for us, quickly, she said, my innocent Śrīnu
47. *ōri*, when this woman gets pregnant, I said, younger brother
48. what kind of innumerable gifts would she give with happiness
49. there will be such joy and happiness, *ōri, ayyo*
50. no thorns of millet will affect their feet
51. I can look after her daughter and her son
52. by taking this *dharma-cakra* (powerful disc)
53. in this creation, the name
54. on the day, when she calls it
55. that innocent daughter
56. with her golden hand
57. whatever she gives, younger brother
58. let us receive it, younger brother
59. three years I gave as a condition
60. three years I gave as a condition
61. *olē*, your seven hills, do not give them [now]
62. with joy you have to climb them
63. *olē*, that child's innumerable hair
64. you have to give to my Rāma Hill
65. you will be made to give to the hill, [through] the younger brother
66. in the previous days, *ayyo*
67. she went once
68. from now on, after three years
69. when she climbs again my Rāma Hill
70. she will certainly go, the innocent daughter
71. without giving her thorns of millet, *olē*
72. I will protect her, the innocent daughter

73. for the first-born daughter, you
74. you spread the edge of your sari at the feet of the goddess, *ammā*
75. you have put it in the Oriya kingdom of the Lord
76. that wish was followed by another wish [for a son]
77. to me, of my beloved daughter, some wish, *ōlamma*
78. of innumerable gifts, I gave one
79. with this wish, *ōlamma*
80. in the Oriya kingdom of the Lord, daughter
81. the earthen pot will be praised,[9] *ōlamma*
82. the earthen pot will be praised, *ōlamma*

Rājamma: Whatever it may be, Lord, well, she came [to listen to] what you said, my elder daughter, but, she doesn't know anything, isn't it, we have to tell her, isn't it, all that you tell.

Gōvinda:

83. in this hell,[10] my mother
84. if anything happens, mother
85. these sinful children, they will not give
86. she wished wishes, which cannot be granted
87. *ōri*, we share this view
88. do not call this hell, *ōlamma*

Rājamma: What are your wishes? We should know.

Gōvinda:

89. we shall not scold you, *ammā*

Rājamma: We will buy it.

Gōvinda:

90. with your wish, to the elder brother, daughter
91. *amma*, you have offered the sari border
92. I put my foot on it, *ōlamma*[11]
93. with this wish, with Gōvinda's name
94. [this wish] I have fulfilled, *ōlamma*
95. *ōlē*, that blessing, *ōlamma*
96. if I give it in the Oriya kingdom of the Lord
97. with that wish, *ōlamma*

98. they who belong to a caste which is not my caste
99. those valuable gifts, *ammā*
100. gave she who does not have to give
101. in the Oriya kingdom of my Lord, the greatness
102. the wishes, I am asked for, will be fulfilled
103. *ōlē*, if not, then it [the greatness] is not there, daughter
104. with my sinful voice
105. even if we say, that we don't have that happiness, *ammā*
106. on that day, from the daughter
107. whatever this woman does
108. even if she gives a green banana
109. we will receive it happily
110. do not be afraid, *ammā*
111. happily, I fulfilled your wishes

Rājamma: Up to three years she needs, well, to climb your hill, well, such a small baby, Lord. (Two women join in and confirm that it is such a small baby, and that therefore we should come only after three years.)

Gōvinda:

112. *ayyo*! What did I say, *ammā*?
113. for you, three years, *ammō*
114. these conditions I gave, *olē*
115. to that little child, *arrā vallā*
116. not to rural places

Rājamma: no, no.

Gōvinda:

117. three years, both of us
118. on this day, [to] the younger brother, daughter
119. with that wish, it is possible to go

Rājamma: I will be dead, by then.

Gōvinda:

120. *ammo*, in this world, that quickly, *ammā*
121. you will not die, the Rāma Hill
122. my Rāma Hill, you

123. without seeing it, you won't die, *ammā*

Rājamma: I will die. Interval of about 10 seconds. A few people of the audience are amused about Rājamma's objections.

Gōvinda:

124. *ayyo*, I granted my boons
125. now you come with your golden voice in front of me
126. with this wish, *ayyo*
127. they came here and ate our leftovers
128. my innocent children, younger brother
129. we, how many times, younger brother
130. have we granted boons happily, *ayyo* [short interval. Sattiyamma began again with her recitation.]

Veṅkaṭeśvara:

131. *ayyo*, incompetent servant[12]
132. *ammo*, what is, daughter
133. *amma*, in your heart
134. *amma*, whatever has happened
135. *ammā*, the hell, *anna*
136. *ammā*, it has to be heard
137. *ayyo*, with your mother
138. *amma*, you can think about it, *ammā*
139. *amma*, the value, *anna*
140. *amma*, in the Oriya kingdom of the Lord
141. *amma*, if it is given
142. *amma*, she who gave a sari, little one
143. *amma*, she who has our justice,
144. *amma*, because of men
145. *amma*, whose caste is not our caste
146. *ayyo*, the child, *annagāni anna*
147. *amma*, her only wish
148. if it is Lord Veṅkaṭaramaṇa
149. *ayyo*, the Lord of a thousand miracles
150. *ayyo*, his elder brother Gōvinda
151. who grants boons
152. *amma*, who will talk
153. *ayyo*, incompetent daughter

154. *ayyo*, incompetent daughter
155. *amma*, with your, *gani anna*
156. *amma*, son, *anna*
157. *ayyo*, how will she bring him, *ammā*?
158. *ayyo*, let me know, *ammā*
159. *amma*, if you let me know
160. *amma*, my child
161. *amma*, tell me in your heart, *anna*
162. I will listen
163. *ayyo*, incompetent daughter
164. *amma*, when I hear it
165. *abbā*, then I, *annagāni, arrā*
166. *ayyo*, the intended services
167. *amma*, the thorns of millet, *anna*
168. *ayyo*, without piercing, I
169. *amma*, I can support, *ammā*
170. *amma*, god of the thousand miracles, *ammā*
171. *amma*, my miracles
172. *ayyo*, those who know them
173. *ayyo*, they should know, *arrā*
174. *ayyo* those who don't know them
175. I will pierce thorns into their feet.

Gōvinda:

176. *ayyo*, innocent daughter, you

Rājamma: well, what else is there to ask? She will come with her boy. I will tell this woman.

Gōvinda:

177. in the Oriya kingdom, you
178. *abbā*, not today, *arrā*, children

Rājamma: (impatiently): of course not today. Whatever you tell her, she will do.

Gōvinda:

179. you come on that day to me, to the temple
180. in fifteen days, *arrō*
181. husband and wife, they

182. I will make them sit on one side
183. this word in my heart will then be known to them
184. whatever my wishes are, are the wishes of the Lord
185. I will answer, my innocent daughter
186. the child who came to me, should not be afraid, *arrō*
187. on my days, bring her to do *pūjā* in the temple
188. I will give golden bamboo sticks to the entire world
189. I am Gōvinda, Gōvinda, Gōvinda
190. my seven hills, three years
191. I gave as a condition, my innocent children, *arrā*
192. The daughter should not be worried, *arrā*
193. What is mine, *arrā*, my innocent one, *ōlamma*
194. With happiness, receive my boons.

Rājamma: She will take the children and their father and will come to your feet, Lord. This section of the divine discourse ends here. After a short interval, Gōvinda spoke to the next devotee.

The Text, Interpreted by the Anthropologist

This text, one might argue, is atypical, since it deals with the case of the foreign anthropologist. The wish for a child, however, is rather common among the Vāḍabalija. Moreover, the fact that the god or the medium deals with the problems of a foreigner helped to answer important questions as, for instance, 'who is the author of the text, the medium or the unconscious or a spiritual entity, or is the text merely a reproduction of standard cultural knowledge? How is the text composed? How does the argumentation proceed? A textual analysis will show the details.

In the first line, in which the foreign devotee is addressed as 'unknown people', Gōvinda speaks to his younger brother Śrīnu (Veṅkaṭeśvara). This is followed by the statement that he, Gōvinda, had granted boons and made those who came to him happy (2-5). But now he misses the respect of the devotees (8-9). He even blames his younger brother for ridiculing him (5-6). The aim of the accusations is not yet clear, the theme of the foreign person who came to the feet of the goddess is introduced rather vaguely and has to be further developed in the dialogue. The section ends with the standard formulation that 'justice is given' (10-14).

In the following interval a certain helplessness among the audience can be observed. Since the recitation deals with a foreigner, nobody tried to put pressure on the god to talk more clearly. Veṅkaṭeśvara's recitation began with addressing his elder brother in a standardized way (15-18). Veṅkaṭeśvara assures his elder brother, that 'the child' would come and that she won't hesitate ('go backward') (19-21). At the same time, Gōvinda is asked to take care of all devotees ('children'), even if they are foreign ('caste without caste'), because he is the almighty elder brother (22-9). Veṅkaṭeśvara reassures that he has given the 'five justices' (the gift of a son) (30-1). Like in other recitations of this god, the devotee is quoted, how she thought during her pregnancy that Veṅkaṭeśvara has given her the child (32-6). Now, the god demands that he should be respected in return (37-9). This is again a dialogue with the elder brother, the foreign devotee is addressed in the third person singular. The demand for a reciprocal gift is formulated in general terms. Both the passages of the gods Gōvinda and Veṅkaṭeśvara refer to the specific case of a foreigner and are in general terms. Several of the elements are found in any other divine recitation as well, as for example the 'five justices', addressing the respective brother, acclaiming one's own power as well as the brother's power. Whereas Gōvinda shows a certain amount of anger about the missing gifts (6-9), Veṅkaṭeśvara, as usual, is benevolent and confident regarding the devotee's intentions (19).

In the next section, Gōvinda repeats what 'he said' two years ago and refers more clearly to the present case. After some standardized phrases about their power, he recounts that both of them 'showed so much justice' (the gift of a son) and expected countless gifts in return which would be given 'with happiness' (47-9). He again acclaims his power and assures that he can protect the daughter in such a way that not even the thorns of millet will hurt her feet (50-2). The gods are prepared to receive the gifts, 'whatever she gives on whichever day' (54-8). With a redoubling of lines it is stated that within three years, the gift has to be given in return to the gods (59-60). Then, the pilgrimage to Tirupati should be undertaken (63-5), and the child's hair has to be given (63-4). Further gifts are demanded, but not specified (65). While the foreign devotee is referred to in the third person singular, it is Rājamma who is addressed in the second person singular. It is again repeated that the foreign devotee has been to Tirupati in the past (66-7). Gōvinda assures that he will protect her during the next three years (68-72). He refers again to the past and states that Rājamma had already once spread the sari for the first born daughter of the foreign devotee (73-4). This story, which was recounted time and again all over the village after I had returned with my two children, referred to the years 1980 and 1981, when I travelled to Andhra Pradesh several times with different Vāḍabalija women who caused me to make offerings to the village god Nūkatāta, asking for a child. Gōvinda's way of addressing Rājamma as the one who spread the sari reflects the different roles in this offering. In fact, I had given offerings, but since I 'did not understand', Rājamma and the other women decided what and when I had to offer. Gōvinda continues and states that the first wish was followed by a second one, which was also granted (76-82).

In the further dialogue, Rājamma doesn't refer to what Gōvinda had recited so far, but mentions that 'the daughter came to listen to the divine words' and that she, Rājamma, would explain because the daughter 'doesn't know anything'. In lines 83-90, Gōvinda continues his very general discourse and repeats that the gods had fulfilled the wishes but that the gifts in return are still missing, while Rājamma asks for details about what to offer. Without answering, Gōvinda narrates what happened two years ago. About 'the one whose caste is not my caste' the god speaks in the third person singular, while Rājamma is addressed directly (90-4). At that time, the foreigner who need not give offerings, nevertheless gave valuable gifts (98-100). The gods have happily granted the boons and would be satisfied with anything the woman gives, 'even if it is a green banana' (104-11). Rājamma's specific question about the god's wish wasn't answered in a specific sense. Instead, the god spoke rather generally about boons and gifts in return. It was actually my question that Rājamma asked for me. I wanted to know exactly what I should give, whereas the Vāḍabalija 'know' what to give in a certain case. Therefore, Rājamma didn't insist on a specific answer, but concentrated on lines 59-60, in which it was said, that I should come to Tirupati within three years. Gōvinda reconfirms that mother and child should both go to Tirupati only after three years. In lines 115-16, my reservations about the pilgrimage with a small baby, which I had expressed in front of

Rājamma and others, have become divine discourse. With a synopsis of seven lines Gōvinda brings this discourse to an end (124-30). He summarizes that he and his younger brother had granted the boon happily and that the devotee came with wishes and ate the leftovers of the gods. Now it is she who has to give gifts in return. Gōvinda's discourse ends at that point.

After a short interval, Veṅkaṭeśvara's medium begins again with her recitation. With the general question 'what is in your heart?' (132-6) it is Rājamma who is addressed. It becomes clear that now I'm addressed when Veṅkaṭeśvara says that I should consider together with my mother which valuable gifts I could give (137-41). In lines 148-52, the topic is again my status as a foreigner ('she wears a sari, but her caste is not our caste'). Finally, Veṅkaṭeśvara talks about 'the child, her only wish' (146-7). In lines 148-52 it is again stated that Veṅkaṭeśvara and Gōvinda are powerful gods who can fulfil wishes. Now the incompetent daughter has to bring her son to the gods (153-6). Veṅkaṭeśvara doesn't give instructions, but proposes that the incompetent daughter should think about it in her heart and let him know (158-63). Then, he promises that he as the 'god of a thousand miracles' would protect the daughter (164-73). Only those who do not respect his greatness will be punished by him (175).

To Rājamma's surprise, Gōvinda begins again to speak. Although the discourse could have ended here, Gōvinda gives the specific answer to Rājamma's initial question. The god proposes, that instead of going to Tirupati I should come to the feet of the gods here in the 'Oriya kingdom' in 15 days (177-80). I had told everybody that my husband would come on a visit around that time. With him I should come to the gods and then they would announce their demands (183-5). The divine discourse finally ends here, after the god had praised again his power, mentioned again the three years, and assured his protection (188-92).

Long stretches of Gōvinda's recitation are of narrative character. Despite the fact that gods (or their media) are dealing with a foreigner, they are able to recite fluently. Formally, the recitation is characterized by a series of repetitions through which the fluency is guaranteed. Each medium has specific phrases, which are repeated several times, sometimes identically, sometimes slightly modified. The phrase 'in the Oriya kingdom of my Lord' is repeated by Gōvinda's medium Māmmalu eight times. Sattiyamma, Veṅkaṭeśvara's medium, uses it only once. Justice (*nyāyamu*) is repeated four times by Māmmalu, twice by Sattiyamma. The expression 'caste without caste' is used three times to characterize the foreigner. Not the foreign devotee, but Rājamma is addressed with the terms 'incompetent daughter/servant' (four times) by Sattiyamma, while Māmmalu uses 'innocent daughter' six times and 'innocent children' three times. Both gods emphasize that they would protect their devotees even from thorns of millet. Gōvinda repeats five times that he has set a time limit of three years to come to his temple. Twice this god refers to the fact that the sari had been spread before him two years ago. Most frequently, however, the term *korika* (wish, plea) is used, fourteen times by Gōvinda's medium and three times by Veṅkaṭeśvara's medium. The fact that the gods have granted the wish for a son is thus made the most important statement. In contrast to this, the demand for a gift in return is mentioned 'only' five times. For the sake of stability and symmetry of the text, Gōvinda's medium redoubles lines three times, whereas Veṅkaṭeśvara's medium uses phrases like 'almighty elder brother' and 'god of the thousand miracles' several times.

The text shows that the media are capable of integrating the story of a foreigner into their divine discourse. The verses in which they recite are not an obstacle, but serve as a kind of framework with the same beginnings and endings within which the story of the foreigner can be narrated. The length of the recitation is caused by the fact that the story is repeated slightly differently several times. The course of the divine argumentation is influenced by the reaction of the audience. Both gods begin with the general statement that they had given 'justice' and granted boons. Gōvinda demands a pilgrimage to Tirupati after three years, and considers my hesitation about the tiring journey with a small child. Rājamma accepted the time limit and confirmed this part of the divine argumentation. However, my specific question 'what is it, that you wish?' is not answered specifically. Obviously, what should be given in return is cultural knowledge and need not be mentioned in detail.

The divine recitation during a state of possession has been represented here in the form of a written text. As such, it can be divided into smaller segments and analysed in detail. As an oral text, the recitation is subject to a different kind of interpretation.

How the divine words have been heard and understood becomes obvious in Rājamma's interpretation of the divine discourse the following day.

The Text, as it was Heard by Rājamma

One day after the possession séance, Rājamma came to my house together with a young woman to tell what the gods had said to me. This conversation has been taped and is therefore of rather formal character. Rājamma spoke with concentration, she wasn't distracted by others, as it would have been the case had we met in her house.

Question: What did the god say?

Rājamma: What god said is the following /1/: I said, that you are my elder daughter /2/. 'Elder daughter, what does it mean? Who is she?', that's what I heard /3/. Another woman said this about you /4/. This is how the other woman talked, I heard it, when she talked like that /5/. Your elder daughter came to me, I gave her bananas with sacred ash (*vibhūti*) /6/. Your elder daughter /7/. A son was born. After he had been born, you gave him my name. It is my name, not the name of another king /8/. It is my name, Gōvinda-*bābu*'s name /9/. If he would get another name in addition, it wouldn't be good /10/. I gave the boy to this woman, she let the fruit ripen and gave my name /11/. I put *vībhuti* into the banana and gave her the banana /12/. I gave it to the woman. After it was given to the woman, she gave birth [to a boy] and gave [him] Gōvinda-*bābu's* name /13/. Your elder daughter /14/. If it is her, then tell your daughter all the words which I have spoken /15/. Your daughter doesn't understand /16/. Go and tell everything to your daughter / 17/. The boy, on my hill, in three years, the boy, to my hill, after two years have passed, in the third year, to me, the mother, the three, the four, have to come /18/. Your husband will arrive in ten days, your husband, here /19/. This, he said /20/. All words which have been told, you have to tell her /21/. Everything that I say, you have to tell your daughter /22/. That's what god said /23/. Therefore, I came to tell you /24/. In the third year you have to come /25/. Your husband, you, the boy, the small boy, the girl, you have to take them and come to my hill /26/. That's what the god said /27/. Because you do not understand these words, I came to make you listen /28/.

[I came] to tell it to you once, so that you understand /29/. The words, which I spoke, make the woman hear them, that's what the Lord said, Ravaṇa /30/.

Question: What did Ravaṇa (Veṅkaṭeśvara) say?

Rājamma: What Lord Ravaṇa said is this: 'what I told you, make the woman hear' /31/. 'What will this woman tell me?' he said /32/. God, the Lord, Ravaṇa /33/. That means, this woman, taking her boy, this boy, the boy Gōvinda, and coming to you, what will you say /34/? 'Then, I will listen and speak, Lord, listen to you,' that's what I said /35/. 'I will listen to you and then tell the woman everything, that the ruling Lord doesn't know and shouldn't talk about. I will also ask the woman and I will let you hear, what she said, Lord' /36/. At the time, when your husband arrives, when your husband comes, when this man arrives, then you have to take this man, this man and the boy, you have to take them /37/. The Lord calls you to his place, what shall I say, inform the woman /38/. That's what he said /39/. Whatever I say, tell the woman, said god /40/. It is Gōvinda-*bābu*'s name, not Ravaṇa, Gōvinda-*bābu* /41/.

Question: What do I have to bring?

Rājamma: You have to buy incense sticks /42/. Then, you take the incense sticks and the boy. When you are coming, buy a coconut, you have to come like this, isn't it, *amma*, buy a coconut, isn't it, *amma*, a bunch of bananas, a dozen /43/. These, incense sticks, bananas, bananas, coconut /44/. These three you carry and come to the Lord /45/. Until then, you don't bring anything /46/.

Question: And a sari?

Rājamma: What we talked about saris, you mean /47/? They will criticize me, *amma*, after a sari was given to me /48/. The people /49/. That's what god said /50/. All will criticize me /51/. If you give me saris and other things /52/. Not now /53/. If you come to our house, then you can give /54/. If you bring and give it next Saturday, then you can worship god and then go away /55/. Isn't it, *amma* /56/? Until then, no sari for me, nor any other things /57/. As long as you don't go back into your village, if you buy and give something in the meanwhile, 'if she gives something to me, people will criticize me'/58/. That's what god said /59/. All will say 'god takes bribes' /60/. Like this, he has spoken to me /61/. These words are right /62/. Not now /63/.

The Power of Listening

Rājamma's interpretation of the divine words provides information about *listening* to oral texts and about what is important in oral tradition: the words, the voice, the performance? What is it exactly that is heard? Is it the words spoken, the ones which are expected or the ones which are associated? To what extent does the heard version differ from what was actually said? In the Vedic culture, the heard, '*śruti*' was supposed to be the divine word, the manifestation of the divine. '*Śruti*' had the highest authority, it transformed the listeners while taking part in the divine words. In the present possession séances the words heard are divine words, too. They have authority, too. How are they heard? People in the audience are not passive members in a communicative event (Burghart 1996: 300). Burghart sees listening as a practice which acknowledges the speaker (ibid.). In listening to him, the speaker gains importance. He has found the right words and the right voice in order to give meaning and authority to what he wants to say. Moreover, a speaker who is heard gets transformed through the act of listening (ibid.). Media become deities for the times they are listened to. Speaking and listening are practices that depend on and influence each other. Critical listening will lead the divine talk into another direction than affirmative listening. In any case, it is the listener who gives meaning to a text. Rājamma's account of what she had heard, shows that the recitations not only have an internal semantic, but that there is also an external semantic through which the text gets a much broader meaning than the words actually spoken would provide. The meaning of the spoken words results from the words themselves as well as how those are heard.

What of the divine recitation was considered important and reported? What was left out, perhaps because it was considered to be well-known or unimportant, or because it was simply forgotten? Do some themes get reported which are not part of the divine discourse? How much cultural knowledge is necessary to understand?

The following themes are mentioned by either Gōvinda or Veṅkaṭeśvara:

1. reference to the fact that the woman is foreign and from a different caste,
2. plea to the respective brother to give justice,

3. praising one's own power, as well as the brother's power,
4. demand of reciprocal gifts for providing a pregnancy,
5. granting protection for mother and child,
6. three-year postponement for the pilgrimage to Tirupati and offering of the son's hair,
7. reference to the past: to the first visit to Tirupati, the plea to the gods for a daughter and then for a son, granting both boons by the gods,
8. general answer to Rājamma's question about the things I should give: 'whatever she gives, even a green banana',
9. specific instruction, that husband and wife, together with the two children, should come to the feet of the gods after fifteen days,
10. final promise of divine protection.

The textualized form of the oral recitation can be divided into ten themes. However, in its oral performance the divine words have been heard differently. This results into a completely different text. Rājamma mentioned the following themes:

1. Explaining the term 'elder daughter', she refers to a woman in the audience, who asked whose elder daughter was concerned here.
2. Gōvinda's report of several important events of the past: he had given bananas with *vibhūti* to the elder daughter two years ago. After that, a son was born. The child got his name, because he, Gōvinda, had given the son.

   This section, in which every statement is repeated at least once, is a correct account of what had happened two years ago. It has not been mentioned, however, in the divine discourse, but Rājamma summarizes here from her perspective what had happened until now. Rājamma evaluates the gift of a banana with *vibhūti*, the birth of the son, and his name Gōvinda as most important. Rājamma refers here to her own memory and presents it as divine quotations. The points she mentioned are the presupposition to understand the divine argumentation, but they haven't been mentioned in the divine discourse. The divine reference to the past mentioned instead the first pilgrimage to Tirupati, the granting of the wish for a daughter and then for a son. Only the divine statement, 'with this wish they ate our leftovers' (126-7), could be considered as a general statement about the gift of a banana with *vibhūti.*

3. The three-year postponement to visit the temple in Tirupati granted by Gōvinda.

   This is a quotation of what had been said in the divine recitation. But while Gōvinda only said, that the mother had to show her son 'to my hill', according to Rājamma he said, that the whole family should come. Such a statement was made neither by Gōvinda nor by Veṅkaṭeśvara. Rājamma's account, however, reflects the usual practice. Naturally, the whole family would go to Tirupati, even though this was not demanded explicitly by the gods.

4. The statement that my husband would come in ten days and that I should bring him and my son to the gods.

   This statement is quoted from the divine discourse. The request is considered to be central and it is repeated by Rājamma emphatically.

5. Gōvinda's instruction that Rājamma should explain the divine words to the foreign woman, and that she should make 'the elder daughter hear' the words which had been spoken by the god.

   This and other supposed statements by Gōvinda and Veṅkaṭeśvara have been repeated by Rājamma several times. This request has been uttered neither by Gōvinda nor by Veṅkaṭeśvara. Instead, Rājamma mentioned this in her dialogue with the gods. It was she who said 'my elder daughter doesn't know anything' and therefore she suggested to pass on the divine utterances to her daughter. Several repetitions of this supposed divine utterance make Rājamma's text powerful and authoritative.

6. Veṅkaṭeśvara's utterance 'what is it that this woman will tell me?'

   After Rājamma mentioned Ravaṇa (Veṅkaṭeśvara) and quoted him with his utterance 'the words that I spoke, make this woman hear them' (30), I asked what this god had said. Veṅkaṭeśvara's utterance 'what is it that this woman will tell me?' is quoted and explained as follows: Rājamma would act as a mediator, when we go to Tirupati. Obviously, the foreign woman would need an interpreter for her communication with the god. Rājamma would act as such an interpreter. She would listen to the god and pass on the divine words to me. She would also ask 'the woman' and tell Veṅkaṭeśvara what she said. Rājamma's explanations refer supposedly to lines 132-3 ('what, daughter, is in your heart?'), or lines 156-7 ('the son, how will she bring him, let me know') and to lines 161-2 ('speak in your heart and I will listen. If I know, I will support you').

7. 'Whatever I say, tell it to this woman.'
   Rājamma quoted several general utterances made by Veṅkaṭeśvara, such as 'the Lord calls you to his place', or 'whatever I say, tell it to this woman.' The rather general character of Veṅkaṭeśvara's utterances is explained by Rājamma: it is Gōvinda's name that has been given to the child, not Veṅkaṭeśvara's name. Therefore, Veṅkaṭeśvara doesn't make specific demands, in contrast to Gōvinda who refers to the situation in a more detailed way.
8. What should be brought as offerings?
   When I asked specifically, what I should offer to the gods, Rājamma cited bananas, coconuts, incense sticks. These are Rājamma's instructions, the gods haven't made these utterances. These are the customary offerings to the gods. Everybody knows it, there is no need to state this explicitly.
9. The offering of a sari.
   My question whether I should offer a sari resulted from several conversations with women in which I was told, that the gods get a sari as a valuable gift in case they grant a wish, and that I should offer a sari. Several times I was told, that one has to give gold coins, ornaments or money to the gods. I had hoped to get clarity about what exactly was expected from me. Rājamma's answer was clear and unambiguous: God had said that people would criticize him, if I offered him a sari. They would say, god is corrupt, that he takes bribes. However, this divine utterance (which wasn't in fact uttered by the gods) was immediately modified by the proposal to bring a sari next Saturday, when I would be going to worship the gods. This again was quoted by Rājamma as a divine utterance although Gōvinda only said 'whatever my wishes are, are the wishes of the Lord, I will answer, my innocent daughter.'

CONCLUSION

In her account of the divine words, Rājamma didn't distinguish between cultural knowledge, associations, own memories of past events and actual components of the divine utterances. Few contents of the two texts are congruent. Standardized utterances regarding the god's own power which are given much attention in the divine discourse, or the pleas to the respective brother for divine support, are not mentioned. They are part of any divine discourse and are used to lend authority and effectiveness to the divine words. These utterances do not refer to the specific situation and therefore they don't have to be quoted. References to the past are based on different personal memories. It is not the god's memories which are recounted, but Rājamma's memories. The words which have been heard are replaced by her own associations and memories regarding a certain theme. The most important divine instructions, however, are repeated identically: the three-year postponement of the pilgrimage to Tirupati, the instruction that husband and wife should come to the gods in fifteen days, and give the gifts in return. While the gods speak allegorically of a green banana, Rājamma 'translates' these utterances into specific instructions. Rājamma produces specific divine answers to my specific questions. Partly they are based on her cultural knowledge, partly on discussions among the Vāḍabalija, in which, among other things, the behaviour of the possessed media is commented and criticized. Everything which is mentioned by Rājamma is reported in detail, enriched with cultural knowledge common to everybody.

If one decides to represent divine recitations which are made by a medium in trance 'with paper and types', one has to take into consideration that oral texts have a 'life of their own'. While their existence as a spoken text is ephemeral, their existence as a 'heard' or 'remembered' text is much more long-lived. The texts are recited in a metrical form. A similar number of syllables in each line, identical beginnings and endings and parallelisms result in a specific rhyme pattern. The texts consist of panegyric passages, narrative elements and directive passages. In the panegyric passages, the power of the gods is praised. These passages are highly standardized and consist to a large extent of formulaic phrases with which cultural knowledge is presented. The utterances are highly assertive in the sense that scepticism regarding the divine power is minimized and confidence is enhanced. There seemed to be no need for Rājamma to pass these passages on to me, since everybody knows how powerful the gods are. In the narrative elements, the gods refer to the past. Here, they transform secular discourse into divine discourse. The media are clearly authors of these textual passages. Rājamma takes up these passages, but sticks to her own version of what happened in the past. It is these passages which make divine words 'true'. Correct reference to events of the past is seen as proof that the deity speaks the truth. The slight difference between Rājamma's memory and the divine memory seems to be of no significance. Most important are the directive passages which are developed in a dialogue between the god and his audience. Instructions about the worship of the gods and the offerings are negotiated between the gods and their audience. The directive elements are passed on in great detail.

The comparison of the two texts, the spoken version and the heard version, shows how the media proceed in their recitations. Panegyric passages assert divine presence and divine power, narrative passages give the divine words truth, directive passages give detailed instructions to the devotees about the worship of the gods. The two texts also show, that effectiveness is not based on speaking alone. It is also listening which gives illocutionary force to an oral text.

NOTES

1. William Francis Allen in his introduction to *Slave Songs of the United States* (Allen, Ware and Garrison [1867]1992: iv-v; quoted from Bendix 2000: 33).
2. For a comprehensive collection of essays see J. Assayag and G. Tarabout (eds.), 1999, 'Possession in South Asia: Speech, Body, Territory', *Collection Puruṣārtha*, vol. 21.
3. This form of possession shall not be considered here.
4. For more details see Schömbucher 2006.
5. In the sense of 'do you think I am blind?'
6. In the sense of 'the wishes will be fulfilled'.
7. The first exclamation 'Gōvindā' was very loud. People in the audience joined these exclamations and repeated the god's name several times.

Sattiyamma repeated the name twice and held the syllable 'ō' for eight seconds.

8. *nāmā*, the *vaiṣṇava* symbol on the forehead.
9. The earthen pot, in which camphor is burnt, while the gods are asked for advice.
10. *narakambu*, lit. 'hell', here in the sense of 'world'.
11. In the sense of 'I accepted it'.
12. *annikāri*, 'doing many different things, without being able to do something successfully'. It is a frequently used expression only of this medium. It is translated here as 'incompetent', in contrast to the gods, who are mighty and powerful.

REFERENCES

Assayag, Jacky and Gilles Tarabout (eds.), 1999, *Possession in South Asia: Speech, Body, Territory, Puruṣārtha*, 21.

Bendix, Regina 2000, 'The Pleasures of the Ear: Toward an Ethnography of Listening', *Cultural Analysis* 1: 33-50.

Burghart, Richard 1996, *The Conditions of Listening: Essays on Religion, History and Politics in South Asia,* ed. C.J. Fuller and J. Spencer. New Delhi: Oxford University Press.

Claus, Peter J., 1984, 'Medical Anthropology and the Ethnography of Spirit Possession', *Contributions to Asian Studies* 18: 60-72.

Jakobson, Roman, 1993, *Poetik: Ausgewählte Aufsätze 1921-1971,* Frankfurt: Suhrkamp.

Schömbucher, Elisabeth, 2006, *Wo Götter durch Menschen sprechen. Besessenheit in Indien*, Berlin: Dietrich Reimer Verlag.

———, 1999, 'A Daughter for Seven Minutes: The Therapeutic and Divine Discourses of Possession Mediumship in South India', in J. Assayag and G. Tarabout (eds.), *Possession in South Asia: Speech, Body, Territory, Puruṣārtha,* 21: 33-60.

———, 1993, 'Gods, Ghosts and Demons: Possession in South Asia' in H. Brückner, L. Lutze and A. Malik (eds.), *Flags of Fame: Studies in South Asian Culture*. New Delhi: Manohar.

———, 1988, 'Equality and Hierarchy in Maritime Adaptation: The Importance of Flexibility in the Social Organization of a South Indian Fishing Caste', *Ethnology* 27 (3): 213-30.

———, 1986, *Die Vāḍabalija in Andhra Pradesh und in Orissa. Aspekte der wirtschaftlichen und sozialen Organisation einer maritimen Gesellschaft*, Wiesbaden: Franz Steiner Verlag.

PART III

The Observer: Reconsidering the Categories of the Observer

8

The Faculty of the Voice

Saskia Kersenboom

The Object

Several years ago I saw Peter Sellers in the movie *Being There*. In a most convincing manner he personified a gardener tending the garden of a huge mansion. His only contact with the world outside was a television and its remote control. His garden was real, the world beyond a metaphor. Culture, to him, was indeed the original Latin *cultura* derived from the verb *colo*—'to plough; to till; to tend'. The soil, the seeds, the seasons and their harvest were his paradigm. The moment his master died he strolled into a universe he did not know; but he continued to measure even this human environment by the standards of his ecological pragmatism. His inversion of social reasoning was embraced as 'in-depth-understanding' cast into stunningly simple, lucid metaphors. For instance, he answered questions on economic recession calmly by the logic of his garden: after summer comes fall and winter is followed again by spring. Decay and seeming barrenness are absolutely necessary for the renewal of nature. His answer was simple: *being there, you'll understand: you'll understand what happens, you'll understand what is necessary to do*; it made him president.

The thrust of the argument is the observation that culture is a matter of 'being there', 'know-how', 'familiarity', 'acting skillfully and strategically'; it equals digging into the soil, planting the seeds, watching the weather, inferring the necessary and tending the processes of growth and fruition. Culture is a process, an ongoing concern, a praxis that takes its meaning only in application, in practices that chisel the presence of culture.

Human culture is such a praxis, rooted in practice and interaction as conditions for the fruition of human knowledge. In a kind of 'radical hermeneutics'[1] the humanities are cultivated in the open, among fellow human beings, taking as their vehicle the four dimensions of shared presence that unite time and place. Human time and human space, man-made presence, are the only rift into 'general, physical time' and 'general, physical space' that opens up to us. All that we can achieve or know, we perform in that 'clearing'; it constitutes our garden, our stage, our opportunity. This performance is the praxis of human culture. The clearing that is belaboured here is not the rich soil of a garden, it is a stage. The harvest does not bring the products of the earth but the products of mankind: human cultures. The performance called 'human culture' is the effort to feel intuitively the hall around its stage and the audience that might be present there; it is our effort to express and open ourselves to an aswer. It is limited, in space, in time and in means; nevertheless, we try to make the best of this opportunity; it is ever unique, acute and fresh to our individual experience. On that stage of our lifetime, lit by the lights of real-life circumstances, we chisel our presence with the limited means we can dispose of. Our bodies are quite capable of such performance: words, sounds and images are all we have, but how rich they are! They form the media of expression as well as the model for a successful reception of our urge. The space around the stage, however, remains dark; it can be felt but not assessed. Still, we act, reaching out with our lives for life, again and again exploring different trajectories. *Human culture is a performing art.* It dwells in the four dimensions of space and time. Only under these conditions can it unfold in full, in the course of performance.

The Challenge

In taking human culture as a performing art, we have to tackle several methodological and theoretical hurdles. The nature of the object of research, culture as performance, enfolds several implications. To begin with: performance is applied knowledge, it is doubly interactive, involving senders and receivers, it unfolds within the dimensions of space and time and is mediated by the five senses; and, as a final feature: performance is goal oriented, therefore it is highly flexible and subject to change.

The live, organic nature of culture is a fact of almost banal, common sense proportions. Still, academic reflection has done close to everything to circumvent this basic given. It dares not tackle this phenomenon in its natural complexity but searches for different principles of organization hidden in, behind or away from, it. Why? I would suggest two reasons that are intimately related: on the one hand, an outdated research agenda that was inherited by the humanities and social sciences, and on the other hand, the traditional media that continue to be employed for the purpose of representing academic knowledge. A 'Radical Hermeneutics' that can truly 'restore life to its original difficulty' needs to orient itself to exactly the opposite horizon that is cherished by the hermeneutics that are until today dominant in academic life. This means the inversion of Ricoeur's classical paradigm 'meaningful action considered as text' into 'text considered as meaningful action'.[2] Asad employs Luria's term 'synpraxic speech' in order to bring out the fact that in the process of translation, the grasping that precedes verbalization, comes with learning to *live* a new mode of life not by learning *about* another mode of life (1986:159).[3] In other words, moving away from the Faculty of Letters to the Faculty of the Voice entails to learn to acquire the perspective that precedes verbalisation as well as the gradual develoment of becoming an eloquent 'speaker' of a mode of life.[4]

The 'Faculty of the Voice' is lucky. It draws its vitality from linguistic anthropology, musicology, theatre studies and communication sciences. Linguistics-at-large proves to be a generous field: it is willing to encompass language both in its verbal and non-verbal aspects. Willingness, however, did not always correspond to capability: to record, describe and analyse non-verbal expressions on paper was impossible. In consequence the major part of practical knowledge and knowledge of familiarity was lost. This type of knowledge remained indeed 'tacit', true to the label it has received in cognitive sciences. But, today, linguistics can finally accept the full challenge of its mission with analytical rigour, representational nuance and theoretical daring as never before. The 'Faculty of the Voice' takes one step further into language and investigates linguistic performance as 'communicative behaviour', that is, stylized behaviour performed through words, sound and images. It aims to familiarize itself with the 'languages of cultures', to train the human voice to 'by-heart' their basic grammatical structures, to apply these in 'cultural utterances' and to build up a 'repertoire' and 'perform these' in order to acquire deeper understanding of their cognitive and theoretical potential. It tries to do so by actively testing these languages, by applying them on a 'stage' set by real time and space, in 'dialogical investigation', in truly interactive communications between senders and receivers.

In retrospect, two great minds saw a similar mission very clearly. In contrast to the widely spread notion that exactly these two giants were the masterminds behind structuralism in its most static forms, the original writings of Ferdinand de Saussure and Roman Jakobson show a different type of structuralism, full of dynamism and organic complexity. Around 1926 Roman Jakobson formulated the imperative research agenda that he envisaged for the twentieth century as follows: 'the overcoming of *statics*, the expulsion of the absolute—here is the essential turn for the new era, the burning question of today'.[5] This fire was ignited by his reading of de Saussure's theory on the antinomy between a state and a change of language, that is, between synchrony and diachrony.

A close reading of de Saussure reveals that his intellectual agenda was much larger and far more nuanced than the static forms of structuralism that have emerged long after his *Cours de linguistique générale* (de Saussure 1931 [1916]). His analytic concepts of *langue* 'language system' and *parole* 'applied language system, speech' do not stand alone. A third, overarching concept was posited by de Saussure but received relatively little attention. This concept, *langage*, was supposed to be the grand target of linguistics. In chapter two (ibid.: 20-2) on the subject matter and task of linguistics, de Saussure states 'la matière de linguistique est constituée d'abord par toutes les manifestations du langage humain (. . .) toutes les formes d'expression', and further 'dans la vie des individus et des sociétés, le langage est un facteur plus important qu'aucun autre'. Here we get a glimpse of the synergetic potential of 'synpraxic speech'.[6] However, he realizes the difficulty in tackling the subject matter of *langage*. First of all he sees *langage* as 'multiforme et hétéroclite', whereas *langue* can be considered homogeneous. (ibid.: 25) Therefore he sees no other intitial step than the gradual exploration of *langage* along the systematicity of *langue*; that is, *langue* as a sign system that unites an acoustic image with a mental image. Its systematicity is considered to be a long-term social product of the human faculty of language, an ensemble of conventions that forms a principle of classification (ibid.).[7] This presumed homogeneity should gradually tame the heterogeneity of the grand project *langage*. De Saussure admits, however, that historically speaking, speech—*parole*—always precedes system—*langue*—; it is from the soil of speech that, system evolves.[8] At the same time he points out that there is nothing collective to be found in speech; its manifestations are individual and momentaneous (ibid.: 37-8). As a result, it seems, in contemporary terms, that both speech—*parole*—and *langage* share a basic quality of heterogeneity moulded by specific temporal and spatial conditions.[9] They also share a basic physical reality, a factual, sensuous presence. It is the actual, individual occurrence of speech that allows us to trace the trajectory of *parole* (ibid.: 27). This trajectory is meant to lead us ultimately into the territory of the social non-corporeal fact, the psychical entity *langue*.[10] This amorphous entity is to be elicited from a mass of individual events; thus it is imagined to transcend the dimensions of space and time into a realm of systematic homogenesis.

That realm, however, is a matter of belief or wishful thinking, not of fact; as stated above, the real, concrete base for *langue*, its *data* to be precise, is *parole*; but, according to the worst fears of de Saussure 'there is nothing collective to be found in speech; its manifestations are individual and momentaneous'.[11]

This quality of heterogeneity and physicality may be dear to our present research agenda but it forced de Saussure to retrace his steps to the more intellectually 'solid ground' of homogeneous principles at work in presumed language systems. His trepidation to tackle his original grand object was caused by the fact that 'le langage échappant le plus souvent a l'observation . . .' (ibid.: 20) made 'le tout global du langage inconnaissable. . .' (ibid.: 38). His working solution for the first problem was '. . . le linguiste devra tenir compte des textes écrits . . .' and to the second '. . . parce qu'il n'est pas homogène tandis la distinction et subordination proposéés (i.e. various langue systems, SK) éclairent tout'.

In short, in spite of observing the dynamic, complex nature of speech, of language-in-performance, de Saussure opts for another research trajectory. Faced by the constraints of collecting and representing data in a lasting manner, followed by their integral analysis, he turns his analytic eye away from the living phenomenon. He does so at the risk of loss of cognitive complexity, dynamic multiformity, purposeful interactivity and empirical experiment. The orignial object of investigation, *langage*, most often escapes his observation. Nevertheless, he continues to consider *langage* the most important factor in the lives of individuals and societies.

Nowadays, the problem that de Saussure had to face can be diagnosed as a basic problem of the representation of knowledge. Apart from the academic preference of homogeneity over heterogeneity current in his times, de Saussure had to work with those representations of living phenomena that were available to him. That means, that next to real time, real space primary events, only representations on paper were available for reflection. As a consequence, his inferential base was a two-dimensional reduction of four-dimensional phenomena. Any physicist, biologist or medical researcher would shudder at this irretrievable loss of synthetic complexity, information, know-how, intimacy on the level of data and of empirical accessibility. The Humanities and Social Sciences at large should be equally appalled.[12]

Today's challenge is exactly that richness and complexity that becomes manifest in the performance of human culture. Performance constitutes the ideal 'analogon' of the human condition, especially in its sophisticated, strategic art forms. The advent of multimedia has made it possible to capture performances of human culture in full. In Saussurian terms, *parole* no longer escapes our observation, we can record it, digitalize it and can return to it as often as we might wish. Word, sound and (moving) image, that form the core-formula of multimedia, constitute at least three manifestations and elements of *parole* that make up *langage*; through multimedial recordings they are now accessible for accurate analysis and reflection. These data capture verbal and non-verbal expressions. Thus 'tacit' knowledge remains visible, audible and articulate.[13] Such digitalized, 'secondary performance' still reveals itself—in *multimedial* representations—as embedded in durable praxis, and, as united by its natural, umbilical cord to its world, society and performer. To study such a document, to author it or to comment upon it demands a hermeneutics that is as radical as its primary, live, real-space, real-time original. It takes 'the faculty of the voice' to grasp, appreciate and explicate its argument in multimedial representations. The larger concept posited by de Saussure, *langage*, is taking a contemporary label in the environment of multimedial representation. Now, the study of *communication* can be tackled, analysed and understood from the more abstract point of view of durable but flexible structures and strategies as well as in its concrete manifold, repeated, individual *performances*. An anthropology that embraces communication-in-performance can finally tread the soil of the grand target of *langage*.

In *prospect* of such new, academic endeavours the epistemic horizon resumes importance. Do we proceed, even now by the turn of this century, with the aspiration for homogeneity or dare we stay right here where life seems to be, and take up the challenge of heterogeneity?

The Faculty of the Voice demands an immersion in heterogeneity, in the world of applied knowledge, of practices that perpetuate and reformulate a culture.[14] Such Anthropology demands a truly 'doubly interactive', 'dialogical', open confrontation with those who live there, creating their world, sharing time and space in a committed presence. This attitude will free us from the accusation of an 'anthropological sleep'.

Foucault diagnoses the 'critical analysis of what man is in his essence' as a condition of sleep—a sleep 'so deep that thought experiences it paradoxically as vigilance', drawing into its analytic dream everything that can, in general, be represented to man's experience (Foucault 1970: 341). This is the *fata morgana* of *homogenesis*. He envisages a solution in the destruction of the 'anthropological quadrilateral' in its very foundations; in the tearing ourselves free from all 'ismic' prejudices, that were formed in splendid isolation, away from the dimensions of space and time, and that represent a lapse into complete solipsism by the workings of entropy. The promised land that stretches behind these feats of growing up is 'nothing more and nothing less than the unfolding of a space in which it is once more possible to think'—which, in fact, shuttles us back right to the start of modernity.

His 'questions about the limits of thought' as well as 'general critiques of reason' are formed out of the same propositional temperament, single interactivity and epistemic aims and are committed to similar forms of representation. Perhaps it is not possible to think radically different thoughts as long as the underlying activity and media of representation remain unaltered. In contrast to purely discursive thought, Anthropology is one of the disciplines that takes us to the field, to the real-time, real-place confrontation with the Other. The enigmatic presence of Foucault's void may turn out to be the vital presence of the Other. The unfolding of the space to think may be revealed in the practices of the Other, in interaction, labour and suffering. Practice and practising the performances of cultures may turn out to be a *conditio sine qua non* to crack the self-confinement in inherited, cherished concepts and to open up the experience of the 'Beyond'; that is, beyond formalization, codification and even articulation.

This type of anthropology does not aspire to unravel what 'man essentially is' cast in terms of universals and general 'meta-systems' but rather what man can be in concrete particulars. Instead of the fixation of 'universal' truths, it needs adequate analogons of presences, of their phenomenal complexity; it needs devices for practice, instruments and occasions for interactivity in order to experience and appreciate the infinite variety of existing 'truths'. To analyse, describe and interpret phenomena is no longer enough: to synthesize them, again, in representations that are in accordance with their natural, inner logic, and with their working order in their cultural context, forms today solid proof for understanding. Such representations allow users repeated experiments until they can imagine and reason along with the organic processes of the phenomenon. Instead of dictating 'general, universal, objective' rules of the performance of human culture, such representations generate a sense of the performance of human culture. It is such sense of human culture that results in apt anticipation, flexible application and improvization. An expertise like that is a contemporary demand.

The challenge of a 'Faculty of the Voice' is in its *différant* ways of collecting, analysing and representing data.[15] Just like the expert gardener who can look forward to a rich crop, the anthropologist who practises in the field of human culture, harvests a rich understanding of cultural performance. So-called 'participant observation' is no longer enough, only 'participant participation' can make us familiar with the actual making, the praxes and aspirations of human cultures. The vocabulary of methods and techniques of research into the 'Voice' includes now drills, skills and competences. These 'objectively' enable us to appreciate and analyse cultural performances. Such attitude puts us where we are as researchers at the stage of fieldwork, namely, as apprentices of another culture. It returns authority and empowerment to the hereditary practitioners of particular cultural performances. We can interpret cultures and improvise on any theoretical implications only on the basis of gradual affinity through practising such performances. No meaning, no authority without practice. No myth comes true without its rite. Participant participation as a faculty of the researcher, the faculty of his or her voice, constitutes such a rite.

The challenge of today's *interactive multimedia* is in the *différant* ways of storing, representing and using human knowledge. They offer the Humanities and Social Sciences new chances to engage themselves in fieldwork and to present their data; the words, sounds and images at play in performance come closer to *langage* and *parole* than any knowledge representation outside the human body ever could.[15] Modern *multimedia* do not only store these parallel processes of performance, they also provide their analyses of form and content as well as commentaries in space and time. At this moment, they are multimedial, dynamic and interactive; the next step will be their increased flexibility.

Today, the demand for flexibility, posited some eighty years ago by Roman Jakobson, generates many, basically heterogeneous, approaches to knowledge. First of all, the recognition that human cognition is only for a small part rooted in the familiar verbal stratum. The written word excels in 'propositional knowledge', whereas non-verbal, so-called 'tacit knowledge' reigns supreme as practical knowledge and knowledge of familiarity. Next to the word, the media of sound and (moving) image regain their place of importance along with the other sensory inroads of perception such as smell, taste and touch. Second, no representation of human knowledge is expected to be 'conclusive', but should, ideally speaking, remain open to 'updating'. Ultimate authority is in the process of applying human knowledge in the world and in the performance of human culture.

The real challenge lies in the world, here and now. Good research should take place there, draw its data from there, in all their complexity. Good representations of knowledge should take us back right there, well prepared, well practised, to experience for ourselves. Culture, once again, resumes its free, organic nature. The human 'clearing' into 'general, physical space' and 'general , physical time' is subjected to intensive human labour. Culture as a performing art keeps us busy. A Faculty of the Voice keeps us awake and alert, as receivers and as senders. It is both theory and method in its praxis, ever cast in the flux of life. What matters is: *Being There!*

NOTES

1. This term is used by me in the interactive, highly flexible setting of the oral tradition of south Indian lyrical poetry, see S.C. Kersenboom (1995); John Caputo (1987) has chosen 'radical hermeneutics' as the title of his work, intending to 'restore life to its original difficulty'.
2. Cf. Kersenboom, 1995, pp. 8-16 for the model of the text of Ricoeur compared to the model of the Tamil performative text.
3. See Kersenboom, 2000, p. 323, fig. 1, depicting the Synpraxis of Speech as a triangle that relates Word, Sound and Image while the Subject is positioned in the middle.
4. See www.paramparai.eu/faculty for the Faculty of the Voice, a dynamic graphic model designed by Kersenboom and realized in FLASH software by Dr. Thomas Voorter where the human Voice develops gradually through the stages of Script, to Utterance, to Role, to performing this role on a Stage set in specific time and space.
5. R. Jakobson, *On Language*, eds. Linda R. Waugh and Monique Monville-Burston, p. 165, quoting his own writings *Iskusstvo* ('Art'), 1919, p. 30.
6. For a synoptic graph of the 'synergy' of synpraxic speech see Kersenboom, 2000, p. 325, fig. 2, and also the dynamic FLASH graphics Faculty of the Voice at:www.paramparai.eu/faculty/ as a whole.
7. Cf. Kersenboom and Voorter, in www.paramparai.eu/faculty/ for: Script—here the grammatical structures (of langue) are in dialectic tension with their phenomenological processes (of parole).
8. Cf. Kersenboom and Voorter; the overall graph develops into five triangles pointing downward and four triangles upward. This dynamic graph was desgined on the basis of the mediational diagram, the Sri Yantra, where the first triangle points downward indicating the concrete, phenomenological appearance of life, immediately followed by reflection

and abstraction. In the Faculty of the Voice this movement upward is seen as the force of abstraction expressed as Theory; this expression is answered by concrete application through praxis which in turn again calls for new reflection and so on. In this milieu parole, manifest speech and praxis are first and last.

9. See Kersenboom and Voorter, in www.paramparai.eu/faculty/ for Utterance.
10. See Kersenboom and Voorter, in www.paramparai.eu/faculty/ for Role and Stage where structures and processes come together in the interactive environment of senders and receivers.
11. See Kersenboom and Voorter, in www.paramparai.eu/faculty/ for the phenomenological perspective as the dot in the centre of the dynamic graph. The original model of the Sri Yantra is visualized as a two-dimensional graph, as a three-dimensional model and as a four-dimensional mediational practice that moves in both directions: from inside to outside and v.v., from down to up v.v. and from concentrated single to manifest diversified and v.v. In this way the Subject evolves into his or her world and within the same framework of reference from his or her world into self-consciousness.
12. And so it is, at least to those who contributed to *Writing Culture: The Poetics and Politics of Ethnography,* eds. James Clifford and George Marcus (1986).
13. Compare today's multimedial digital records with the courageous attempts of Dennis Tedlock (1983): 'performable texts' and oscillograms of the voice of his informant story teller.
14. Pierre Bourdieu has coined an excellent working concept for this circular but flexible presence of culture in the term *habitus*. His notion of *habitus* is his reinterpretation of the concept *habitus* as found in the vast Aristotelian and Thomist heritage. Bourdieu's *Outline of a Theory of Practice* (1990, 7th edn.) finds a methodological follow up in William Hanks (1996), and, in the Design of my own multimedial publication the Compact Disc Interactive *Bhairavi Varnam* inserted into the folio publication *Word, Sound, Image,* Kersenboom (1995). Following multi-media experiments are 'Devadasi Murai, Remembering Devadasis' (1997), especially the interactive chart of the temple ground uniting the categories, ritual time, ritual space and ritual offerings and the Shri Yantra design for the Faculty of the Voice, Kersenboom & Voorter (2001).
15. Derrida, J. (1978) plays with the notion that 'writing', that is to say 'absence', creates a cognitive shift '*différance*' that opens different possibilities from the possibilities that inhere 'real presence'; the central argument of this paper, that is the epistemic fertility of performance

and of its roots in praxis, challenges Derrida's notion of 'writing and difference' by studying 'presence' through presence and writing 'presence' in a multimedial absent yet present way. As a result of new modes of 'writing' reflection, interaction, hermeneutics and the fruition of understanding enter a new era of conceptualization.

REFERENCES

Bourdieu, P., 1990, *Outline of a Theory of Practice*, Cambridge: Cambridge University Press, 7th edn.

———, 1990, *In Other Words*, Oxford: Polity Press.

Caputo, J., 1987, *Radical Hermeneutics*, Bloomington: Indiana University Press.

Clifford, J. and G. Marcus, 1986, *Writing Culture: The Poetics and Politics of Ethnography*. Berkeley: University of California Press.

Derrida, J., 1978, *Writing and Difference*, Chicago: University of Chicago Press.

Fabian, J., 1983, *Time and the Other: How Anthropology Makes its Object*, New York: Columbia University Press.

Foucault, M., 1970, *The Order of Things: An Archaeology for the Human Sciences*, New York: Pantheon Books.

Hanks, W., 1996, *Language and Communicative Practices*, London: HarperCollins.

Jakobson, R., 1990, *On Language* eds. Linda R. Waugh and Monique Monville-Burston, Cambridge: Harvard University Press.

Kersenboom, S., 1995, *Word, Sound, Image: The Life of the Tamil Text* with Compact Disc Interactive (CD-i) Bhairavi Varnam, Oxford: Berg.

———, 1997, *Devadasi Murai: Remembering Devadasis*, CD-ROM by IGNCA and Parampara, New Delhi, Utrecht.

———, 2000, 'It Takes Three to Epistemology', in *Subjectivity*: *Avant Garde Critical Studies*, eds. Willem van Reijen and Willem G. Weststeijn, pp. 315-30, Rodopi, Amsterdam, Atlanta.

Kersenboom, S. and Th. Voorter, *Faculty of the Voice*, Flash graphics, www.paramparai.eu/faculty/

Saussure, F. de, 1916, *Cours de Linguistique Générale*, Paris: Payot.

Tedlock, D., 1983, *The Spoken Word and the Work of Interpretation.* Philadelphia: University of Pennsylvania Press.

9

To Enjoy Playing with Play

Heike Moser

To My Master Teachers[1]

HE, BY WHOSE GOODNESS I WAS REDEEMED, HAVING SLIPPED THROUGH THE CLUTCHES OF THE DEMON AND FALLEN . . . [2]

THE INTER-PLAY—THE TEACHING—THE MASTER

Kūṭiyāṭṭam—'inter-play'—is the name given to India's sole surviving Sanskrit theatre; it is based on a repertoire established for centuries.[3] The highly educated traditional audience drawn to this theatre is not looking for new narrative pieces and plays, but rather for the extremely delicate *bhāva-rasa* inter-play, the 'imbibing' of ultra-subtle emotional impulses, evoked by the mastery of the actors. Some acts are singled out from the plays, given separate names and performed. Lengthy interpolations round off preliminary and secondary episodes and comment on the dialogues; they stretch the staging of a single act up to 41 days of hour-long performances,[4] thereby creating plenty of space for the high play of feelings striven after. 'Inter-play' can be interpreted on many levels: high-caste actors of the *Cākyār* community act together with the similarly highly placed actresses of the *Naṅṅyār* caste and the *Nampyār* drummers; the Sanskrit text of the play is transformed during recitation into a stylized, extremely detailed language of hand gestures, with text, body and voice 'playing' together; important are the fine 'threads', which are spun to fit in with the audience's mood. The list could be extended at will: the powerful inter-play of eye and gesture, the first infusing the second with life;[5] the play of the actors with their roles; the gravitation towards a new social

Fig. 1. The king of demons Rāvaṇan (Paiṅkuḷam Ceriya Rāman Cākyār) and his frightened garden keeper Śaṅkukarṇṇan (Śivan Nampūtiri) in *Tōraṇayuddham*, 3rd Act *Abhiṣēkanāṭakam* (Paluṅkil Temple, Kiḷḷimaṅgalam, 11 Feburary 1997; source: the author, I.97.5-18).

ambience that has recently been forging ahead, and so on. In this essay the inter-play between the teacher and his pupil, i.e. the learning process as such, will be elucidated, as will be too the matter of role understanding.

But first some basic information on *Kūṭiyāṭṭam*—by way of interpolated commentary as is usual in this theatre. *Kūṭiyāṭṭam* is indigenous to the south-west Indian state of Kerala and springs from this in many ways unique culture. Its historical development is lost in the dark; only since the reform of the regional Sanskrit theatre by King Kulaśēkhara Varmman in the eleventh-twelfth century do we possess firm evidence bearing on its evolution and repertoire. Down to the 1950s *Kūṭiyāṭṭam* was exclusively performed in prosperous Brahmanized temples as a ritually important theatre of the elite (Brahmins and nobles). For a variety of reasons Kūṭiyāṭṭam declined over recent centuries. In the twentieth century temples once rich in real estate lost their holdings in the wake of land reforms and performances were drastically curtailed. Also, the new times produced fewer Sanskrit scholars, such as could properly follow a theatre cultivated by an educated elite and develop an appreciation of its subtly mediated messages.[6] In order to survive, *Kūṭiyāṭṭam* had to quit the protective environment of the temple playhouse (*kūttampalam*) with its scholarly public and present itself on 'secular' stages to audiences who were uneducated in the traditional sense. Pupils from other castes, even foreigners like me, are now inducted into this theatrical art; only with difficulty can young talents be recruited from the traditional actor families for a poorly remunerated art-form, a theatre now stripped of its traditional audience. Now as in former times it is the detailed language of hand gestures (which expressly contains signs for case, number and gender),[7] the actual recitation somewhat reminiscent of Vedic presentations by the *Nampūtiri* Brahmins,[8] not to mention the narrative skills involving the eyes, that are at the core of *Kūṭiyāṭṭam* performances. In this very differentiation, however, lies the problem of exclusivity. The three main institutions, by name Mārgi (Tiruvanantapuram), Kēraḷa Kalāmaṇḍalam (Ceṟuturutti) and Ammannūr Cāccu Cākyār Smaraka Gurukulam (Iriññāḷakuṭa), are experimenting with different ways of addressing this problem: especially tailored courses for a broad public are devised and explicatory teaching demonstrations held; long-forgotten acts are revived in the finest detail for a small expert audience, with attempts being made to keep up the annually recurring performances at the very few remaining temples and to participate in experimental performances at the international level. Notwithstanding, the no more than 30 or so active actors and drummers face an uncertain future. If, after escaping from doldrums presided over by traditionalists, it wishes to regain its footing, *Kūṭiyāṭṭam* must be prepared to accept further deep-going changes. What remains is the justified hope for a new audience, keen to enter into the play of emotions, especially at the present moment.[9]

The following essay attempts something like a thick description of the teacher-pupil relationship and the actor's identification with his role.[10] *Kūṭiyāṭṭam*, to be sure, presupposes life-long study by the pupil. Controlling the body is only the first step to real mastery. I have devoted myself since 1995 to the study of *Kūṭiyāṭṭam*; only after years am I gaining a feel for what such mastery might involve.

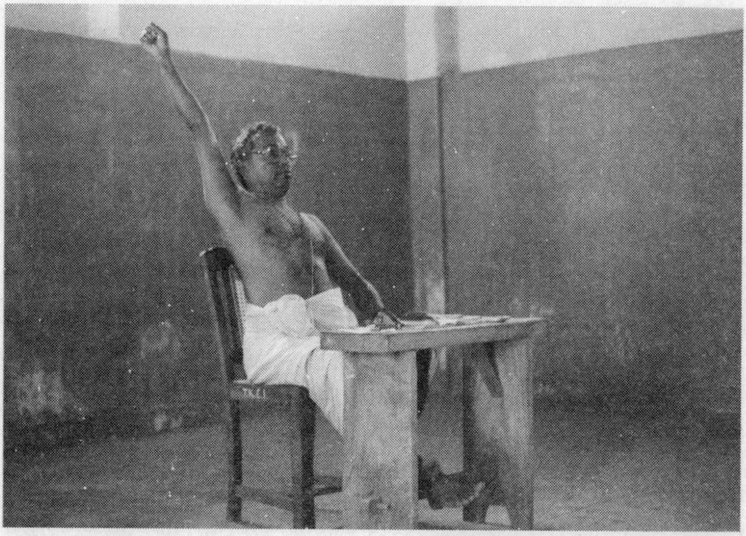

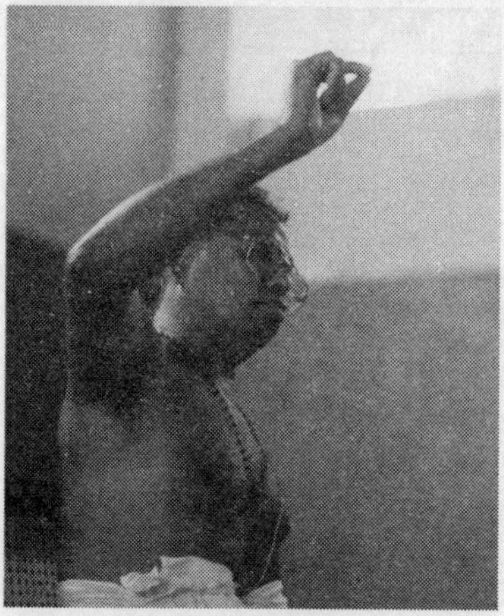

Figs. 2-4. Paiṅkuḷam Ceriya Rāman Cākyār teaching the author (Kēraḷa Kalāmaṇḍalam, January 2001; source: author, I.2001-5, 11, 16).

The difficulty of writing an essay on inner processes of learning is to put into words what cannot be communicated in that medium. Demonstration and imitation, seeing and repeating, feeling, intuition and reproduction, but not lengthy explanations, are the true means of teaching and learning.

How am I, then, to put into words what was not communicated to me in words? A good question! Yet it is worth a try. Using an unconventional style of writing, even playing with words. As a homage to my teachers and their high art.

INTER-PLAY

Move your eyes. Follow my hand. Only your eyes.
Listen and sing after me. Approach me and listen carefully.
Watch my hands and do likewise. Let my hands lead yours.
Imbibe my face, the mood I'm in, my breath, my heart. Feel with me.
Observe my body. Move yours in unison.
Collect your thoughts. Who is Rāman? A god, a teacher, a human being. A masterpiece.

Look, listen, feel, taste, become aware of what cannot be clothed in words. Become a tiny monkey, a parrot, become more than that. Become my mirror image, so that I can become yours. Move in tune with me. Breathe in my rhythm, feel with me, become my twin.
I shall beat you, shall wound you with words. Banish from me what I love. You must learn.

THE TEACHING

Move in accordance with the Kūṭiyāṭṭam rules. I have taught you steps, gestures, pose, mime, recitation, now make use of them. Turn into Rāman for me. Embody him.

What do you know of Rāman? Of Śrīrāman? Of the divine prince in his forest exile? Oh, yes, he is a hero. But what kind of heroic courage is fitting? Feel the peace in his heart, his satisfaction at leading a simple and freely chosen life with his consort and brother among the animals and plants of the forest. At one is Rāman with his fate, indeed for this he was born. Proud he is, the King's son, yet free from arrogance.

No! Sīta is his consort! Does a divine prince given to ascetic ways look thus at the beloved consort entrusted to him? Śūrppaṇakha desires, Rāvaṇan is almost driven out of his mind by his lust—but not Rāman. Look! Not like that! Like this . . .

Let me correct this movement. May I touch you? Relax now and let me lead you.

Your eyes. Everything must repose in the eyes. Sit on the stool. Vīram. Don't move. Speak to me only with your eyes. Summon what is inmost and put it in your eyes. Speak to me . . .

You are Rāman. Now learn to withdraw your feelings. Otherwise you can't leap from a hero's wrath to a girl's bashfulness, leap from Rāman to Sīta to Rāman. Learn how you affect the audience. Learn and withdraw.[11]

Rāman repeats Sīta's words. No, in days of old she, the beautiful one, who eludes embodiment, was not portrayed on stage. Do you know Udyānapravēśam?[12] *Sīta, the radiant one, the goddess, is represented by an oil lamp. What does she say? Take your legs from the stool, become Sīta, the consort.*[13] *Śṛṅgāram. Tender, small, fitting gestures. Smile, move your eyebrows. Look to Rāman from the corner of your eyes. Lovingly, without desire. Trustingly. Yes, just like that . . .*

No, no, no! How often have you reeled under the blows of the stick? And yet bad habits still constrain you! Look here! Listen! Did I teach you that? Get out! Get out of my kaḷari! It is useless, I'm not going to waste my energy, my love, on you any longer . . . Get out of my sight!

The Master

Let your eyes grow large! Open them wide! Put all your striving in your eyes! Look . . . Ah well, perhaps in my case it can't really be seen . . . Yes, you've grasped it! You're doing it right.

Smile, tenderly. Relax the corner of your mouth, don't keep raising and lowering it! I know I often do that myself . . . but it's not good.

The teacher takes his pupils to him. Daughters. Sons. He gives of himself, his body, his heart. And receives both back from them, his intimates.

Girija. Rāman. The others. Āśānmār. Grew up with Kūṭiyāṭṭam. With their master. And are themselves master teachers. My master teachers. Naturally they have their weak points that plague them in daily life, while playing. Weak points it pains them to detect in their pupils, their mirrors. Weak points that may be overcome by a pupil, now their master teacher.

In daily life? Like all of us. In the kaḷari? Well, when there are no distractions, when peace reigns, when the pupil is a pupil and the teacher is a teacher—then there is inter-play. Such instruction no one would disturb.

Fig. 5. Paiṅkuḷam Ceriya Rāman Cākyār portraying a war elephant eavesdroping on a challenge to a duel (rehearsal for the *Dūtavākyam*, Paḷuṅkil temple, Kiḷḷimaṅgalam, 27 September 1996; source: author, I.96.17-2).

Eyes, ears, limbs and heart build pillars, undivided attention sustaining beams. These can be built upon. A bridge. The master teacher reaches the audience through his pupils. A vessel he has painstakingly cleansed of filth and filled with his teaching. A vessel from which sweet love, hot rage, trembling fear, infinite sadness can be poured and tasted. A magic vessel. A cornucopia.

During my time as an Indology undergraduate and as a *Bharata Nāṭyam* pupil I became acquainted with *Kūṭiyāṭṭam* through a few photos and video sequences taken by my professor in Tübingen, Dr. Heidrun Brückner. In 1994 I accompanied her to Kerala to see *Kūṭiyāṭṭam* for myself. Then began my love for this almost forgotten theatre. My application for a study grant found favour with the

DAAD and ICCR. In June 1995 I commenced a two-year traineeship at the Academy of Kēraḷa Kalāmaṇḍalam under P.N. Girija.

Ceremonial acceptance as a pupil by Girija and Rāman Cākyār, Śailaja, Śivan Nampūtiri and Īśvaranuṇṇi involves the initial handing over of a betel leaf along with a nut and a rupee, kneeling before all five and before the oil lamp which stands, in this case, for Paiṅkuḷam Valiya Rāman Cākyār, their master. The blessing is followed by first eye movements, hand gestures, recitation, steps and mime. Testing one's command of the elements. Next day begins the month-long individual tuition, five hours a day for five days of the week.

Fig. 6. P.N. Girija teaching (Kēraḷa Kalāmaṇḍalam, September 1995; source: author, I.95.13-24).

Working every day with the body, the eyes, the hands, the voice, the face. First the individual muscles, then a gesture in tandem with the right facial expression, the correct posture. *Marayilkriya, Purappāṭu.*[14] First small narrative sequences. Instruction together with Sindhu, Sōphi, Lata, Jyōti, with Kṛṣṇakumār and Kanakakumār.

After three months came the stage debut, *Pūtanāmōkṣam.*[15] Something involving expression, not just technique. She is talented

Fig. 7. The author as Laḷita, the beautiful demoness Śūrppaṇakha, in *Śūrppaṇakhāṅkam*, 2nd Act of *Āścaryacūḍāmaṇi* (Paluṅkil Temple, Kiḷḷimaṅgalam, 1 January 1996; source: author, I.96.1-11).

Fig. 8. The author (right) as *nāyika* (heroine) Malayāvati, together with Kṛṣṇakumār as Jīmūtavāhanan in *Nāgānandam*, 3rd Act (Kathakali Club, Trichur, 24 September 1996; source: author, I.96.12-12).

at this, set yourself above tradition and get her to present Pūtana's redemption rather than *Puṟappāṭŭ*. Then the female roles follow, first those of Laḷita and Sīta in *Śūrppaṇakhāṅkam*, then all the minor roles of Sīta in *Jaṭāyuvadham*, of Vijaya in *Tōraṇayuddham*, of Tāra in *Bālivadham*.[16]

Performance of the *nāyika* in *Nāgānandam* with my teachers.

Followed by further sequences from the Cēṭi-*Nirvvahaṇam Naṅṅyār-Kūttŭ*. And any amount of making myself useful during performances, i.e. playing *tāḷam* cymbals, entrance verse recitations,

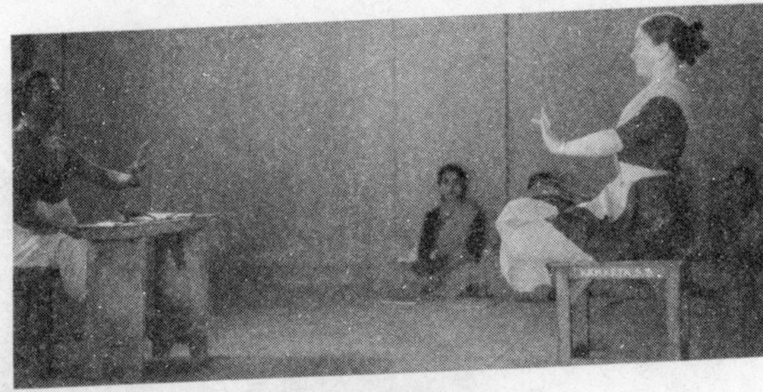

Figs. 9-11. Paiṅkuḷam Ceriya Rāman Cākyār and the author during instruction (Kēraḷa Kalāmaṇḍalam, January 2001; *s*ource: author, I.2001.1-6, 7, 12).

on camera. Days of living on top of each other while touring or performing in traditional temple contexts. In a word, inter-play.

A painful farewell in April 1997 is followed by many shorter visits; in 1999 I complete my MA thesis. Finally, in 2000-1, comes another training stint lasting several weeks. With Paiṅkuḷam Ceriya Rāman Cākyār. I play a male role. Śrīrāman. The second act of *Āścaryacūḍāmaṇi*, the wondrous crest jewel.[17]

This rainy season I intend to return. Then I plan to complete my doctoral thesis on *Kūṭiyāṭṭam*.[18]

So much for myself and my training track to date.

How is a Pupil Turned into a *Kūṭiyāṭṭam* Actor?

First, the pupil must master the tools of the trade. Bodily control. Starting with the muscles: face muscles, eye muscles, limbs, vocal chords. Instruction in the morning, at nine or ten. Standing at rest, at a half-squat with knees and feet turned outward. Elbows raised, circular movements of the wrists are described before the upper belly. At least six verses on Mukāmbika are slowly recited. For twenty minutes or half an hour. Those who cannot endure squatting any longer, whose trembling knees give way, are given a taste of the stick. As punishment? True, but the main point is to boost a flagging of self-discipline, that is, to re-energise sluggish limbs.

Then come further exercises to warm and limber up the body, such as moving the shoulders in a circle, or squatting with legs astraddle, first lean to one side, then to the other, or leaps in which the conjoined big toes should ideally touch the forehead.

Then *Marayilkriya*, *Purappāṭu*. Then a narrative sequence or other, ever recurring elements such as *Paṭappurappāṭu*, *Kāmaśaram*, *Kōppaṇiyippiykkuka*.[19]

Until the lunch-break at twelve or 1 o'clock.

At 3 o'clock every day begins twenty minutes of eye training. Eyes wide-open and large, the eyeballs are first moved from right to left and back to right, then they are rolled in an upper semi-circle, then in a lower semi-circle, rolled in a full circle in both directions, in diagonals, in a recumbent figure of eight, working up and down. Mechanically. All the while sitting upright, the arms folded across the chest, the head motionless.

Then it's the turn of the face muscles. Eyebrows working up and down, flutter the lower eyelid, wobble the cheeks, turn the corner of the mouth up and down.

What must always be performed for the nine *rasas*? Eyebrows up and down, smiling all the while, eyes not too large for love, *śṛṅgāram*. Eyes large and replete with power, brows raised, heroic courage, *vīram*. Corner of mouth working up and down, eyebrows severely puckered, eyes replete with power but not too large for sadness, *karuṇam*. Eyebrows raised, corner of mouth smiling downwards, eyes turned sideways for the disdainful variant of humour, *hāsyam*. Eyes as large as possible, eyebrows working up and down, wobbling your cheeks, smiling for rapture, *adbhutam*. Corner of mouth inclined slightly downwards, eyebrows raised, perhaps gently puckered, eyeballs wander restlessly from left to right and back to left with the head moving gently in time—fear, *bhayānakam*. For disgust, *bibhatsam*, wrinkle and pucker the nose, mouth and eyebrows, while making the eyes large. Work the lower eyelid up and down, keep the eyes large, incline the eyeballs downwards slightly for *raudram*. The whole face is immobile and peaceful, at one with *śāntam*'s peace. The much invoked breathing technique? It comes automatically as soon as a feeling is 'grasped', does not require focusing on.

Then come the hand gestures. The twenty-four basic gestures with examples of their use. *Rāmāyaṇasaṁkṣēpam*.[20]

Then voice training. Verse recitation in the various registers.

And this goes on month after month.

Costumes? Face paint? No rehearsing is permitted in costumes, which weigh several kilos and feature wooden adornments and heavy wooden crowns; nor is there any rehearsing of the use of green make-up to highlight the facial expressions, or of the use of rice beards, or of the use of seeds to redden the eyes. All this must await one's stage debut.

Is Instruction Today Different From, Say, a Hundred Years Ago? Is One Taught Differently in Terms of Curriculum and Final Diploma at the State-run Kalāmaṇḍalam School than, Say, at the Ammannūr-Cākyār-Gurukulam?

The core of instruction has not changed. It remains what it always was: inter-play. *Kūṭiyāṭṭam*. True, Paiṅkuḷam Valiya Rāman Cākyār has refined a teaching strategy at the Kalāmaṇḍalam, a sort of institutionalized *gurukulam*. He has compressed the time of basic training with one's uncle or mother—practising in any spare time—into several years and fashioned it into a full-time training course. The basic principles, the ways and means of teaching and learning, abide, as does the training phase, which cannot be measured by the number of hours of instruction imparted, or by the six or eight years it may take to get one's diploma, or by the number of years one has spent at the Gurukulam. It can be gauged by master and pupil alone and it varies in every case. What can be said, though, is that four or six or eight years are not long enough to produce a new master. Not by a long stretch.

How is a Role learnt? What Elements go into the Role as a Whole?

Basically, the Sanskrit/Prakrit dramatic texts must be learnt by heart in the *Kūṭiyāṭṭam*-specific recitative mode—and this means all the roles. They must be learned by heart and they must be understood. Sitting on the grass mat. Then listening repeatedly to the recitation of the role-related texts for memorisation and reciting after the master. The vocal registers are merely the frame for transmitting the content. Joined next by hand gestures bearing on the text. Then by the *āṭṭaprakāram*, the unspoken Malayalam commentary translated into hand gestures. Notetaking and memorizing on the grass mat. All with eyes and mime and heart.

Gradually the role is mastered: first the text, then the matching hand gestures, then the eyes, the mime, the atmospherics. The commentary in the same order. Now the pupil may rise and, at last, commit his whole body to posture and movement. The point has been reached where the body's elements are fused. This 'technical body' must now be filled with ever more life; it must be so charged with feelings that the audience can sense them. Understanding the role grows through correction, working in from the outside, from how the elbows are held to eye movements, from eye movements to the heart. Spirit, essence are added by a process of osmosis. Very slowly, not at all points, and not always. Mastery takes years of grappling with the roles, takes year-long practice.

Who is Rāman? Read the myths, the Rāmāyaṇam. Study the retrospective nirvvahaṇam episodes. Learn who Rāman is. Ponder and repeat your whole life long. Repeat with your master, repeat with your students. Repeat, improve, refine, learn.

Repeated, improved, refined to the point of mastery—perhaps, or perhaps not. The audience knows a master when they see, listen to, 'feel' one, by his demonstrated power to move them. The actor ponders how a performance has gone, ponders aloud with other actors and with the learned public; he himself knows it when his acting attains mastery and when not. The heart must grow; the ability to express this regularly on stage, as a stage presence maintained for hours on end, must be acquired. The *Kūṭiyāṭṭam* repertoire is limited for good reason; its strict rules are not devised arbitrarily but with a view to shaping individual dramatic talent into a subtle and unique whole. True masters are rarely younger than forty or fifty. Or even older.

Śrirāman, at the Start of the 2nd Act of the Play Āścaryacuḍāmaṇi

This is an exemplary verse with a short explanation appended, but without the detailed repetition by division of the latter, furnished with a commentary in the prose word-order, *anvayam*; and without possible lengthily commented passages, the *upaślōkas*. Both may or may not be inserted. Two hours of performance time for a single verse is no rarity, although the same verse can also be covered in fifteen minutes. Here therefore is a short version.

Three teaching texts—here telescoped for simplicity's sake—in chronological order.[21]

- *Recitative dramatic text simultaneously rendered into hand gestures (nāṭakam/grantham)*
- Unspoken commentary text explaining the dramatic text and only communicable with hand gestures and body movements (āṭṭaprakāram)
- Stage instructions (kramadīpika)

[. . .] *vaidēhi, vidūrē sarvvaṃ vismayanīyatayā śrūyatē.* enna granthaṃ colliyāṭi atinṯe arttham āṭū. allē sītē! vidūrattiṅkaluḷḷa

vastukkaḷ okkeyuṃ vismayattōṭu kūṭe kēḷkkuṃ cennu kāṇunna samayattiṅkal itō mumpuˇ kēṭṭatuˇ—ennuˇ nissāratayuṃ tōnnum. oriykkal kūṭi coḷḷi. *paśya*—ennuˇ colliyāṭi atinṯe arttham. atuˇ entuˇ? nī tanne vaḻipōle vicāriccāluṃ.
śailāyāmibhir ambuvāhanivahacchāyais triyāmācaraiḥ
sēvyā pañcavaṭīti mē matir abhūd udvēlakautūhalā |
sēyaṃ dēvi, cirōcitām upanayaty udyānayōgyāṃ śrīyaṃ
śrōtur [v]vismayanīyavastuviṣayāḥ śailāṭavīsāgarāḥ ||
ennuˇślōkattinṯe arttham āṭū. ī pañcavaṭi parvvatam pōle taṭiccuruṇṭuˇ nīṇṭuˇmēgham pōle kaṟuttiriykkunna rākṣasanmārēkoṇṭuˇniṟaññirippōnnatāṇuˇ—ennīvaṇṇam mumpuˇmaharṣimār paṟaññu kēṭṭa samayattiṅkal rākṣasarē kāṇānuḷḷa āgrahaṃ hētuvāyiṭṭuˇ enṯe manassil ēṟṟavuṃ kautukaṃ varddhiccu vaśamāyi. allē dēvi, ā pañcavaṭi iviṭe vannu kaṇṭa samayattiṅkal vaḷare kālam paricayicciṭṭuḷḷa udyānattinṯe śōbhaye vahiykkunnu. atu hētuvāyiṭṭuˇparvvataṅṅaḷuṃ vanapradēśaṅṅaḷuṃ samudraṅṅaḷuṃ dūrattiṅkalninnuˇ kēḷkkunna samayattiṅkal cennu kāṇunna samayattiṅkal itō mumpuˇkēṭṭatuˇ—enna nissāratayuṃ tōnnum. *uttarārddhaṃ colli* sītayuṭe cūrṇṇi kēṭṭāṭi nēre irunnuˇ aṇiyaṟayil pōrū.

[. . .] *O Sīta, one hears of all that is far off as were it something amazing.* Recite this text and enact the meaning with hand gestures.
O Sīta! All things far off are heard of with amazement; but when one arrives [there] and sees [these things], are they as one has been led to expect? Rather they disappoint. Recite again. Look—Recite this text and enact its meaning with hand gestures. How is that? Ponder it in the same way [I will set out for you]!
"Huge as mountains, [dark] as storm-clouds—Pañcavaṭi must be haunted by such nocturnal spirits!—this is what I thought and could barely tame my curiosity".
Now I am here, my lady, and [Pañcavaṭi] seems like a long-familiar garden of delights.
As long as we have [only] heard of them, they excite us all the more, the mountains, forests and seas.
Thus [recited and enacted with hand gestures] enact the meaning of

> the verse. "This Pañcavaṭi is replete with demons that are as wide, broad and high as mountains and as black as clouds"—thus spoke the Ṛṣis before. When I heard this, great curiosity arose in my heart, born of the desire to see a demon. My lady, after we have arrived, we see that Pañcavaṭi here decked out *in the delights of a* long-loved *garden*. Therefore [I ask:] do mountains, forested areas and seas one has heard of while [still] far off live up to expectations when one draws near and sees [them]?—Surely one thinks them disappointing. *Recite the second half of the verse* [and enact its meaning with hand gestures], listen to Sīta's prose, sit upright [in Rāman's pose], descend into the room behind the stage.

The text is recited in the vocal register called *indaḷam*. In the *Kūṭiyāṭṭam* recitative mode, the pauses are placed as follows: When the following word begins with a vowel, final consonants combine with the latter, while words ending on a vowel or words beginning with a consonant are generated thus: *śailāyāmibhi-rambuvāha-nivaha-cchāyai-striyā-mācaraiḥ.* Metre plays no role. Prose (as also verse in every metre) is pegged by the speaker, by the meaning of what is said and by the situation to one or other of the *Kūṭiyāṭṭam*'s recitative registers. Here it is *indaḷam*. An heroic character in a peaceful mood. A notation? With each speaker *indaḷam* sounds a little different. Practising is not the same as in costume. Tonal frequency analyses? These I have already performed.[23] But what about the voice's power as the lines go up and down. What goes on in the body that goes with the voice?

The hand gestures for the first prose sentence might appear in a pupil's notes as follows:

Text	*Meaning*	*Hand gestures*
vaidēhi	Sita!	1. right 'name' 2. both hands 'goddess' 3. left 'vocative', addressing one's peers or the slightly lower-ranking
vidūrē	far off	1. right pallavam, 'far' 2. left locative case 'saptami'

sarvvaṃ	everything	two mudrākyam, 'all'
vismayanīyatayā	as something amazing	1. both hands, face 'adbhutam' 2. two muṣṭi 'yōgyam' 3. 'iti' 4. left instrumental case 'tṛtīya'
śrūyatē	is heard	1. both hands 'hearing' 2. 'kriya' (action as indicated by the verb)

Fig. 12. Śrīrāman (Kṛṣṇakumār) and Sīta[22] (Lata) in the *Śūrppaṇakāṅkam*, 2nd Act of the *Āścaryacūḍāmaṇi* (Paḷuṅkil Temple, Kiḷḷimaṅgalam, 1 January 1996; source: author, I.96.13).

Hand gestures for case endings, for modality, for gender, for number. Abstract gestures and graphic gestures, culturally specific and readily understood by all. Invariably stylized. Then comes mimicry, eye movements, working with the body. The eyes follow the hands; large, replete with power, staring into the distance. A pupil might try to make notes of what must be learnt. On paper. But the pupil doesn't do this. Except perhaps someone as wedded to a note-taking culture as I am. As I tried to do above in the case of hand gestures. Though covered with scrawl (and often sketches), paper as a medium quickly reaches its limits, becomes second-rate as a guide. One's bodily memory, however, is far-reaching and reliable; it memorizes texts in the context of recitation or of gestures; it files away what is essential in a steadily growing, portable archive that can be accessed at will. The intellect is called on for interpretations, for the decorative element, but the scaffolding is supplied by what the body itself has internalized. It is interesting, academic that I am, to have this turn into bodily awareness. Any full-scale attempt at a description, at analysis, at writing a book would always be fragmentary, for what is intended for the stage belongs on stage. Text, voice, body, costume, heart, audience.

But What About Role Identification?

As I said, it is a part of learning. It requires great mastery, it paves the way to the highest mastery. A kind of embodiment, of deep emotion that spills over to the audience, not so far removed from what is generally called possession.[24]

So What, then, is True Mastery?

It is to observe oneself, one's perfected ability to move the audience, in all awareness of *bhāva-rasa* inter-play. To *act*, mind you, not to embody. To channel one's own emotion through the role and overcome it, the better to be seized by an even higher, a sublime emotion, that of artistic perfection. What matters is not to *be* Śrīrāman, but to *portray* him perfectly for the audience. To enact him. To play. To deploy one's trained body, in full awareness, down to the least quiver of the muscles. To hover over the stage, the role, the audience. To apprehend the least vibration in each member of the audience. To knowingly tug on the audience's heart-strings, drawing them in until they are ensnared, captivated. To enjoy what I call playing with play.

To enjoy playing with play.

This experimental essay, not formulated in the dry language of the scholar and not regurgitating current theories or ongoing research, attempts to acquaint readers of diverse backgrounds with the inner meaning of the Sanskrit theatre known as *Kūṭiyāṭṭam.* Are not my readers just as colourfully mixed as the new public that *Kūṭiyāṭṭam* is winning over—what with indigenous experts, so-called devotees,[25] simple, unsophisticated members of the audience, experimental theatre insiders, Indologists all rubbing shoulders? The divinity so central to a *Kūṭiyāṭṭam* performance can, however, hardly be numbered among my readers; likewise the inter-play between stage and audience is quite different from the relationship struck up between author and readership. And yet it is my hope that both processes—those relatively easy to reproduce in factual terms and those of a more inward kind, which are far from easy to put into words—have been welded in this all-too-limited paper-bound medium to the point of fusing into a single—if schematic—image, namely that of *inter-play.*

NOTES

1. To my teaching master P.N. Girijadēvi. To my teaching master Paiṅkuḷam Ceriya Rāman Cākyār.
2. Subhadra's words as repeated by her servant-confidant Cēṭi in due perspective, *Subhadrādhanañjayam* 2nd Act. In cases of Sanskrit quotations and appellations I use the conventional orthography and pronunciation of Kerala. Acknowledgments: This contribution has originally been written in German and was translated into English by Dr. Bruce Allen, Tübingen. I thank Heidrun Brückner for her invitation to reflect on this topic and to contribute to the present paper.
3. The *Kūṭiyāṭṭam* repertoire contains the following plays: Harṣan's *Nāgānandam*, Kulaśēkhara Varmman's *Subhadrādhanañjayam* and *Tapatīsaṃvaraṇam*, the plays attributed to Bhāsan (esp. *Pratimānāṭakam, Abhiṣēkanāṭakam, Pratijñāyaugandharāyaṇam*), the two Prahasanas *Mattavilāsam* and *Bhagavadajjukam*, as well as Śaktibhadran's

Āścaryacūḍāmaṇi and Nīlakaṇṭhan's *Kalyāṇasaugandhikam*.—As part of revival efforts now under way, the actress and choreographer Mārgi Sati published a new acting manual, Sīta's flashback in Bhavabhūti's *Uttararāmacaritam* (Mārgi Sati 1999).

4. *Mantrāṅkam*, 3rd Act of *Pratijñāyaugandharāyaṇam* (Moser 2000); see also the disapproval of such comprehensiveness in *Naṭāṅkuśa*, the Goad of the Actors, a critique of the *Kūṭiyāṭṭam* Sanskrit theatrical practice dating from the fifteenth century (Paulose 1993).
5. An actor might sit for hours on a stool and stirringly narrate an inserted side-episode using only his hands and face.
6. Even earlier the number of genuine Sanskrit scholars was not that high; many Nampūtiri Brahmins were able to recite the Veda and a number of Sanskrit texts, but were quite unable to understand their proper meaning. The role of the Malayalam-speaking Vidūṣaka has developed to the point where he is now a kind of 'translator'.
7. The hand-gesture language itself enables an interpretation of hidden meanings or ambiguities contained in the recited dramatic text and can—as in *Mantrāṅkam*—reveal a further text level (Moser 2000).
8. The dramatic text is chanted in a recitative style, the tonal registers of which vary with the character and the situation.
9. Very recently, on 18.3.2001, *Kūṭiyāṭṭam*, together with 18 other outstanding cultural spaces or forms of expression from the different regions of the world, was awarded the title of Masterpiece of the Oral and Intangible Heritage of Humanity by the UNESCO. What this declaration means for the study and performance of *Kūṭiyāṭṭam*, the future will have to show.—Further introductory literature on the *Kūṭiyāṭṭam* complex may be found in the works listed in the bibliography; the reader is especially referred to the special edition of the journal of Sangeet Natak Akademi (1995), where articles on all aspects of *Kūṭiyāṭṭam* have been collected in English translation.
10. This is neither the first attempt to describe the process of learning in *Kūṭiyāṭṭam* (see for example Pfaff 1997, Venu 2002 or the unpublished works Johan 1997/8: 72f and Johan 1999/2000: 92-180), nor is it the first time that the verse *Śailāyāmibhiḥ* is explained in all detail (see for example again Johan 1997/8: 112-61 and Johan 1999/2000: 154-7 or Sowle 1982: 148-51); but it is the first essay trying to mediate in a literary way.
11. *Kūṭiyāṭṭam* tends to an epically evocative interlocking of different episodes. The actor acts as a kind of narrator in side- or/and pre-episodes inserted into the main story-line; his task is to portray in solo performance all the beings that are encountered therein: humans, gods, animals, demons and the like. Still he always has to bear in mind his

main role, if only because of the costume and make-up he is wearing. The technical expression for this technique is *pakarnnāṭṭam*. The rapid switches between the various narrative roles, their respective characters and emotive states, require great mastery to carry conviction.

12. *Udyānapravēśam*: a play segment famous in *Kūṭiyāṭṭam* that has been taken from the *Aśōkavanikāṅkam*, 5th Act *Āścaryacūḍāmaṇi*. Sīta is a prisoner in the garden of Rāvaṇan, who spends hours in solo performance praising her beauty and begging fruitlessly for her love. Thus rebuffed, he threatens to smite Sīta with his sword; only at the last moment is he restrained from so doing by his consort Maṇḍōdari.
13. Similar considerations to those already set out for *pakarnnāṭṭam* in case of side-episodes hold for the adoption of the text by role figures, who are really intended to appear on stage but at various points in the *Kūṭiyāṭṭam* tradition do not do this. The text evokes a switch from the real role figure of Śrīrāman to that of his consort Sīta, who does not appear on stage. This technique is called *kēṭṭāṭṭuka*—portraying what is heard. Śrīrāman, who appears directly here as role figure (i.e. in the dress and make-up for Śrīrāman), first poses with a series of hand gestures the question, 'What did she (Sīta) say?' then he switches to the pose of Sīta, 'speaks' her lines (again using nothing but gestures) only to return, with a terminal hand-gestured question, 'Is that what she said?', to his real role as Śrīrāman. Variants of this technique are possible: sometimes Sīta's text is recited by the cymbal-playing *Naṅṅyār* sitting beside the stage. This technique of the non-appearance of various figures in *Kūṭiyāṭṭam* theatre is criticized in *Naṭāṅkuśa* (Paulose 1993).
14. *Maṟayilkriya*: the movements behind the curtain is performed by way of introducing key role figures when they first take the stage. Behind a curtain held up by two stage assistants, purely technical combinations of steps accompanied by hand-movements of the same kind are performed, these being variously fixed for each type of character. The curtain is by no means large, so that the audience can see both the actor's feet and the tip of his headgear. Mainly during the *Maṟayilkriya* the actor is turned towards the two copper drums (*miḻāvu*˘), the principal instruments in *Kūṭiyāṭṭam* that are played at the rear of the stage.—*Puṟappāṭu*˘ is the name given to the extended introduction of a role figure after the curtain is removed, whereupon a solo retrospective (*nirvvahaṇam*) ensues.
15. *Pūtanāmōkṣam* is an episode from the *nirvvahaṇam* retrospective (lasting many days) by the Cēṭi in *Subhadrādhanañjayam*, 2nd Act. Inserted as a solo performance by an actress is the entire history of Śrīkṛṣṇan, down to his sister Subhadra's marriage with his friend Arjjunan-Dhanañjayan, this being the latest point reached in the play proper.

This retrospective requires all the skills an actress can muster (she traditionally comes from the *Naṅṅyār* community) and is known under the names *Śrīkṛṣṇacaritam* and *Naṅṅyār(amma)-Kūttu*˘(see Nārāyaṇan Nampyār 1984 and Rajagopalan 1997: 88-182).

16 *Śūrppaṇakhāṅkam* = *Āścaryacūḍāmaṇi* Act 2.—*Jaṭāyuvadham* = *Āścaryacūḍāmaṇi* Act 4.—*Bālivadham* = *Abhiṣēkanāṭakam* Act 1.—*Tōraṇayuddham* = *Abhiṣēkanāṭakam* Act 3.

17. Traditionally, women take the female roles and men the male ones (an exception is the demoness Śūrppaṇakha—in her terrible demonic apparitional form she is played by a man). That I, as a woman, was permitted to study a male role can be put down to the determination with which those actively teaching today embrace experiment and innovation. The same passage of Śrīrāman (see below) was first played by a woman—none other than my teacher P.N. Girija—on 24 December 1998 in Mumbai (on 9 November 1995, my fellow student Kalāmaṇḍalam Sōphi became the first woman to play a male role on stage, playing on that occasion Lakṣmaṇan in the *Jaṭāyuvadham*, Act 4 *Āścaryacūḍāmaṇi*).

18. This was written in the year 2001; I did return; the thesis was submitted in October 2004 (Moser [2006]).

19. *Paṭappuṟappāṭu*˘, the soldiers' preparations for battle (putting on their armour, readying their weapons, etc.); *Kāmaśaram*, the effects of the darts of the god of love, Kāmadēvan; and *Kōppaṇiyippiykkuka*, the sumptuous attiring and making-up of a heroine by her servants subsequent to bathing – these are three examples of choreographically fixed sequences performed using gesture and mime that can be inserted in appropriate contexts.

20. A Malayalam version of the entire *Rāmāyaṇam* epic cycle known as *saṃkṣēpam* – or summary – is translated for training purposes into the language of gestures. Here the pupil is inducted not only into the mythology, but also into the permutations and combinations of gesticulatory lore.

21. In the following three different typefaces are used to isolate three textual levels. These are recitative dramatic text, stage instructions and commentary communicated by gesture.

22. In recent years Sīta has been portrayed on stage in *Śūrppaṇakhāṅkam*.

23. Moser 2002.

24. Schömbucher 1993.

25. *Darśan*, religious 'watching', feeling one's way into a figure drawn from mythology, can be the motive behind attending a *Kūṭiyāṭṭam* performance. It is no rarity on such occasions for individuals to pause briefly before prostrating themselves before the stage, or even to ritually

encircle the latter. It is not a performance-centric uplifting of the aesthetic faculties that is being sought here or, for that matter, the narration of a story-line.

SELECTED BIBLIOGRAPHY ON *KŪṬIYĀṬṬAM* (PLUS CITED WORKS)*

Brückner, Heidrun, 2000, 'Manuscripts and Performance Traditions of the So-called "Trivandrum-Plays" Ascribed to Bhāsa—A Report on Work in Progress', *Bulletin d'Études Indiennes* 17-18 (Paris), 501-50.

Byrski, Maria Christopher, 1967, 'Is Kudiyattam a Museum Piece?' *Sangeet Natak Akademi Journal* 5: 45-54.

Daugherty, Diane, 1996, 'The Nangyār: Female Ritual Specialist of Kerala', *Asian Theatre Jounal* 13/1: 54-67.

———, 2000, 'Fifty Years On: Arts Funding in Kerala Today', *Asian Theatre Journal* 17/2: 237-52.

Johan, Virginie, [1997/8], 'Decouverte et apprentissage du Kutiyattam: Recherche sur le langage de l'acteur', Paris: Institut d'études théâtrales de Paris III [unpublished M.A.-thesis].

———, [1999/2000], 'Kuttu—Kutiyattam: Presentation de ces theatres dans leur contexte keralais et recherche sur La transmission du savoir chez les Cakyar', Paris: Institut d'études théâtrales de Paris III [unpublished M. Phil. thesis].

———, 2002, 'Kūttu, Kūṭiyāṭṭam, Théâtres Classiques du Kerala', *Revue d'Histoire du Théâtres* (Paris) 4: 365-82.

———, 2004, 'Intrigue et représentation dans le théâtre Kūṭiyāṭṭam, exemple du "Toraṇayuddham" ("la bataille de la porte" acte III de l'Abhiṣēkanāṭakam de Bhāsa) et de son Purappāṭu (entrée) de Śaṅkukarṇa', Toulouse: Publication de Centre de Recherches Appliquées au Théâtres Antique/CRATA, 38-75.

Jones, Clifford Reis (ed.), 1984, *The Wondrous Crest-Jewel in Performance: Text and Translation of the Āścaryacūḍāmaṇi of Śaktibhadra with the Production Manual from the Tradition of Kūṭiyāṭṭam Sanskrit Drama*, New Delhi: Oxford University Press.

Kunjunni Raja, K[umarapuram], 1964 [1960], *Kutiyattam: An Introduction*, New Delhi: Sangeet Natak Akademi.

* Moser [2007] contains an elaborate bibliography, including Malayalam works on *Kūṭiyāṭṭam*.

Mādhava Cākyār, Māṇi, 1996 [1975], *Nāṭyakalpadrumam*, Ceṟuturutti: Kēraḷa Kalāmaṇḍalam.

Mārgi Sati, 1999, 'Śrīrāmacaritam naṅṅyārammakkūttŭ': Avataraṇa-prakāram', Kōṭṭayam: Karanṯ Buks.

Moser, Heike, 2000, 'Mantrāṅkam: The Third Act of Pratijñāyau-gandharāyaṇam in Kūṭiyāṭṭam', *Bulletin d'Études Indiennes* (Paris) 17-18 (1999-2000), 563-84.

———, 2002, 'Versrezitation im Sanskrit-Theater Kūṭiyāṭṭam (Kerala / Südindien)', In: *Meter, Rhythm and Performance—Metrum, Rhythmus, Performanz,* ed. Christoph Küper, Frankfurt/M.: Peter Lang (Linguistic International, 6), 457-67.

———, 2007, *Naṅṅyār-Kūttŭ—ein Teilaspekt des Sanskrittheaterkomplexes Kūṭiyāṭṭam. Historische Entwicklung und performative Textumsetzung,* Wiesbaden: Harrassowitz (Drama und Theater in Südasien).

Nārāyaṇan Nampyār, P.K. (ed.), 1984, *Śrīkṛṣṇacaritam naṅṅyārammakkūttŭ* Kōṭṭayam: Nāṣanal Bukksṯṯāl.

Nārāyaṇappiṣārōṭi, K.P. (ed.), 1988 (1967), *Āścaryacūḍāmaṇi. Śaktibhadramahākaviyuṭe āścaryacūḍāmaṇi nāṭakavum atinṟe abhinayattinuvēṇṭi racicciṭṭuḷḷa kramadīpika, āṭṭaprakāram, tuṭaṅṅiya āṭṭakrama viśadīkaraṇaṅṅaḷum*, Tṛśūr: Kēraḷa Saṅgītanāṭaka Akkādami.

Panchal, Goverdhan, 1984, *Kuttampalam and Kūṭiyāṭṭam*, New Delhi: Sangeet Natak Akademi.

Paulose, K.G. (ed.), 1993, *Naṭāṅkuśa: A Critique on Dramaturgy,* Tripunithura: Govt. Sanskrit College (Ravivarma Samskṛta Granthāvali, 26).

———, 2000a, *Bhagavadajjukam in Kūṭiyāṭṭam: The Hermit and the Harlot—the Sanskrit Farce in Performance,* Delhi: Bharatiya Book Corporation.

———, 2000b, *Bhīma in Search of Celestrial Flower: Nīlakaṇṭhakavi Kalyāṇasaugandhikavyāyoga.* Sanskrit Text with English Translation, Delhi: Bharatiya Book Corporation.

——— [and Margi Madhu], 2003, *Improvisations of Ancient Theatre: [Documentation of the text and performance of Kaanchukeeyam, from a 11th century Sanskrit text],* Text and performance by Margi Madhu. Tripunithura: International Centre for Kutiyattam.

Pfaff, Walter, 1997, 'The Ant and the Stone: Learning Kutiyattam', *The Drama Review* 41/4 (T 156): 133-62.

Rajagopalan, L.S., 1997, *Women's Role in Kūḍiyāṭṭam,* Chennai: The Kuppuswami Sastri Research Institute.

———, 2000, *Kūḍiyāṭṭam: Preliminaries and Performance,* Chennai: Kuppuswami Sastri Research Institute.

Richmond, Farley, 2002, *Kutiyattam: Sanskrit Theater of India,* Multimedia-CD-ROM. Ann Arbor: University of Michigan Press (Digital Publishing at the University of Michigan Press, CD-ROM 0-472-00263-5).

Sangeet Natak Akademi, 1995, *Kūṭiyāṭṭam,* ed. K. Ayyappa Paniker, *Sangeet Natak Akademi Journal* (New Delhi) 111-14 [special issue].

Schömbucher, Elisabeth, 1993, 'Gods, Ghosts and Demons: Possession in South Asia', in *Flags of Fame: Studies in South Asian Folk Culture,* eds. H. Brückner, L. Lutze and A. Malik, New Delhi: Manohar (South Asia Institute, New Delhi Branch, Heidelberg University, South Asian Studies, 27), pp. 239-67.

Sowle, John Steven, 1982, 'The Traditions, Training, and Performance of Kūṭiyāṭṭam: Sanskrit Drama in South India, Berkeley: University of California (unpublished Ph.D. thesis).

Unni, N.P. and Bruce M. Sullivan, 1995, *The Sun God's Daughter and King Saṃvaraṇa: Tapatī-Saṃvaraṇam and the Kūṭiyāṭṭam Drama Tradition: Text with Vivaraṇa Commentary,* Delhi: Nag Publishers.

———, 2001, *The Wedding of Arjuna and Subhadrā: The Kūṭiyāṭṭam Drama Subhadrā-Dhanañjaya: Text with Vicāratilaka Commentary, Introduction, English Translation and Notes,* Delhi: Nag Publishers.

Venu, G., 1989, *Production of a Play in Kūṭiyāṭṭam: Text and Translation of the First Act of Abhiṣeka Nāṭaka of Bhāsa with the Kramadīpika (production manual) and the Āṭṭaprakāraṃ (acting manual) from the Sanskrit Drama Tradition of Kerala,* Irinjalakuda: Natanakairali (Documentation of Kūṭiyāṭṭam Series, 1).

———, 2002, *Into the World of Kutiyattam with the Legendary Ammannur Madhava Chakyar,* Irinjalakuda: Natanakairali (Documentation of Kūṭiyāṭṭam Series, 3).

10

Embodying the Lion's 'Fury': Ambivalent Animals, Activation, and Representation

Phillip B. Zarrilli

INTO THE LION'S GAZE: THE LOOK AND FEEL OF 'FURY'

It was during my initial trip to Kerala, south-western coastal India, in 1976-7 that I first encountered what can be described as 'the lion's gaze'—the look and feel of 'fury'. Inspired by Jerzy Grotowski, I had travelled to Kerala to study the now internationally known Kathakali dance-drama of Kerala, and to see whether I might find it possible to adapt its exercises in training Western performers. While undergoing intensive training in Kathakali's preliminary exercises and massage at the Kerala Kalamandalam, I discovered that the precursor of these remarkable exercises and psychophysiological processes, *kalarippayattu* was still being practised (see Zarrilli 1998, Chapter 1).[1] It was during my second encounter with *kalarippayattu*, while observing twice-daily classes at the C.V.N. Kalari, Thiruvananthapuram, that I experienced 'the lion's gaze'. Then forty-five-year-old master, Gurukkal Govindankutty Nayar, began to practise sword and shield, the most advanced weapon in the repertory, with one of his most well-trained and remarkably agile students, Rajashekharan Nayar. After 'saluting' each other by performing a series of prostrations with the entire body and touching their swords and shields to 'pay respects', they began an exchange of jumps, turns, and slashing cuts both in set forms and free style, moving back and forth across the *kalari* floor (Figs. 1-2).

Fig. 1. The late Gurukkal Govindankutty Nayar practising sword and shield. (Photo: author)

Fig. 2. Gurukkal Govindankutty Nayar and Rajashekharan Nayar practising sword and shield. (Photo: author)

The master's eyes opened wide, sparks literally flew from the student's shield from the tremendous force of the torrent of blows toward the neck, head, ribs, and ankles he delivered as he backed the student into the corner of the kalari, before relenting. The exchange momentarily took my breath away.

At the time, and for many years afterward, I could not explain why. I did not have an appropriate language with which to express what I had witnessed. Indeed, it has taken me over twenty years of research, practice, and reflection to articulate some of the assumptions, meanings, and interpretations of the 'lion's gaze'.

In retrospect, my breath was taken away, not out of a sense of danger for either myself or the student practising since he was able to withstand the forceful torrent of the powerful slashing cuts, but for the fluidity and virtuosity of the exchange, the single-point focus, as well as the manifest power and 'danger' in the master's attack. This was a 'danger' different from that I had experienced in another *kalari* where, observing practice with weapons I had been afraid *for* the safety of the students, not *of* the manifest but controlled power that was being unleashed. In the context of a routine daily class, Govindankutty Nayar and his student had suddenly embodied an extraordinary intuitive sense of control, and a remarkable actualization of ' the power of fury' capable of destruction that was gut-wrenchingly palpable.

What I witnessed then, experienced later in my own training, and saw only a handful of other times, is a concentration of the powers of practice in this optimal state of actualization manifest in the eyes of the master (Fig. 3). In India the eyes are understood to be a vehicle for gaining 'knowledge' or affecting something or someone (Eck 1981: 6-7). When a devotee takes even a momentary glimpse (*darshan*) of a divine image, there is contact and *an exchange*, not a simple 'looking at'. The eyes are the window to one's internal state or condition. They are a conduit and zone of modulation between forces outside (such as the 'evil eye') and inside (using one's mental power, *manasakti*). When in a state of possession, the *teyyam* ritual performer's wide-open eyes manifest the deity's power (s*akti*) and presence in the performer-as-vehicle.[2]

I had experienced a practice so concentrated with 'mental power', and so 'single-minded' (*ekagrata*) and manifest in the master's eyes and entire body, that as an observer I felt the 'terror' of a state

Fig. 3. The lion pose in the C.V.N. style. Ġurukkal Govindankutty Nayar. (Photo: author)

of (transformative) 'fury' that *could have done* terrible harm, but at the same time was completely 'controlled' and thereby protecting the practitioner and/or the one on whose behalf he might exercise that power. Not surprisingly, the ambivalence implicit in my reaction to the manifestation of the power of the 'lion's fury', the sense of destroying and/or protecting, is reflected in the ambivalence of leonine elements of the Hindu pantheon, mythology, and performances (Napier 1986, passim; Emigh 1996, Chapter 2), and is paralleled, as we shall see later, in the 'fury' of village goddesses who can either protect or destroy (Caldwell 1995).

Theoretical and Methodological Concerns

Like other 'extra daily' modes of disciplining or cultivating the body-mind, *kalarippayattu* and Kathakali are two modes of cultural praxis through which experience and meaning are constantly (re)shaped and (re)positioned through practice of their corporeal techniques. The practice of either discipline cannot be reduced to its obvious set of virtuosic body-techniques; rather, modes of cultural practice exist as a set of potentialities of 'self', 'power', 'agency', and 'behavior' inherent in the complex set of practices, discourses, and representations through which a practitioner's experience is historically and contextually negotiated. Ideally, the practitioner's self is reconstituted through long-term practice to achieve a certain type or quality of agency, power, and/or behaviour which can be deployed personally, socially, even cosmologically. This essay assumes with Bryan S. Turner a constant dialectic between the lived experience of the body (*Leib*) and 'the body as representation' (*Körper*) (1992: 57). Therefore, I assume that practitioners speak from their own experience of the body-in-practice (*Leib*), that these explanations are discursive representations of the body (*Körper*), and that there is a constant process of negotiation between experience, the set of discursive formations available, and how an individual thinks and talks about the experience of practice at any given moment.

Although embodied practice of *kalarippayattu* or *kathakali* techniques are the primary modes of entrainment, the experience and meaning of practice cannot be reduced to their obvious sets of virtuosic body-techniques; rather, modes of cultural practice like these exist as a set of potentialities inherent in the complex set of practices, discourses, and representations through which a practitioner's experience is historically and contextually negotiated, or in Bourdieu's sense, a form of 'tactical improvization' (Jenkins 1992: 51). This essay is one such improvization written between *kalarippayattu*, Kathakali, and my own experience of practice.

Second Encounter: The Lion's 'Fury' on the Kathakali Stage

It is the penultimate moment in one of the most popular plays in the Kathakali repertory, *The Killing of Duryodhana* by Vayaskara Aryan Narayanan Moosad (1841-1902). Based on the Mahabharata epic which recounts the conflict between the five Pandava brothers led by Dharmaputra, and their cousins, the evil Kauravas led by Duryodhana, *The Killing of Duryodhana* enacts two of the epic's most important events—the banishment of the Pandavas after their defeat by the Kauravas in a game of dice, and their ultimate victory

Fig. 4. *Raudra* Bhima in *The Killing of Duryodhana*. Margi Gopi.
(Courtesy: Heidrun Brückner)

over the Kauravas years later on the great battlefield of Kurukshetra. As part of the addictive game of dice, played between Dharmaputra and Duryodhana at Duryodhana's court, Dharmaputra is induced to wager, and ultimately lose, everything in the Pandavas' possession—army, palace, wealth, kingdom, his four brothers, their collective wife (Draupadi), and finally, himself. Gloating over his victory, Duryodhana orders his younger brother, Dussassana, to bring Draupadi to court and disrobe her by unwrapping her cloth. Dussassana's attempt to humiliate and violate Draupadi is thwarted by her prayerful devotion to Lord Krishna who miraculously provides her with an endless stream of cloth. Draupadi curses the Kauravas, and vows that she will not tie up her hair again until it has been washed in Dussassana's blood.

In the penultimate scene of *The Killing of Duryodhana* on the great battlefield of Kurukshetra, the strongest of the Pandava brothers, Bhima, is about to kill Dussassana to avenge his transgression of Draupadi at court. The actor who has been playing Bhima until this point in the all-night production, exits behind the hand-held curtain, and is replaced by a senior actor playing '*Raudra*

Bhima'—Bhima transformed into his 'furious' (*raudra*) form (Fig. 4). *Raudra* Bhima appears in special leonine-style make-up used only for this role, accentuating his state of 'fury.' The dramatic text provides the following description of *the result* of Bhima's act of killing Dussassana:

When the angry Bhima/man-lion (Bhima/Narasimha) drank Dussassana's blood,
Draupadi's heart was drained of anger, and filled with excessive joy and love. (*Sloka 37.* Menon, 1962, Part II: 367, translated by V.R. Prabodhachandran Nayar)

In the performance tradition for the scene, the dramatic action clearly marks both Bhima's 'transformation' into the state of fury, and Dussassana's reaction to it:

After the last part of the dialogue (*padam*) is enacted . . . there follows the special fighting steps [between Bhima and Dussassana], the fight with maces, fighting with fists, and then after the final circling of the stage is completed, Bhima moves stage-right, sits, and meditates for a moment, transforming himself into Narasimha [the 'man-lion' avatar and fourth incarnation of Lord Vishnu]. From that moment, Dussassana is unable to take even one step forward since his end is evident and beyond any doubt. Immediately, Bhima catches hold of Dussassana, throws him to the ground, and kills him by ripping open his chest, just as the demon-king Hiranyakasipu was put to death by the Narasimha incarnation. (Menon 1962, Part II, 367, translated by V.R. Prabodhachandran Nayar)

Both the textual reference and the tradition of enactment of the scene make clear that Bhima's transgressive act of disemboweling Dussassana with his hands and mouth, and the subsequent washing/purifying of Draupadi's hair in Dussassana's blood, are undertaken as leonine acts. Entering this state of 'fury', Bhima has *become* Narasimha.

There are two primary iconographic and mythological sources for this leonine transformation in Indian antiquity—the *kirtimukhas* or the 'face/visage of glory' associated with Siva, and the 'man-lion' figure of Narasimha, associated with Visnu.[3] A *kirtimukha* serves mainly as 'an apotropaic demon-mask, a gruesome, awe-inspiring guardian of the threshold' (Zimmer 1972: 182) adorning numerous temples and serving as protective icons. Common throughout India and Bali, they are ubiquitous to Kerala where they appear in both small northern Kerala *teyyam* shrines (Fig. 5) and major temples such as Sri Mahadeva temple in Kaviyur (Bernier 1982: 99, and Plate 192). Rodney Needham explains that the *kirtimukha*

> represents a creature of Siva, in his form as Rudra, 'the Roarer', when the god was asked to give up to Jalandhara his exquisitely beautiful wife Parvati. At this insolent demand, Siva produced from the region of his spiritual third eye a being 'resonant like thunder', with the appearance of a man-lion. The creature immediately rushed as the messenger, Rahu, who desperately begged the protection of Siva. The demon, foiled of his prey, pleaded piteously for something to eat; the god commanded him to consume his own body, which he did until all that remained was the head. Siva was greatly pleased by this demonstration of obedience; he gave the demon the title *Kirtimukha* and appointed him as his door-keeper, 'very heroic and terrible to all wicked persons'. ('Foreword' in Napier, 1986: xvi)

As the 'man-lion' incarnation of Lord Visnu, Narasimha is the form Visnu assumes in order to vanquish the demon-king Hiranyakasipu when he is about to kill his son, Prahlada, who has become a devotee of Visnu against his father's wishes. The *Bhagavata Purana* describes Narasimha and his 'fury' much as they are represented iconographically in temples and in performance:

> . . . there emerged from the pillar in the assembly hall the Lord who had assumed a form that bore no semblance to man or beast . . . Narasimha . . . with eyes fierce and fiery like molten gold, and a face that was inexpressibly haughty, with its matted locks and quivering mane, projecting tusks and razor-sharp tongue that flashed like a sword, and an intimidating scowl on it; with pointed ears that stood erect, a mouth and nostrils wide as mountain-caverns . . . covered with hair white as the moonbeam, a short-thick-set neck, broad chest, and small belly; with a multitude of arms reaching out in all directions, with claws for weapons . . . Hari let off a peal of titanic laughter which grated harshly on the ear and struck terror into all hearts, and moving with lightning speed, caught Hiranyakasipu who had closed his eyes. As he writhed helpless in his grasp, like the rat in the grip of the snake, Hari laid him across his thigh . . . and ripped him open as playfully . . . With eyes dreadful to behold in their blazing wrath, his mane and face red with drops of blood, like those of the lion that has killed an elephant, He, who wore the entrails like a garland, and was licking the corners of his mouth, threw aside the body of the Asura whose heart-lotus he had plucked out with his pointed claws . . . . (Raghunathan 1976: 610-11)[4]

Fig. 5. A typical *kirtimukha* above the entry to a *teyyam* shrine in northern Kerala. (Courtesy: Heike Moser)

The story is enacted both as a spectacular ritual trance/possession performance in the Orissan *Prahlada Nataka* (Emigh 1996: 35ff) and in the Kathakali dance-drama, *Prahlada's Law* by Matavoor Kelu Asan (1857-88). As Vishnu's man-lion incarnation created to kill Hiranyakasipu, Narasimha 'naturally' enters a state of wide-eyed fury to kill, and then indulges in a leonine display of satiation as he licks the blood of his victim in the *kathakali* enactment of this scene. No doubt the staging of Hiranyakasipu's death served as the basis for the staging of Bhima's killing of Dussassana.

Throughout Kerala and in *kalarippayattu* in particular, this state of fury engendering violence is most popularly associated with the goddess. In all Hindu *kalari*, the most important deity is the guardian worshipped in the south-west corner of the space—either a form of the goddess (Bhagavati, Bhadrakali, Chamundi or Durga), or a combination of Siva-Sakti such as Kalabhairava and Kalabhairavi. In the *kalari* Bhagavati manifests her 'ferocious' personality (see Caldwell 1995, passim). When propitiated by Kurup ritual specialists in special propitiation ceremonies, she is conceived in elaborate multi-coloured floor drawings as 'an even more intense form of the *ugra* class of fierce deities' notable for her 'energized eyes', and with an expression evoking 'the *rasa* of *vira* or valour, supported by *raudra* or fury' (Jones 1981: 73). Bhadrakali is her violent form. She is the goddess of war and weapons and is popularly known as that form of Kali which possesses boundless powers of destruction. In her form as Bhadrakali, the 'fierce virgin' is the heroine of *mudiyettu*, one of a series of ritual arts and possession performances based on the legend of 'the killing of Darika' performed in Bhagavati temples during annual temple festivals (Caldwell 1995: *passim*). Masters associate the goddess with Sakti, the divine embodiment of the active principle of power/energy. As Sakti, the goddess embodies the dangerous, unstable feminine energy and is associated with the generation of a powerful, 'furious', heated condition, and therefore inspires terror. Since both the leonine and the goddess embody, like warriors, the ability to protect or to destroy, it is not surprising that the iconography of the 'ferocious' in all cases displays energetic, activated, wide-open eyes ready to do violence.

As represented most graphically and explicitly within the Kathakali repertory in *The Killing of Duryodhana*, the 'heroic' is a state dramatically marked by the hero's sacrificial act of blood-letting, usually accomplished when one or another demon or demon-king is dispatched by the end of the performance as in *The Killing of Kichaka*, *The Killing of Narakasura*, *The Killing of Baka*, etc. South Asian scholar Chris Fuller's assertion that in South Asia 'warfare itself is a reiteration of the idea that an ordered cosmos is created by sacrificial destruction' (1992: 124-5), is played out time and again on the Kathakali stage, traditionally toward the end of the play at dawn when these 'killings' take place—ritual blood-lettings which support anthropologist Rich Freeman's assertion that in medieval Kerala battle was a 'dominant metaphor for conceptualizing relations of spiritual and socio-political powers' (1991: 588).[5] Especially during scenes like this where stage blood is used for the disembowelment of Dussassana, Kathakali reflects Kerala's 'harvest of war' where 'blood becomes the central metaphor for the essential fertilizing fluid of life' thereby promoting 'the health and fertility of the kingdom' (Freeman 1993: 289).

As early as the writing of the Indian encyclopedia of dramaturgy,

Natyasastra (*c.* second century BC-second century AD), the state of anger or fury (*raudra*) was especially associated with the behaviour and actions of demons and demonesses since they are those who engage in 'anger, rape, abuse, insult, untrue allegation, exorcising, threatening, revengefulness, jealousy and the like' and undertake such normal actions as 'beating, breaking, crushing, fighting, drawing of blood', etc., that result from anger (*Natyasastra* VI.63, Ghosh 1967: 113). But it was acknowledged that a state of anger or fury, and the resulting violence, arises not only in demons, but in other characters as well (VI.68. Ghosh 1967: 115). Indeed, in the Kathakali repertory nearly all the epic heroes as well as the greatest of the sages like Durvasa in *King Ambarisha's Law* (Aswati Tirunal Tampuran 1756-94) and Parasurama in *Sita's Marriage Selection* (Kottarakkara Tampuran 1555-1605) seem to be in an almost constant state of anger and/or moral outrage. Such 'human' anger is normal. But fury is quite a different matter. Unlike demons, demon-kings, the 'man-lion', or the goddess Bhagavati in her 'terrifying form' for a state of agitation or 'fury' is 'normal', and therefore for whom violence, killing and blood-letting are 'normal', when heroes must engage in violence and kill to fulfil their duty, their entry into the state of being/doing required to let blood and kill is occasionally marked by signs of a 'transformation', most literally in Bhima's transformation into Narasimha.

When characters like Bhima, Narasimha, or King Rugmamgada embody a state of *raudra*, the 'fury' refers not to the heroic/divine character's state of mind, but rather to the witness's/victim's experience of 'terror' at the manifestation of this state that now stands before them. I have argued at length elsewhere for an interpretation of this as a state of 'transformative fury' (Zarrilli 2000: 169-74). It is a state of being/doing quite different from 'anger' *per se*. This distinction between anger and the more heightened state of fury is reflected in everyday Malayalam life. Typical human 'anger' (*deshyam*) can be controlled, and is differentiated from *kopam*, a fundamental state of 'excitement' or 'agitation' where anger becomes an uncontrollable fury or 'wrath' (Madhavan Pillai 1976: 307). *Kopam* is characteristic of demons, or the goddess in her heated, agitated, ferocious forms. It is that state of fury that will result in violence inevitably being visited against the object or cause of the state of excitation or anger. If a god is *not* propitiated properly, his/her 'fury' will be visited on those who have prevented or disrupted the act of propitiation.

From the perspective of Narasimha or Bhima, entering a state of 'transformative fury' is to enter a state beyond emotion *per se*. It is a state of concentrated, single-minded activation. In *King Rugmamgada's Law* by Mandavapalli Ittiraricha Menon (*c.* 1747-94), King Rugmamgada is only able to overcome all the emotional obstacles in the way of drawing his sword to (sacrificially) kill his son when he enters a state of 'transformative fury' by loosening his hair, and taking on the look of the 'lion's fury' with his wide-open eyes. In this state of activation, heroes such as Bhima or King Rugmamgada are as terrifying as the goddess when she appears in her terrifying forms (Kali or Bhadrakali) or as Narasimha. The terror is in the eye of the beholder because of the 'terrible' things that happen when the power (*sakti*) concentrated in this state is unleashed. Dussassana, Hiranyakasipu, and Mohini the enchantress in *King Rugmamgada's Law*, are all witness to the violence about to be done, and therefore as terrified of this wide-eyed 'wrathful' form manifest before them as villagers are 'terrified' of what the goddess might do.

One of the characteristic features of all these examples of the manifestation of divine/heroic rather than demonic 'fury' is the 'freezing' of the witness and/or victim of 'fury'. Dussassana is terrified, and 'unable to take even one step forward'. When Hiranyakasipu sees Narasimha emerge from the pillar, even this demon-king is terrified at the horrific form of the man-lion before him. Like Dussassana, he is rendered defenceless in the face of this transformative and divine 'fury'. When Mohini witnesses King Rugmamgada's transformation, she responds with fear and distress, and is frozen with terror as he tells her, 'Watch what I do!' (Zarrilli 2000: 168) Dussassana sees that Bhima *will* kill and disembowel him. Hiranyakasipu likewise sees that the man-lion incarnation of Vishnu *will* kill and disembowel him. Similarly, but as a witness rather than the victim, Mohini sees that Rugmamgada in his transformative state of fury *will* complete this bloody sacrifice of his only son before her very eyes.

Third Encounter: Embodying the 'Inner Life' of Animal Forms

The teacher's verbal command to 'take position' ['*amarnnu . . .*' Fig. 6] begins each repetition of body exercise sequences (*meippayattu*) performed back and forth across the training space. The feet begin just beyond shoulder-width, with the *external* focus across the space at eye level. Sensing down through the soles of the feet, into the earth, the hands and arms trace an arc outward and upward through space, above the head, shaped there into two fists. At the moment the impulse to move sets this sequence in motion, the external focus shifts from the point ahead to the fists above the head, and then travels with the fists downward as the *entire* body continues to move in a wave-like motion, tracing the arc of the wave literally between the legs and behind the body, scooping down 'under' the earth/floor to focus ahead once again—eyes returning to the point at which they began across the space, just above the fists.

During the brief one to two seconds it takes to assume this position, the '*internal* eye' sensed in the lower abdominal region

Fig. 6. The elephant pose in the C.V.N. *Kalari* style. Final position with the energy out/forward and back/down from the lower abdominal region. Debbie Romeo, Jean Adamak, and Adam Oliensis in training with the author. (Photo: author)

simultaneously continues to maintain a connection with the point ahead where the external focus began, the relationship to the earth through the soles of the feet, and the opening through the head at the top of the spine. When the final pose is assumed one should be as 'immovable' or 'sturdy' as an elephant. One's energy in this dynamic form creates and accentuates a sense of opposition sensed from the lower abdominal region at the root of the navel (*nabhi mula*)—outward/ahead through the eyes/fists, and backward/down through the soles of the feet and along the spine, into the earth. The virtuosic practitioner is not representing, but inhabiting the kinesthetic 'musculature' of an elephant. Indeed, the 'position' one has assumed in this description is known as the 'elephant pose' (*gajavadivu*) as performed at the C.V.N. Kalari, Thiruvananthapuram, Kerala, India. It is one of the basic animal poses, usually numbering eight (see chart below), integral to the practice of *kalarippayattu*, and is only the first move in a lengthy 'body exercise sequence' (*meippayattu*) which combines the animal poses with kicks, steps, jumps, and gymnastic turns performed in increasingly difficult and complex combinations back and forth across the *kalari* floor.[6]

The above description is based on my personal repetition of this pose somewhere between 400,000 and 500,000 times over more than twenty years of practice and teaching, on the corrections I received from my primary teacher, Gurukkal Govindankutty Nayar, during over seven years of training, and on extensive ethnographic research in Kerala. Repetition. Correction. Reflection. More repetition. More correction. More reflection. Necessary to the inhabitation and internal actualization of what is potential within any particular pattern of movement. Taking time to bring 'actualization' to the potential of this and other animal forms—to build, over time, in space, a kinesthetic awareness where the perceiving consciousness is not a looking at, but a mode of intuitive embodiment where the 'body becomes all eyes' and is able to respond, like an animal, immediately to stimuli in the environment. The optimal state of a martial artist. The optimal state of a performer?

Just as postures (*asanas*) are central to yoga training, the animal poses are at the core of *kalarippayattu* training. The poses are not static forms, but configurations of movements which embody both the external and internal essence of the animal. Styles differ considerably. The chart below lists the poses identified by two different masters. Although the basic positions and movements are similar, except for the elephant and serpent, the names are different, as are interpretations.

Kalarippayattu Animal Poses: Two Styles

Gurukkal Govindankutty Nayar and the C.V.N. Style :

elephant pose (*gajavadivu*, Fig. 6)
lion pose (*simhavadivu*, Fig. 4)
horse pose (*asvavadivu*)
wild boar pose (*varahavadivu*)
serpent pose (*sarpavadivu*)
cat pose (*marjaravadivu*)
cock pose (*kukkuvadivu*)
fish pose (*matsyavadivu*)

Gurukkal P.K. Balan

horse pose (Fig. 7)
peacock pose (*mayuravadivu*, Fig 8)
serpent pose (Fig. 9)
cock pose (Fig. 10)
elephant pose
cat pose
lion pose
wild boar pose

Behind the fluid grace of the gymnastic forms is the strength and power of movements which can, when necessary, be applied with lightning-fast speed and precision in potentially deadly attacks. 'Hidden' within all the preliminary exercises and basic poses are complex combinations of offensive and defensive applications which are eventually embodied by constant practice. As Gurukkal P.K. Balan explained, 'When any animal fights, it uses its whole body. This must also be true in *kalarippayattu*. Only a person who has learned these eight poses can perform the *kalari*-law, and go on to empty hand combat, weapons, massage, or applications to the vital spots.' Each pose has its own specific fighting applications:

The horse is an animal which can concentrate all its powers

centrally, and it can run fast by jumping up. The same pause, preparation for jumping, and forward movement [that are in a horse] are in *asvavadivu* (Fig. 7).

When a peacock is going to attack its enemy, it spreads its feathers and raises its neck, and dances by steadying itself on one leg. Then it shifts to the other leg, and attacks by jumping and flying. The capability of doing this attack is known as *mayurvadivu* (Fig. 8).

A snake attacks its enemy by standing up; however, its tail remains on the ground without movement. From this position, it can

Fig. 7. The horse pose as taught by P.K. Balan Gurukkal. (Photo: author)

Fig. 8. The peacock pose as taught by P.K. Balan Gurukkal. (Photo: author)

turn in any direction and bite a person. This ability to turn in any direction and attack by rising up is known as *sarpavadivu* (Fig. 9).

When a cock attacks he uses all parts of his body—wings, neck, legs, fingernails. He will lift one leg and shake his feather and neck, fix his gaze on the enemy, and attack. This is *kukkuvadivu* (Fig. 10).

Fig. 9. The serpent pose as taught by P.K. Balan Gurukkal. (Photo: author)

Fig. 10. Gurukkal P.K. Balan in the cock pose. (Photo: author)

P.K. Balan's explanations above emphasize the more obvious, mimetic aspects of embodying the animal poses for attack and/or defence. What is even more important than copying the external form of each animal, is the subtler process of inhabiting the 'inner life' (*bhava*) of the form. At first the exercises are 'that which is external', but as the forms 'come correct' students ideally begin to manifest physical, mental, and behavioural signs (*laksana*) indicating change.[7] Like long-term practice of postures (*asana*) in *hatha yoga*, the forms bear the 'fruit' (*phalam*) of practice and become 'that which is internal' as one is able to assume difficult forms, remove mental distractions, and actualize one-point focus (*ekagrata*).

But what constitutes 'correct practice?' Kallada Balakrishnan explained how 'Each movement, step, and pose has its own "inner life" (*bhava*) which must be exhibited when practising *kalarippayattu*.' *Bhava* is a term commonly used to refer to the actor's psychophysiological embodiment of a character's states of being-doing in Kathakali. Gurukkal Govindankutty Nayar compared the martial artist's process of 'becoming one' with the 'original qualities' of the forms of practice with that of the actor 'becoming' his role. 'Take the role of Duryodhana. He lives that part by becoming it.' For the Kathakali actor 'becoming the character' is a process in which the actor controls and circulates his inner energy (*prana vayu*) into and through the stylized and codified forms he has come to embody and thereby uses to create the character (see Zarrilli 2000, Chapter 4). Just as the actor 'becomes' the character by embodying the various *bhavas* required by the dramatic context of the play such as Bhima's embodiment of 'fury', so does the martial artist 'become' by embodying the *bhava* appropriate to each form.

Govindankutty Nayar explained how the 'inner life' of each movement is assumed to be present as the seed of the form, implanted by the master during each first lesson. 'In due time', training and careful correction nurtures this seed, helps it sprout and grow. The student slowly discovers the correct form and its application. The practitioner himself does not create the benefits or powers which are eventually realized through practice of a discipline; rather, practice is a means of bringing such powers 'to their maximum efficiency' (Varenne 1976: 134). The *Amritabindu Upanisad* illustrates the idea that knowledge in a discipline of practice is assumed to be 'already there', hidden, waiting to be discovered:

> And knowledge is hidden
> in the depth of each individual
> just as in milk
> the butter we cannot see is hidden;
> this is why the wise practitioner
> must carry out a churning operation within himself,
> employing his own mind without respite
> as the churning agent. (Varenne 1976: 59)

Each form and weapon is assumed to have its ideal dimensions and dynamic mode of fulfilment. Govindankutty Nayar explained how

> All the arts have their prescribed forms, and they should be done according to those forms, like a fine carving which should be made of one piece of wood according to the dimensions recorded in the sacred texts. Or, for an ivory carving, to have its 'life force' it can only be taken from a live elephant to have that life force necessary for use in worship (puja). If you take the ivory from a dead animal, it cannot be used. It will not have its life force (*prana-vayu*).

The master himself becomes one with the inner life of a pose (*vadivu*), embodying the qualities of the animal for which each pose is named, and manifests this quality in his practice. Becoming accomplished in the pose through repetition and correction is to 'become one with its original qualities'. If one is unable to achieve such oneness, then the martial form 'becomes nothing' or 'loses its actuality'. The potential of a form to manifest power (*sakti*) or to be of practical use in combat is never awakened or realized.[8]

Entering a State of 'Transformative Fury'

The leonine apotropaic images of the lion's fury, Narasimha, the ferocious goddess, as well as the 'Furious' Bhima all emphasize the state of fury as witnessed from the outside, i.e. from the perspective of the potential for violent destruction. A quite different picture of this state emerges when we examine it from the perspective inside. Emigh and Napier provide three complementary observations on the nature of this leonine state of being/doing, and for the 'arresting presence of leonine apotropaic faces' (Emigh 1996: 71):

(1) this particular configuration, with the enlarged eyes, mouth pulled back, nostrils flared, and tongue distended 'does not correspond to any of the recognizable sets of characters that have been identified with displays of "primary" human emotions' identified by Ekman and Friesen (1975), and therefore might be considered as a state with its own unique features;
(2) following Oohashi Tsutomu's research, this state bears a 'striking resemblance to the "threat display" as identified by ethologists . . . a transitory expression made in response to danger—all senses alert, caught between fear and fury—that

serves as a warning and may precede a ferocious attack, or, for that matter, a grudging retreat' (Emigh 1996: 71);

(3) finally, 'apotropaic figures characteristcally exaggerate *all* the instruments for gaining sensory information: eyes, ears, nostrils, tongue, and fingers are commonly rendered larger than "natural". . .' (Emigh 1996: 71). This exaggeration may have to do with the human brain's monitoring of sensation (Napier 1986: 205), suggesting that these leonine images reflect a state of heightened, intense, raw sensation that 'commands attention precisely because it thwarts our apprehensions about what its meaning might be . . . The message it offers is, in fact, a warning . . . It says "hands off" in an unambiguous way, but it does so through its own expressive ambiguity' (Napier 1986: 200).

Interpreting this state of 'transformative fury' as a special state of 'heightened, intense, raw sensation', reflects commonplace Malayali assumptions about the ideal state of the *kalarippayattu* practitioner. The common Malayalam folk expression, 'the body becomes all eyes' (*meyyu kannukuka*) encapsulates the *kalarippayattu* practitioner's idealized state of actualization achieved through long-term practice of the animal poses and other exercises, where the body-mind is in such a concentrated state of acuity and awareness that, like Brahma, the 'thousand-eyed', one can 'see', sense, and respond to any stimulus in the immediate environment. It is an animal-like state of 'instinctual' awareness, loss of voluntary control, and of any social/personal inhibition. This optimal, idealized state of actualization is seen in the master's eyes (Figs. 1, 3), in the activation of the practitioner's inner life-force (*prana vayu*), and is traditionally understood to awaken, activate, and raise the 'serpent power' (*kundalini sakti*) understood to lie dormant within the subtle body as understood in yoga which a master embodies, circulates, and utilizes either to heal through therapeutic massages or to do violence (Zarrilli 1998, Chapters 5 and 6). When utilized in fighting, this 'power' is traditionally understood to take on the furious, wrathful (*raudra*), or destructive aspect of the goddess either alone or in combination with Siva as the fearful (*kala-bhairava*). As P.K. Balan Gurukkal explained, in fighting the practitioner should manifest this 'special power of fury' (*raudra*).

From the perspective of the martial practitioner, this 'special power of fury' is comparable to the state of single-minded 'transformative fury' actualized by King Rugmamgada described above—a state similar to that described by J. Richardson Freeman regarding Kerala's *teyyam* ritual performers. Freeman has observed that their body-mind state in performance 'entails no loss of consciousness, or "dissociation" in psychological terms, but rather a *heightened* sense of consciousness . . .' in which 'one's consciousness has not travelled somewhere else, shaman-like, but that instead, one's own body and mind are taken over and animated by a higher and more powerful [and I would add more concentrated] form of consciousness' (1993: 131). Some *kalarippayattu* masters point out that the combination of self-confidence, doubtless heroism and internal fury manifest in the raising of *kundalini sakti* does not lead to emotional upset or anger, but rather to a state of intense concentration of energy (*aveshakaram*), 'the power generated from concentration'. In *teyyam* this heightened sense of consciousness takes the shape of 'performative acuity with regard to the rituals' (1993: 131). For the martial practitioner, it is a single-minded performative acuity with regard to wielding the weapon.

It was not until a number of years later in my own training, when, as an advanced practitioner with a weapon in my hands, that I began to experience from the inside this single-minded state of transformative 'fury'which I had only observed at first, frightened, from the outside. When I began my training in 1976-7, I considered myself a pacifist, and abhorred violence of all kinds. I still do. But at that time my 'pacifism' was only a belief to which I adhered—it was not a state of being I could embody.

I was loath to pick up a weapon of any kind. But pick up a weapon I did as part of the ongoing training—day in and day out. Over years of training in the basic forms and weapons, I gradually began to defend myself against increasingly violent, furious attacks—attacks which unleashed tremendous 'power' in blows, cuts or thrusts that, if not defended, could kill me.[9] This is an experiential state that, in polite society, we usually do not want to visit—that arena of darkness where we could, we might undertake violence ourselves. As I entered more and more advanced weapons training, and gave myself over to the process, I had to defend myself, and in doing so, I had to enter a state of tremendously heightened awareness, acuity, single-minded focus, and responsivity. Experiencing the heightened state of acuity, awareness, perception, and readiness necessary when wielding a 'live' weapon was initially not only disconcerting, but disturbing. Responding to the 'attacks' from Gurukkal Govindankutty Nayar, it took me into a new experiential arena that I was not sure I wanted to visit. I was not prepared for the deep and profound resonances that this experience of 'fury' and potential violence demanded. Clinical psychologist Stephen Diamond explains that:

> anger and rage—like sexuality in Sigmund Freud's Victorian era—have come to be regarded as evil, sinful, destructive, uncivilized, pagan, and primitive passions, much better buried than openly admitted. The volatile emotions of anger and rage have been broadly 'demonized', vilified, maligned, and rejected as purely pathological, negative impulses with no real redeeming qualities. As a result, most 'respectable' Americans habitually suppress, repress, or deny their anger. . . . (1996: 7)

In retrospect, it was only as I began to experience my own ability to do violence—as I learned I had the ability to actually kill another human being with a weapon in my hand—that I began to explore this transformative state of fury, and 'be pacified' not just in words, but in my entire body and mind.[10] Only by embodying the 'lion's fury' could I begin to more fully understand the nature of this activated state of being/doing.

NOTES

1. Interviews with *kalarippayattu* masters were conducted as part of long-term ethnographic research in Kerala between 1976 and 1993. I went on to train intensively in *kalarippayattu*, and have developed my own system of training actors, making use of *kalarippayattu*, *t'ai chi ch'uan*, and yoga (see Zarrilli 1995, Chapter 13). The animal forms discussed in this essay, and the perspective about the use of such forms in training actors, is quite different from most other uses of animal forms in actor training. For example, Lee Strasberg regularly used an 'animal exercise' derived from his experience of Maria Ouspenskaya's classes when he developed his training at the Actor's Studio in order to enable

developing actors to step outside the 'human sphere', to develop observational skills, in order to enter into 'the problem of physical characterization', and eventually to explore 'emotional or mental rather than the physical characteristics of the animal' (Hethmon 1965: 104-5). See also the rather standard approaches in Penrod (1974: 147-8), and Manderino (1985: 71-5).

2. *Teyyam* is a traditional ritual performance genre in northern Kerala which serves as the locally most popular form of Hinduism through which hundreds of pan-Indian and local deities are propitiated, including local heroes.
3. The major deities of the Hindu pantheon include Brahma (the creator), Visnu (the preserver, manifest in his ten primary incarnations), Siva (the destroyer), and various forms of the goddess such as Kali, Durga, Bhagavati, Sakti, etc.
4. Narasimha has been worshipped at least in some Kerala temples for centuries, and appears as the major deity at the Pulliyur Narasimha Temple in Chengannur, Alleppey district. A major niche wood carving illustrates the central event in the story of Narasimha where he rips out the entrails of Hiranyakasipu. Even in Narasimha's *yogasana* sitting posture, his face is represented in typical leonine, ferocious aspect with blazing eyes wide open, and protruding tongue (Bernier 1982, Plate 177).
5. The Malayalam title of all these plays includes *vadham*, which literally means the act of 'killing.'
6. Animal forms are common in a number of Asian martial arts. During the Later Han dynasty (AD 25-220) in China, Hua To developed a series of exercises based on the movements of the tiger, deer, bear, monkey, and bird (Draeger and Smith 1969: 16). See also Dukes for a discussion of animals in Buddhist practice (1994: 272-5).
7. See Zarrilli (1998, Chapters 4-5) for a full discussion.
8. A few masters still use *mantram*—repetition of a series of sacred syllabels or words—in order to access or unlock the 'highest' power 'hidden' within an animal pose. For the 'lion pose' this would mean repeating Narasimha ('man-lion') *mantram* (Zarrilli 1998: 144-5).
9. Excellent master-teachers do *not* unleash a blow or cut with force beyond what a particular student can safely defend; therefore, some students may not advance very far if they are either technically unable to master basic animal forms, or if they are unwilling or unable to enter and explore a 'state of fury' where they might do violence.
10. Rollo May reminds us that 'for the self-respecting human being, violence is always an ultimate possibility—and it will be resorted to less if admitted than if suppressed' (1972: 97).

REFERENCES

Balakrishnan, P., 1995, *Kalarippayattu: The Ancient Martial Art of Kerala*, Trivandrum: St. Joseph's Press.

Bernier, Ronald M., 1982, *Temple Arts of Kerala*, New Delhi: S. Chand.

Caldwell, Sarah Lee, 1995, 'Oh Terrifying Mother: The Mutiyettu Ritual Drama of Kerala, South India', unpublished Ph.D. dissertation, Berkeley: Department of Anthropology, University of California.

Diamond, Stephen A., 1996, *Anger, Madness, and the Daimonic: The Psychological Genesis of Violence, Evil, and Creativity*, Albany: SUNY Press.

Draeger, Donn F. and Robert W. Smith, 1969, *Asian Fighting Arts*, New York: Berkley Publishing Co.

Dukes, Terrence (Shifu Nagaboshi Tomio), 1994, *The Bodhisattva Warriors*, York Beach: Samuel Weiser, Inc.

Eck, Diana L., 1981, *Darsan: Seeing the Divine Image in India*, Chambersburg: Anima Publications.

Ekman, Paul and Wallace V. Friesen, 1975, *Unmasking the Face: A Guide to Recognizing Emotions from Facial Expressions*, Englewood Cliffs: Prentice-Hall.

Emigh, John, 1984, 'Dealing with the Demonic: Strategies for Containment in Hindu Iconography and Performance', *Asian Theatre Journal*, 1, 1: 21-39.

———, 1996, *Masked Performance*, Philadelphia: University of Pennsylvania Press.

Freeman, J. Richardson, 1991, 'Purity and Violence: Sacred Power in the Teyyam Worship of Malabar', unpublished Ph.D. dissertation, University of Pennsylvania.

———, 1993, 'Performing Possession: Ritual and Consciousness in the Teyyam Complex of Northern Kerala', in Heidrun Bruckner, Lothar Lutze and Aditya Malik (eds.), *Flags of Fame: Studies in South Asian Folk Culture*, New Delhi: Manohar, 109-38.

Fuller, Chris, 1992, *The Camphor Flame: Popular Hinduism and Society in India*, Princeton: Princeton University Press.

Ghosh, Manmohan (ed. and translator) 1967 (1951), *The Natyasastra* (vols. I-II), Calcutta: Granthalaya Private Ltd.

Hethmon, Robert H. (ed.), 1965, *Strasberg at the Actors Studio*, New York: The Viking Press.

Jenkins, Richard, 1992, *Pierre Bourdieu*, London: Routledge.

Jones, Clifford Reis, 1982, 'Kalam Eluttu: Art and Ritual in Kerala', in *Religious Festivals in South India and Sri Lanka*, ed. Guy R. Welbon and Glenn E. Yocum, New Delhi: Manohar, pp. 269-94.

——— 1981, '*Dhulicitra*: Historical Perspectives on Art and Ritual', in *Kaladarsana: American Studies in the Art of India* ed., Joanna G. Williams, New Delhi: Oxford and IBH Publishing, pp. 69-75.

Manderino, Ned, 1985, *All About Method Acting*, Los Angeles: Ned Manderino Books.

Menon, K.P.S., 1962, *Kathakaliattaprakaram*, vol. II, Quilon: S.T. Reddiar & Sons.

May, Rollo, 1972, *Power and Innocence: A Search for the Sources of Violence*, New York: W.W. Norton.

Napier, A. David, 1986, *Masks, Transformation, and Paradox*, Berkeley: University of California Press.

O'Flaherty, Wendy Doniger, 1973, *Siva: The Erotic Ascetic*, Oxford: Oxford University Press.

Penrod, James, 1974, *Movement for the Performing Artist*, Palo Alto: Mayfield Publishing Co.

Pillai, Madhavan C., 1976, *NBS Malayalam English Dictionary*, Kottayam: National Book Stall.

Raghunathan, N., (trans.), 1976, *Srimad Bhagavatam*, vol. I, Madras: Vibhneswara Publishing House.

Turner, Bryan S., 1992, *Regulating Bodies: Essays in Medical Sociology*, London: Routledge.

Varenne, Jean, 1976, *Yoga and the Hindu Tradition*, Chicago: University of Chicago Press.

Zarrilli, Phillip B., 2000, *Kathakali Dance-Drama: Where Gods and Demons Come to Play*, London: Routledge.

———, 1998, *'When the Body Becomes All Eyes:' Paradigms, Practices, and Discourses of Power in Kalarippayattu*, New Delhi: Oxford University Press.

——— (ed.), 1995, *Acting (Re) Considered: Theories and Practices*, London: Routledge.

———, 1986-7, 'From Martial Art to Performance: *Kalarippayattu* and Performance in Kerala', pts. 1 and 2, *Sangeet Natak*, 81-2: 5-41; 83: 14-45.

Zimmer, Heinrich, 1972, *Myths and Symbols in Indian Art and Civilization*, Princeton: Princeton University Press.

11

Creating Presence: Performing the Oral Narrative of Devnārāyaṇ

Aditya Malik

The narrative of Devnārāyaṇ[1]—which has frequently been classified as an 'epic'[2]—is one of the most well-known folk narratives in Rajasthan.[3] The narrative and Devnārāyaṇ's cult covers a large area extending over most of Rajasthan and Malwa, the north-western region of Madhya Pradesh. Together with the 'epic' narratives of Pābūjī, Gūgājī, Tejājī, Rāmdevjī, Gopi Cand and Bharthari, it belongs to a rich and significant corpus of oral narratives current in Rajasthan today.[4]

One of the chief concerns of a study of a folk narrative is not only to understand the structure and content of the narrative and the context in which it is performed, but also to understand in depth and take seriously the notion of narrative and performance that is offered from within the cultural framework of the 'cult'. How are narrative and performance defined and perceived? Are there distinct and articulate notions of what constitutes a narrative and performance? How do these notions depart from a notion of narrative and performance derived from the researcher's own cultural framework? Thus, as Ricoeur (1981: 51),[5] writing on the goal of hermeneutics, points out:

> . . . hermeneutics comprises something specific; it seeks to reproduce an interconnection, a structured totality by drawing support from a category of signs which have been fixed by writing, or by any other process of inscription equivalent to writing. So it is no longer possible to grasp the mental life of others in its immediate expressions; rather it is necessary to reproduce it, by interpreting objectified signs. This *Nachbilden* (reproducing) requires distinct rules since the expressions are embedded in objects of particular

nature . . . . it is philology—the explanation of texts—which provides the scientific stage of understanding.

But as Kersenboom (1995: 5f.) writing with reference to the 'Tamil text', points out, this notion of the hermeneutic goal outlined by Ricoeur (and others) is questionable, since

In moments of actual encounter with alien textual activity, this agenda proved to be a hidden one: phenomena were not studied in order to detect their individual coherence and autonomy, but rather for the sake of something hidden behind them: a *universal-validity-of-interpretation-upon-which-all-certainty-in-history-rests.* This cascade of concepts was bewilderingly strange to Tamil experts . . . structured totality, fixation, *Nachbildung, Auslegung* and *Interpretation,* produced constructs that had no physical shape or presence, but were nevertheless there, influencing the quality of life. Orientalism developed a life of its own, reigning supreme in the West and as an obnoxious reminder of difference in the East. The agenda of Tamil experts was a straightforward one: their language, and *eo ipso* their literature, were of divine origin, or divine substance and directed at a divine aim.

If, as in Kersenboom's study of the 'Tamil text', the very notion of text and its relationship to the actual world within the so-called 'alien' cultural context of research diverges from the scholar's own point of reference, would it not be necessary to set up an entirely different framework within which to ask questions? Would it not indeed be necessary to explore a whole new set of questions that may not tally with the researcher's well-treaded paths of analysis and explanation? As Piatigorsky (1985: 215) with regard to the analysis of Indian religion notes:

It is therefore of great importance to identify the main conditions under which terms corresponding to 'religion', or 'ritual', or 'cult'—where such exist—are used in a religion investigated as meta-concepts for its objective understanding of itself. . . . In the Indian case these terms of reflexive understanding developed within speculative structures of consciousness which neither codified the religion (as in theology) nor existed separately from it (as in philosophy) but analysed the religion from within the religion itself.

Following Piatigorsky's observation on Indian religion, we could analogously ask whether there are corresponding terms such as verbal narrative, visual narrative, performance, performer, etc., found within the narrative (and religious) tradition of Devnārāyaṇ. Although these may not be codified into a 'theory' of the text or of performance, they nevertheless do exist as meta-level concepts used and transmitted by the community of devotees for whom the narrative is of fundamental importance. And, it is as meta-level concepts used to describe the narrative and its performance that such terms and concepts need to be taken seriously.

In this essay I successively examine the categories of performance, remembrance and memory, song and declamatory chant, repetition, dialogue, and reported speech. Each of these features individually and collectively build the context for the communicative act of telling and listening to the oral narrative. As in the case of conversational dialogue, meanings emerge and vanish here with the appearance and disappearance of *sound* in different instances of the narrative's recitation. The oral 'text' is marked for performance, and therefore does not fall within the parameters of 'writer' and 'reader'. It is part of an entire event that itself is geared towards engendering an equally tenuous quantity, namely 'divine presence' (*prakāś*). Thus the notion of 'text' (both oral and visual) is bound to a larger context. Unlike the written text, neither the oral nor the visual narrative exist as self-contained objects.[6]

PERFORMANCE

The narrative of Devnārāyaṇ or, more precisely, sections from the narrative are performed in religiously determined contexts. Most usually a performance is part of a *jāgraṇ* or 'night-wake'.[7] The purpose of a *jāgraṇ* is to evoke the presence (*prakāś*) of Devnārāyaṇ.[8] Performances are called *'paṛ vā̃cṇo'* ('speaking/reading the *paṛ*') implying the use of an elaborately structured 8.5 m. × 1.50 m. painted scroll on which characters and scenes of the narrative are depicted. Performances of this kind take place in three distinct places: (a) the home of a devotee, (b) in front of a Devnārāyaṇ or Saval Bhoj temple, and (c) in front of the community meeting place, *'hathāī'*. Performances can take place any time of the year except for the period called *'caumāsā'* or the rainy season. During this time Devnārāyaṇ (and other Hindu deities) are supposed to be asleep. Performances begin on the eleventh day of the bright half of the month of *Kārttik* which falls in October-November. During the '*caumāsā*' period the painted scroll called *paṛ*, which is a central element in performances, is never unrolled. Narratives and songs may be sung, but in the so-called seated posture (*baiṭho gāṇo*) without the use of the *paṛ* and other dance techniques operative during 'regular' performances.

The space marked by the scroll when it is unfolded and held up is 'sacred'. The scroll itself is considered to be a 'portable' temple in the centre of which there is the life-size figure of Devnārāyaṇ seated together with his four brothers in his royal court (durbar). A makeshift altar is set up in front of his image. Here incense sticks are burnt, and offerings of grain and money are made. Each time an offering from a member of the audience is made the Bhopā or his co-singer blows a conch (*saṅkh*) and proclaims the devotee's name and the quantity and item offered by him. The performance is interrupted here. Besides such interruptions there are other pauses during which the singers are offered tea or tobacco and are asked to be seated.

Such pauses can be relatively frequent so that from a total time of about nine hours, six are spent in narrating and performing the story. The singers wear a particular costume (*bāgā*) and use a stringed instrument called *bīṇ* or *jantar*. This double gourd instrument is worn by the main singer who plays on it while singing the narrative and pointing to corresponding sections of the scroll. His partner carries an oil lamp which illuminates the scroll during the performance that involves a series of movements back and forth along the length of the scroll and between the two singers. The main singer may also undertake a series of pirouette-like steps at specific moments during the recitation. There is a great deal of interaction between singers and the audience. The audience members often comment on the episode concerned or the singers' performance itself. The singers are also apt to comment on the audience's degree of attentiveness and wakefulness. Audience members may also claim to know more than the singer who must claim and reclaim his authority as a 'specialist' by successfully answering 'critical' questions. At times, during pauses, members of the audience may also entertain the audience by performing a few lines themselves.

The sequence which such a performance follows can be summarized as follows:

(a) Purificatory rites.
(b) Setting up the *paṛ*.
(c) Wearing the costume by the Bhopā.
(d) A *seva* for consecrating the *paṛ*.
(e) Invocations of many deities.
(f) Prosimetric narration of the story.
(g) Donation during frequent pauses.
(h) An *ārati* for deities and characters on the *paṛ*.
(i) A *sevā* at the end of the performance when the *paṛ* is rolled together again.[9]

The first term that provides us with a correspondence to 'performance' is *paṛ vā̃cṇo*. Thus, the external description of song, narrative, dance, pointing to the *paṛ,* audience participation etc., is—for Bhopas and devotees (*bhaktas*) alike—simply called 'speaking/reading the paṛ'. The performance is not, as one might expect from a textual perspective, described as 'narrating or telling Devnārāyaṇ's story.' The focus here is not on the 'text' as such, but on the scroll, which is an icon of the deity, and of the text. However, the scroll is not self-explanatory: it needs to be 'spoken' or 'read', i.e. it needs to be 'decoded' and rendered meaningful by a specialist, namely, the singer. Each performance thus involves a deconstruction of the entirety of images on the *paṛ*, and a simultaneous reconstruction of its meaning. The meaning of the images becomes distinct or rather emerges through the juxtaposition of spoken and sung narratives together with visual images located on the *paṛ*. The *paṛ,* therefore, is not spoken or read like a picture-book, it is read, on the contrary, through a narrative which manifests on account of its own recitation. The Bhopa does not decode the images on the *paṛ* according to his own interpretation like an art historian may do, he is bound by the interpretation of the images encoded in the narrative. The *paṛ,* according to the definition provided by the term *paṛ vā̃cno,* is not, therefore, simply an illustration of verbal, narrative content. It is, in fact, that which gets revealed through the interpretative framework provided by the narration. It would appear then that the imagery and iconicity of the *paṛ* is much more central to a performance than is the narration itself. This iconical emphasis can also be traced in sentences such as *paṛā̃ kā lekh,* meaning 'writing of the *paṛ*', that the singer Śrī Hukamārām Bhopā used to prove the existence and authenticity of specific passages and episodes from the narrative. The *paṛ* was 'proof' of the oral text, and not vice versa. Visual imagery and iconicity are thus considered primary to verbal expression. But without verbal expression, the meaning(s) of the images do not reveal themselves.[10]

Before moving further, one point needs to be clarified here, and that is the use of the term image. This again is an external category used to describe the pictures on the scroll. The term image suggests a static visual representation or symbol of a real or imagined object. However, the 'images' on the *paṛ*, are, as I have mentioned, 'icons' in a special sense of the term. Once again, they are not icons in the sense of only being traditionally conceived visual representations of religious themes,[11] they are, in fact, the iconic or visual *presence* of characters and scenes from the narrative. A term often used by singers when pointing to deities, persons, animals on the *paṛ,* is *birājmān,* i.e. they are 'present', 'seated', or 'manifest'. The images of deities, persons, animals, etc., therefore, *are* those deities, persons, animals, etc.[12] There is no distance created between the symbol and thing. While this correlation undoubtedly results from the sacred nature of the scroll, it is also a product of the 'oral' and 'aural' culture built into the tradition of Devnārāyaṇ. As Jardine (1996: 6f.) observes:

> An oral culture can hardly conceive of words as labels of some sort, as literate people tend to do, since spoken words are not 'things' that can be picked up and 'attached' to other things; a word must be an event or an action. Further, sound for oral peoples is dynamic also in the sense that it is linked to power: it must be driven by power from a source of some kind, which is why words (i.e. dynamic actions, events) themselves are understood to have great, even magical, power. . . . Since oral cultures communicate mainly through sound, which is irreducibly dynamic, they lack the capacity to 'stop' the dynamism of the life-world and subject it to abstract analysis. Oral thought processes, in other words, are always highly contextual.

This correlation of word or image and thing is also evident in the case of the visual narrative that, as has been pointed out above, is also conceived in terms of the metaphor of 'written text' or 'script' (*lekh*).[13] Thus it is not as though the *paṛ* is simply a picture book spread out to accompany the narration. The *paṛ* and its imagery are a concrete expression of the presence of the content of the imagery. This is particularly evident in the case of Devnārāyaṇ himself, who is seated on his 'python throne' in the centre of the *paṛ*. The presence of Devnārāyaṇ in the two-dimensional image is as real as the presence of a deity in *mūrtis* in Hindu temples.[14] There is no contradiction in the fact that there may be simultaneous performances of Devnārāyaṇ, done by different Bhopās using different *paṛs*, because the presence of Devnārāyaṇ, like that of other deities, is manifest in both a universal and localized form.[15] The presence of Devnārāyaṇ and other deities or persons on the *paṛ* is of central importance because the entire performance is focused on manifesting Devnārāyaṇ's *prakāś* ('presence', 'radiance', 'light', 'splendour'). Thus on another level the activity of 'speaking/reading the *paṛ*' which also involves not only the narration of the text, but also dancing, musical instrumentation etc. occurs within the larger framework of 'presencing' Devnārāyaṇ. The narration does not stop at revealing or decoding the meaning of the *paṛ*. The decoding in reality continues further than the semantic and cultural meanings into the domain of experiencing 'presence' (*prakāś*). The culturally specific sense of both 'speaking/reading' (*vā̃cno*) and 'the written' (*lekh*) in terms of visual images of the *paṛ* (and not the verbal expression of the narrative) thus extends into the realm of presencing the divine.[16] Thus the meanings of the images ultimately make sense within the context of the manifestation of divine power.

Remembrance

In this section I briefly examine the meaning of the act of remembering with which a recitation always begins. Rather than regard this preliminary segment of the narrative situation as a 'formulaic', and therefore insignificant, recurrent beginning, my intention is to relocate it as a primary source of knowledge. My contention is that this source, which is almost unintelligible or unimaginable to the rationalized users of the printed word, is of prime importance to a wide variety of expressive traditions in India, ranging from story-telling to dance, theatre, and music. Similarly, the efforts of scholars, who themselves no longer cognize through the oral and aural, to understand oral narratives in terms of 'mental texts', 'memorization', 'formulaic language', etc., are drastic attempts at making orality intelligible. Nevertheless, by virtue of being cut off ourselves from the source of creative inspiration as it is perceived in different expressive traditions, we tend to gloss over its validity and authenticity.

Typically, the narration of Devnārāyaṇ begins with an invocation of different benevolent and auspicious deities that are also present on the *paṛ*. In the invocation, the deities are revered and remembered. The verb used here is *siṃvarṇo* which is cognate with Hindi *sumiraṇ* or *smaraṇ* and means 'remembering', 'recollecting', 'calling to mind', 'memory'.[17] The deities invoked during the invocatory section are Devī Śāradā, Gaṇeś, Devnārāyaṇ, Bhairūnath, Sarasvatī, and one's guru. The deities are invoked in order to provide protection, learning, and wisdom. Thus for example, two lines tell us that without one's guru there is no knowledge, and without Mother Sarasvatī there is no song or voice. By remembering Śāradā (a name of Sarasvatī or Durgā), the singer begins by saying she will always reside in the heart. The goddess Sarasvatī also resides in the singer's voice (*kaṇṭh;* literally: 'throat'), inspiring him to sing. By remembering Gaṇpat or Bināyak one gains happiness and satisfaction. And, again, whoever reveres Devnārāyaṇ, the god worshipped in the form of bricks (*ī̃ṭh*),[18] will never have a scarcity of milk or cereals. The important point here is not only of course that the protective and inspirational qualities of different deities are being invoked, but also that they are being 'remembered'. There is an invitation to remember. In other words, the singer is 're-membering' or 're-attaching' himself to the source from which the recitation flows.

In fact, the reference to remembrance at the beginning of the narrative marks out the very nature of the work of narrating which is an exercise in bringing forth from an epistemological domain presided over by the goddess of learning, creativity, and wisdom. It is not, from the point of view of the singer, an exercise in bringing forth from memory, in the sense of an internalized, 'mental' act of the retrieval of knowledge. The domain of knowledge and inspiration from which a singer draws out the song is in a sense external to him. It is an 'objectified', phenomenological sphere that grants him knowledge. This understanding of oral narration is, from an epistemological point of view, contrary to the understanding that oral narration is the result of complex processes of learning and memorization. Thus, for example, Finnegan (1992: 114-17), in her chapter on composition, transmission and memory, points out that in earlier models narratives were 'pictured as coming down automatically irrespective of human agency', but that later critical studies move 'away from the idea of storing verbatim memories to one of people reconstructing and organizing on the basis of what they know and do, so that remembering means not drawing on rote memory but a creative and organizational activity by the user.' The emphasis in more recent work is, thus, an 'memory as a social process'.

But while the questions posed by Finnegan above are important from the researcher's perspective, they nevertheless tend to overlook the cultural categories used by singers and performers to describe their own activity. Thus '. . . the Indian notions of *smara* (Sanskrit) and *marapu* (Tamil) combine love, memory, tradition and worship. They refer to reverential acts of ritual attendance, and also to the passionate longing of love. . . . *Smara,* "memory", "love", "worship", constitute "tradition", that which is handed down from one generation to the next (Skt. *parampara*). The heritage one receives from the elders is kept alive and fostered in love, for its beauty, value and concrete "indexicality"'.[19] Moreover, the Sanskrit category of *smṛti* refers to the remembrance of revealed knowledge, *śruti.* Marwari *siṃvarṇo,* Hindi *sumiraṇ,* and Sanskrit *smara* in the context of oral narratives and written texts, thus all refer to the *source* of religious literature. In the case of Devnārāyaṇ it is also this source that allows the oral narrative to manifest itself. The invocation of deities at the beginning of a recitation need not therefore be reduced to a matter of 'formula' or ritual prescription of some kind. It is a matter of becoming 're-connected' to a sphere of inspiration and knowledge.

Song and Declamatory Chant

Let us now turn to the formal structure of the narrative, while keeping in mind that the formal structure, by virtue of also being a reflection of what the singers do, provides us with an insight into the larger communicative framework of the narrative. As mentioned above, the Bhopa begins the narrative with an invocation (*remembrance*) of various deities, most notably Śāradā and Sarasvatī, the goddesses of learning, music, wisdom, speech and creative inspiration. Following this he begins with the narrative *per se*. The narrative itself is a weave of verse and prose on the one hand, and song and declaimed speech, on the other. In addition to the interaction between these textual forms and delivery modes, there is the interaction between the main singer and his partner. The dialogic form of the delivery is furthermore also to be found in the narrative itself, which proceeds through a series of dialogues between different characters or voices. Before turning to this central element of the narrative, let me first deal with the verse and prose sections.

Gāv and Arthāv

The verse sections of the text, which incidentally are also called *gāv*,[20] on account of their being sung, consist of four lines and a refrain. In some cases the sung sections comprise more than four lines. These exceptions will be discussed below. The *gāv* is sung by both singers simultaneously. In many instances they begin with an extended vowel 'on-line': 'e. . .'. The first line ends with an extended *auvũ raī* or simply *raī*. The last word in the second and fourth lines invariably rhyme, but not in the first and third lines. The refrain usually consists of (*bhalā̃ jī bhalā̃, Dev bhalā̃*) [Very good, sir. Very good, Dev]. When not referred to in terms of song (i.e. *gāv*), the verse sections are called *karī* which literally means link in a chain, 'connection', or 'sequence'. Thus the verse sections are understood to be links in the narrative chain. And, in fact, the narrative moves from one set of *kaṛīs* to the next. Each set of *kaṛīs* contains a short, compressed monologue spoken by a particular character. In the prose section following a verse, this 'monologue' is almost repeated verbatim. The difference of course lies in the form of delivery which is now 'declamatory'. The prose sections which are declaimed are called *arthāv*, literally meaning 'explanation' or 'meaning' (Hindi: *arth*). In contrast to the verse sections, here there is a definite spacing of the singers' voices. While the lead singer begins the sentences, his partner may rejoin in a number of alternate ways: (1) he may complete a sentence ended half-way by the lead singer, (2) he may simply repeat the lead singer's text, (3) he may add a line of his own, and (4) he may simply acknowledge the lead singer's text with remarks such as *mhe* or *vāh vāh*.

After the lines of the verse section have been faithfully repeated in the declaimed prose section, the singer and his partner continue the narrative in the dialogic manner mentioned above till it is time to sing another *kaṛī*. The declaimed section invariably ends with lines such as *Let's see what news x has to say/says* and *By saying it, know it, let's see*. These lines denote (1) that a person is about to speak and that (2) whatever is to be *known* is to be revealed by saying it or by speaking it. The word used for 'news' is '*samcār*'. Thus *x* always begins his speech to *y* in the form of a first person sung 'news'. Logically then, that which is to be known through *x*'s speech, and by implication the continuation of the narrative, becomes apparent in telling it/saying it/speaking it aloud. The emphasis on the connection between speaking and knowing is significant because it underlines the oral nature of the narrative. The singers do not say, for example, 'know it, by reading it or 'know it by understanding what is written'. The reference throughout is to speaking and telling. This aspect importantly underscores the emergent nature of knowledge for this particular oral tradition. Since there is no knowing before someone speaks, we cannot take recourse to 'frozen' receptacles of knowledge such as scriptures, inscriptions, palm leaves, books, etc., to preserve and reveal knowledge.

Conversational Discourse

The dialogic interaction between the lead singer and his partner is matched on an internal level by the dialogical structure of the narrative. By this I mean very specifically that the narrative is fundamentally nothing more than a series of conversations or dialogues between different voices.[21] There are hardly any extended third-person descriptions of events or scenes offered by the singers themselves. Whatever happens in the narrative takes place through the voices of various characters. Thus the narrative both in its internal structure as well as external expression comes closest to the speech genre of conversation. The analysis offered here and in the subsequent sections on repetition, dialogue, and reported speech, therefore, focuses primarily on the nature and occurrence of utterances as a fundamental unit of speech, rather than on linguistic features such as grammar, or even 'formulaic' language in order to understand the oral composition of the narrative.

While describing the features of conversational discourse in everyday situations,[22] Tannen (1994: 25f.) points out that

. . . conversational discourse frequently represents what others have said ('reported speech') as dialogue ('direct speech' or 'direct quotation') rather than third-person report ('indirect speech'), and that 'direct speech' is more vivid, more effective. But why is dialogue more vivid? I believe it is because the creation of voices occasions the imagination of a scene in which characters speak in those voices, and that these scenes occasion the imagination of alternative, distant, or familiar worlds, much as does artistic creation. Finally, the casting of ideas as the speech of others is an important source of emotion in discourse.

Whereas the conversations in the narrative are situated in the present, giving us a scene of a current event, the commentary offered by the singers is situated in the past. For example, such a commentary may be inserted between dialogues to spell out time and place:

The time they reached Sindhbaḍā (mhe), both Bhairavnāths took hold of the trunk. They shook the trunk./ The Jogiṇīs were sitting on the leaves./ One by one they all tumbled and fell down, (sir said.)/ By Durbar's command, there was a well nearby (mhe). They all went and fell into the well./ Bhairavnāth said 'Śrī Mahārāj'.

Repetition

Finnegan (1977: 90) states that 'the most marked feature of poetry is surely repetition'.[23] Furthermore, she observes that:

. . .repetition in some form is a characteristic of oral poetic style: repetition of phrases, lines or verses; the use of parallelisms; recurrent formulae. Oral poetry is necessarily ephemeral. Repetition has a real point in such circumstances. It makes it easier for the audience to grasp what has been said and gives the speaker/singer confidence that it has understood the message he is trying to communicate. In antiphonal forms, refrains, choruses or the direct repetition of a leader's lines, repetition offers an opportunity for an audience to take part with ease in the act of performance, to a degree not possible without some measure of repetition (ibid., p. 129).[24]

The oral style of Devnārāyaṇ's narrative is repetitive on many levels. One obvious form of repetition is the verbatim declamation of sung sections. Then there is the refrain at the end of each verse section, and the use of certain stock descriptions to mark 'battle scenes'. In addition there is repetition in the case of certain passages where a specific action is repeated by different people. Thus, for example, in the search for Bhuna, each family member, in consecutive sung sections entrust Chochu Bhat with a letter for Bhuna. Here we find a degree of repetition in the phrases used, which describe, as mentioned, the same act carried out by different persons. The use of repetition here adds to the emotional and poetic quality of the moment which in terms of the narrative bears the promise of a reunion with a family member. Whereas these examples relate to the poetic structure of the narrative, the kind of repetition mentioned above involving the singers can be said to relate to the style of delivery. In this case it is not that lines from the sung sections are repeated in the declaimed section, but that lines in declaimed sections are repeated by the lead singer's partner. 'Internal' repetition is thus paralleled by 'external' repetition. And the 'internal' dialogue of the narrative as a series of spoken encounters between different characters is paralleled by the 'external' dialogue of the singers.

But repetition even in this case is quite varied and may involve a wide range of possibilities. However, given the nature of repetition itself as something that is not necessarily produced but 'reproduced', this would mean that even though there may be many options available to the singer, the ultimate choice of utterance is determined by the first singer's speech. Creativity on the part of the second singer then lies in choosing from a range of given responsive modes. But the second singer's response is not limited to repetition. He also may bring in his own text, which is either a commentary on the foregoing line or an addition that propels the narrative forward.

The Function of Repetition

Tannen (1994: 47f.) while analysing repetition in conversation asks the following fundamental question:

> Why is there repetition in conversation? Why do we waste our breath saying the same thing over and over? The various purposes simultaneously served by repetition can be subsumed under the categories of production, comprehension, connection, and interaction. The congruence of these functions of discourse provides a fourth and overarching function in the establishment of coherence and interpersonal involvement.

In the case of production, she points out that 'repetition enables a speaker to produce language in a more efficient, less energy-draining way. It facilitates more language, more fluently' (ibid., p. 48). Comprehension is facilitated by repetition 'by providing semantically less dense discourse. If some of the words are repetitious, comparatively less new information is communicated than if all words uttered carried new information' (ibid., p. 49). Connection is established through repetition because 'it serves a referential and tying function. Repetition of sentences, phrases, and words shows how new utterances are linked to earlier discourse, and how ideas presented in the discourse are related to each other' (ibid., p. 50). Tannen continues to point out that the function of repetition in relation to production, comprehension, and connection 'refer(s) to the creation of meaning in conversation. But repetition also functions on the interactional level of talk: accomplishing social goals, or simply managing the business of conversation' (ibid., p. 51).

Having so far discussed the various possibilities of repetition within the narrative, let us now turn to the function and role of repetition under the four headings stated above. The first category is that of 'production'. Repetition in this case facilitates 'more language, more fluently'. Certainly this feature is apparent in the *arthāv* sections where the second singer repeats parts of the first singer's lines. Undoubtedly 'more language' is created here by using more of the same words while providing information. As a whole the narrative is enlarged and extended through repetition, and the production of 'more language' does actually also contribute to its lengthy 'epic' dimension. However, the production of more language, here, is closely linked to the second category, namely comprehension. Thus the repetition of the *gāv* passages in the *arthāv* sections facilitates a better understanding of the sung verses. In fact, the term *arthāv*, which means 'explanation', 'meaning', 'commentary', itself implies that the repetition of verses in declaimed prose is meant to provide a clearer comprehension of the former.

Here again we find that a term is used that suggests a conceptual, meta-level perception of the narrative and its narration from within the tradition. Thus the passages following the *gāv* sections are not called 'prose' as against 'song', but, significantly 'meaning' or 'explanation'. This distinction enables us to again visualize how the narrative is conceptualized. According to the terms used, the narrative of Devnārāyaṇ in this case consists of sung sections, which are then laid out and 'explained'.[25] Of course, this form of 'explanation' does not involve answers to 'how and why' questions. It does not 'explain' the sung sections in different words. Rather it explains by repeating the same words in a different mode of delivery. It is repetition itself, as Tannen observes, that lays bare the meaning of the words and sentences, since in the initial lines of the *arthāv* practically no new information is supplied. New information is supplied in subsequent lines. But here too there is repetition, as a consequence of which it is easier to comprehend the import of the first singer's utterance. But more than facilitate simple semantic comprehension, repetition within the *arthāv*, which often involves only some, select words, functions as an instrument of emphasis. The few words that are repeated (sometimes the whole line in transposed form) carry within them the core of what the first singer intended to mean in his speech. Thus repetition, involving the *arthāv* and sections within it, facilitates/serves not only comprehension, but also emphasis.[26]

Tannen's third category is 'connection'. This category, it would appear, is more linked to everyday conversation than to the situation relating to the narration of Devnārāyaṇ, in which there is less of ideas and more of scenes and events that are presented and linked with one another. The linkage of scenes and events is, of course, partially created through repetition, but more so this is afforded by the structure of plots and subplots in the narrative.

As Tannen points out, these three functions ultimately relate '. . .to the creation of meaning in conversation [and] accomplishing social goals, or simply managing the business of conversation' (ibid., p. 52). It is quite evident that repetition, in the special case of the narrative, also relates to the production of meaning. The creation of meaning is guided in this case not towards the singers themselves, but towards the audience which listens to the performance of the narrative. However, meaning does not emerge only at a purely linguistic or semantic level. It emerges here also at an 'experiential' level through the 'bringing-forth' of the content of the narrative which revolves around the life and deeds of Devnārāyaṇ, and the devotees' participation in the evocation of his power. The various forms of repetition, inherent to the narrative and its telling, are transformed from being literary features to partaking in the realm of *praxis*. Together with the various other aspects of the whole performance they too take on a causal character in the production of meaning as an interplay of semantic, sensory, cultural, and religious elements.

DIALOGUE

As pointed out above, the narrative is 'repetitive' on (at least) two levels: the level of form (verse and prose, etc.) and the level of delivery (lead singer and second singer). Furthermore, it became clear, that the narrative is also 'dialogic' in two senses: the sense in which dialogue between characters occupies a central position as a narrative strategy and the sense in which the singers are engaged in a dialogue with one another (and, of course, also with the audience producing a third sense of dialogue). As indicated previously, a full understanding of the narrative as a communicative event would not only involve an understanding of its language, but also an understanding of the nature and relationship of utterances as a vehicle for constructing oral narrative structure,[27] and, also for the dialogic structure of the world represented in the narrative.

Given the centrality of the fact that the narrative delivery of Devnārāyaṇ is essentially constituted by two voices who spin out the narrative content through an exchange of utterances, it is worth while to examine the nature of this dialogue. As pointed out above, it is possible to locate this form of dialogue within the umbrella category of speech genres we call conversation. Naturally, the kind of conversational dialogue which occurs during a narration of Devnārāyaṇ is contextually distinct from the kind of conversational dialogue which may occur in 'everyday life'. Whereas conversations of everyday life are centered around a variety of subjects and may develop in a variety of forms, the conversation occurring during a narrative of Devnārāyaṇ is focused and determined by the content of the narrative. Also, the form of the conversation or exchange between the singers is quite regularized. It is to be limited to a set of options which have been discussed above. Above all, however, the conversational nature of the exchange between the singers has a distinguishing feature that 'everyday' conversation does not possess. Whereas in everyday conversation there is always the possibility that the respondent will become speaker, and the speaker will take the place of respondent, in the case of the narrative, the identity of the respondent is always fixed. The second singer is the one who provides the rejoinder to the first singer's utterances and not vice versa. The role of listener and speaker is, therefore, predetermined by the narrative style. Although the dialogue between the singers thereby involves a certain level of inflexibility, it also provides a set of options in terms of which the second singer's rejoinder may be expressed.

At this point it should be noted that the narrative tradition of Devnārāyaṇ itself has a notion of 'rejoinder'. This is called *hũkāro (hũkāriyo* being the person who responds) and means a verbal expression of assent or of comprehension and agreement,—urging the narrator to carry on speaking. Thus there is conceptual awareness here of the fact that a speaker always requires a listener. In other words, human communication is considered to be essentially 'dialogic' rather than monologic. The speaker or singer cannot express himself in a vacuum. It is the active comprehension of the listener expressed through the *hũkāro* that draws out the singer's lines and ultimately facilitates the progress of the narrative. This notion of the active listener or respondent comes close to Bakhtin's understanding of speech communication:

> . . . when the listener perceives and understands the meaning (the language meaning) of speech, he simultaneously takes an active, responsive attitude toward it. He either agrees or disagrees with it . . . , augments it, applies it, prepares it for execution, and so on. Any understanding of live speech, a live utterance, is inherently responsive, although the degree of this activity varies extremely. Thus all real and integral understanding is actively responsive, and constitutes nothing other than the initial preparatory stage of a response (in whatever form it may be actualized). (1987: 68-9)

Given the importance of a response for all 'live speech', it is not surprising that the narrative tradition of Devnārāyaṇ with its focus on orality should involve a lead singer and his respondent. It is remarkable that such a notion should in fact be formalized (institutionalized) to such a degree.[28]

So far we have pointed out the role of dialogue, and of speaker and respondent in relation to the actual narration of the narrative. But what implications, if any, does such a narrative form have on the structure of the text? How is a text constructed through a series of utterances (and not 'sentences')? What kind of text emerges in this way? Given the spoken nature of the narration as a series of utterances, the text is composed of a body of sometimes complete and sometimes only partially complete sentences, (in the case of *arthāv)* of exclamations, of monosyllabic rejoinders, etc. The text as a whole is thus made up of grammatically fragmented linguistic units (such as the sentence). These broken units only make sense due to the fact that they are utterances in an oral narrative and not written sentences in prose. The oral nature of the narrative allows for the 'incompleteness' of the grammatical structure of the text. And, as has been pointed out above, within the chain of 'incomplete' sentences there is a chain of grammatically incomplete repetitive utterances created through the second singer's response to the lead singer's words. The text contains within itself a repetition of itself. As a series of dialogic utterances, it responds to and imitates itself. Thus the 'text' created by the second singer does not lay importance on being 'autonomous' or 'original'. It is caught up in a perfect 'intertextual' flow with the text of the first singer. In other words, it exists on the boundaries of the lead singer's text by referring to, and in fact reproducing, it.[29]

Reported Speech

It was mentioned above that the delivery of the narrative and the narrative itself are dialogic in two different senses. The first sense is in which the recitation proceeds on the basis of an interchange between the two singers. This interchange—a communicative event situated in a performance setting—is directed at setting up and establishing a corpus of meaning for the audience who listens (and also interacts) with the singers. The second sense of dialogue involves the construction of the narrative in terms of dialogues between characters of the story. Thus it was shown that the central sections of the story (*gāv*) are units of speech or conversation uttered by one character and directed towards another character. Given these two senses of dialogue one could state that the 'inner' dialogue of the narrative occurs within the 'outer' dialogue of the singers, which in fact provides the frame for the narration. But in what sense are we to understand the relationship between the 'outer' and 'inner' dialogues? How is the inner dialogue part of or built into the outer dialogue? Once again the line of inquiry I will take up here rests on the assumption that the recitation of the narrative is a particular speech genre that comes closest to that of 'everyday' conversation following an interchange between two speakers. But before proceeding with this inquiry, I shall refer to an understanding of what in linguistic terms can be called a dialogue. A dialogue, in the sense Bakhtin refers to, arises from the fact that all utterances are in fact *polyphonic* in nature: 'Utterances are not indifferent to one another, and are not self-sufficient; they are aware of and mutually reflect one another. . . . Each utterance is filled with echoes and reverberations of other utterances.' (Bakhtin 1986: 91). A special form of dialogic utterance is an interchange which involves the reporting of another's speech. 'Reported speech' can have two forms.[30] One, which involves a direct quotation such as 'He/she said: I did that.' The other which involves an indirect quotation such as 'He/she said that he/she did that/had done that'. The assumption behind reported speech as 'direct quotations' is that the utterance of one person can be faithfully repeated by someone else in a content other than the original one in which the utterance was spoken. Thus there is the belief that the utterance and its meaning content can remain untouched regardless of the speaker and spoken content.

However, as Tannen (1994: 133) points out:

> 'reported speech' is a misnomer, an abstraction with no basis in the reality of interaction. When speakers cast the words of others in dialogue, they are not reporting so much as constructing dialogue. . . . Dialogue is not a general report; it is particular, and the particular enables listeners (or readers) to create their understanding by drawing on their own history of associations. . . . The constructing of dialogue for framing as reported speech reflects the dual nature of language, like all human behavior, as repetitive and novel, fixed and free, transforming rather than transmitting what comes its way.

From the point of view of the narrative of Devnārāyaṇ, we find that what the singers are doing—at least on the surface—is to continuously 'report' what characters in the narrative said (to one another). By inserting the name of the person who speaks before each dialogue the singer identifies his/her voice. The singers do not, for example, personify characters or speak in the first person as characters might do in a theatre. On the contrary, they are involved in reporting to the audience or listeners what went on or what was spoken. In this sense it is the singer who claims access to the scenes and events of the narrative, just as a third person who witnesses a conversation between two people, and then reports the conversation to a fourth person. However, as Tannen points out, 'reported speech' is not just repetition but also construction. How does the singer's activity of reporting dialogue involve construction? If it does involve construction is this the same as saying that the singers 'improvise' while narrating? What consequences follow if we begin to view the 'constructed' nature of the narrative rather than its 'improvisational' nature? Supposing we were to perceive the singers' task not as 'recitation' but as 'reporting'? How would our understanding of the communicative event alter from this perspective? Would our search for fixity (formula, repetition) and free play ('creativity/improvisation') be altered? For example, as Tannen argues, '. . . the construction of dialogue represents an active, creative, transforming move which expresses the relationship not between the quoted party and the topic of talk but rather the quoting party and the audience to which the quotation is delivered.' In other words, it is the context in which the act of reporting is done that determines the sense which the 'quoted' speech is to take. If a reported speech does involve the creative and transforming aspect Tannen refers to, then it would seem obvious that singers alter what they say according to who they perceive the audience to be, and the relationship they have to the audience. A simple example of this alteration or, in fact, choice in telling can be seen in terms of the episode a singer 'reports' to the audience. He does not always 'report' episodes of his own choice, but also those wished for by the audience. By placing the communicative act of singer and audience within the framework of 'reported speech' we can conceptualize the process of selectivity involved in a different way. Selectivity in reporting is not just a question of desires or wants, but also of being in rapport with the 'listening' of the audience, just as a speaker reports what he/she has heard selectively depending on the intention he/she has in 'reproducing' an utterance in a specific social or interpersonal context. But what exactly is meant by 'listening'? How is listening different from verbal response? Listening, we may state, is an internal state of the listener that provides the context for the speaker's utterence to unfold and make sense. Therefore, it is a non-verbal *activity* that engenders speech.[31] Thus the activity of singing and speaking is not solely bound to the singers' agency, but to the audience's particular agency evoked through listening. Depending on this interrelationship between the audience and singer, the singer would tend to 'report' the narrative in varying ways. This would explain why performances are never exactly the same. However, it would also shift the emphasis from 'improvisation', i.e. an explanation of variation in terms of a singer's individual capability, to 'construction', or the creative building up of narrated dialogue in a specifically interactive situation in which listening plays a vital role. In such a situation it would be natural that there is a movement between fixity, i.e. the use of 'formula' and 'free play' (or creativity?). Thus the problem of formulaic language and improvisation during a performance need not refer solely to the phenomenon of 'memorization', and 'improvisation', etc., but to the question of 'construction', and the 'interaction' based on listening.

By viewing a performance or recital of the narrative as an example of extended 'reported' speech, we can also begin to appreciate the nature of the singer's work. The singer's work is not simply to sing, recite or perform the narrative, rather it is to mediate or report what happened and what was said to the audience. Implicit in the singer's work is a knowledge of past events which are then passed on in a specific content as dialogue in the present to the audience. It is the singer's privilege then to have 'overheard' or gained knowledge about Devnārāyaṇ that is then communicated to his devotees.

Conclusion: Creating Presence

While studying the oral narrative of Devnārāyaṇ, one is confronted with a number of questions. Most immediate amongst these are: How is it recited or performed? Who are the performers? How is the oral recitation structured? What is the relationship between verbal narrative and visual narrative? However, beyond these questions the concern here is also with the ways in which the categories of 'text', 'performance', 'performer', 'visual narrative', 'orality', 'communicative event' and so on are defined from within the tradition itself. For example, are there categories that correspond to these conceptual terms? If this be the case, then what kind of understanding of the narrative do they represent? Does this understanding perhaps warrant a revision of our own conceptual categories? Moreover, does the tradition represent a coherent 'system' of communication? And, if so, is there a specific framework in which the arrangement of terms and components can be placed? In this essay I have attempted to show that the communicative context of the narrative is composed of epistemological categories such as 'remembrance' on the one hand, and aspects of 'speech genres' such as 'repetition', 'dialogue', and 'reported speech' on the other. These categories and genres themselves serve another overarching purpose, and that is to create, invoke and celebrate the presence of Devnārāyaṇ, the deity, whose story is being told.

NOTES

1. This essay is a revised version of a chapter from my book on Devnārāyaṇ. See Malik (2005).
2. See, for example, Blackburn (1989), Malik (1993), Miller (1994), Singh (1993), Smith (1991). Blackburn furthermore classifies the narrative under the category of so-called 'martial epics' in India that emphasize 'group solidarity' and are 'concerned with power, social obligation, and social unity; they turn on themes of revenge, regaining lost land, or restoring lost rights. . . . Martial epics celebrate external—often military or political—conflict and a warrior ethic.' (1989: 5).
3. A synopsis of the contents of the narrative that has two main parts is offered in Chapter Four of my book (Malik 2005).
4. See Binford (1976), Blackburn (1989), Gold (1992), Lapoint (1978), Smith (1991).
5. Cited in Kersenboom (1995: 5).
6. Thus as Kersenboom (1995: 16) with reference to the 'Tamil text' observes: 'While the nature of the Western text is static, an object of analytical abstraction, and takes the form of a document, the Tamil text is organic in nature, a process of synthetic absorption, living a reality of performance. The application of both differs as well: while the document adds to a database that eventually will produce the ultimate interpretation as truth, the performance offers a becoming, an embodiment, of life, here and now. These extremes are substantiated in their material representations.'

7. Thiel-Horstmann (1985) provides a complete documentation of the *jāgrana* in the context of worship conducted by the north Indian bhakti sect, the Dadupanth. In her preface she notes that the *jāgrana* is, temporally speaking, the most extended form of worship that occurs in front of the community. During the course of a *jāgrana* a number of texts are either sung or declaimed. The purpose of these texts is to 'awaken' the devotee, and to motivate him or her to be free of *saṃsāra.* She also notes that the documentation in published form denies the reader many other components of the night-wake, such as '. . . die musikalisch-ästhetischen Freuden der Veranstaltung, ihre zeitliche Geschlossenheit, das Milieu des *satsanga* und den verdienstlosen Triumph einer doch glücklich überstandenen Nachtwache . . .' (ibid., p. 10). Again, the implication here is that the texts are embedded in a larger aesthetic, 'performative' situation, in which their meaning unfolds, thereby motivating singers and listeners.
8. Since my intention here is to provide an understanding of the 'concept' of performance, I do not describe the performance itself in great detail. The main features are summarized below. A complete documentation of a single night's performance would, as Thiel-Horstmann's study mentioned above shows, entail a monograph in itself. For details on the performance situation of Devnārāyaṇ, see further Miller (1994).
9. See Mair (1988: 102) and Miller (1994).
10. Similarly, Smith (1991: 17) writing on the related 'picture story-telling' tradition of Pābūjī points out that: '. . . the use of the phrase "reading the *paṛ*" is a valuable indication of the way in which *bhopos* conceptualize their work. They do not speak of "singing an epic"; they refer not to singing or narrative but to performance, and their term for performance invokes the cloth-painting. . . . We approach Pābūjī through his *paṛ,* and we approach the *paṛ* through the *bhopos* "reading" of it.'
11. Miles (1985: 34) distinguishes between religious images that are either iconic, representational, impressionistic, or abstract. According to her, of these four types, iconic images are 'most denotative . . . that is, organized according to traditional depiction whose every detail . . . may be 'read' by the worshipper in terms of a particular content of scriptural or historic significance. . . . The interpreter of images, like the interpreter of texts, must determine the denotation of the image as a preliminary step to suggesting the spectrum of meanings it was likely to have had for the different members of its historical community.'
12. Thus even to claim that these images are strongly denotative in the sense of being icons, would be to fall short of their meaning.
13. On the other hand, the written word represents an abstraction or distancing from the real world: 'With its connection to existential

events broken, an alphabetically written word becomes a set of abstract symbols in static, quasi-permanent space rather than a dynamic event. The context, which is so important to oral communication . . . tends to recede greatly into the tacit or even unconscious background' (ibid., p. 9). In this connection see also the important work of Ong (1982).

14. *Mūrtis* are strictly speaking not 'images' of a deity, they are a concrete manifestation of a deity and its divine power.
15. Bolle (1969: 127ff.) points out that: '. . . unless one understands the primacy of the *place,* the nature of the sacred in most of Hinduism remains incomprehensible, and the plurality and variety of gods continues to form an unsolvable puzzle. *God is universal because He is there. . .*'.
16. It is interesting to note that the notion of 'speaking/reading' and 'writing' should relate to visual images in a predominantly oral tradition. The orality of the narrative does not allow for a notion of reading and writing connected to the written word, i.e. to the symbolic manifestation of language in script. Since there are no symbols to place language 'inside', reading and writing are used with reference to visual 'text'. It is, of course, surprising that concepts of reading and writing at all emerge in such a context. In other words, we would have to understand that reading and writing as concepts are not possessions of senders and receivers of *'Schriftsprache'* alone. Naturally the occurrence of such terms could also be attributed to the fact that we are not dealing here with a primary oral culture, but with one that exists in relationship to written culture.
17. This is very similar to the oral poetry of the Hāṭkar Dhangars of Maharashtra who begin compositions (*ovīs*) with '*sumbarāna māṇḍilā*' or '*sumbārana devācā*' ('the remembrance is set', 'the remembrance of god') (Sontheimer 1989: 9). The oral narrative of Devnārāyaṇ involves memory in two senses. One sense, of course, is that in which the singer himself sings from 'memory' (although this is not what singers claim. More frequently a singer talks of being 'inspired' or 'energized' by Sarasvatī or Devnārāyaṇ). The other sense is that in which the singer is involved in recreating and re-expressing the past in the present. When concerned with the meaning of the narrative it is also imperative to look into this latter aspect of 'memory' and 'remembrance', although from the point of view of oral transmission the first sense of memory is equally important. Memory in the sense of the recreation of history brings us squarely onto one of the central concerns of the narrative, namely, a discourse on historicity.
18. The aniconic representation of Devnārāyaṇ in the form of a row of

large upright bricks is taken up in more detail in the chapter on 'Visual Narrative' in my book (Malik 2005).

19. Kersenboom (1995: 19 and 94f.).
20. From the verb *gāvṇo:* 'to sing'.
21. These may involve humans, gods, demons, animals, and even trees.
22. On discourse and conversational analysis, see also Goodwin (1981), Gumperz (1982), Wardaugh (1985).
23. Cited in Tannen (1994: 20).
24. Notwithstanding the common occurrence of repetition in oral forms of poetry, Finnegan concludes, however, that 'the exact significance of repetition in oral poetry is not, therefore, clear' (ibid., p. 132).
25. This system of terse, compact verse followed by a commentary reminds one of Indian philosophical and literary schools which reproduce texts verse by verse, each of which are followed by a longer, detailed commentary. The distinction between such philosophical and literary commentaries and the oral narrative of Devnārāyaṇ lies of course in the fact that in the latter case the narrative also progresses in the *arthāv* sections which themselves anticipate the next *gav* and so on.
26. This becomes easier to comprehend when actually listening to the second singer's spoken style of repeating the first singer's lines.
27. The distinction between language and utterance is comparable to the distinction between *langue* and *parole* made by Saussure. Thus '. . . the language, thought of an abstract pattern or scheme, and speech (to adopt the usual, somewhat unsatisfactory, translation of *parole)* are individual uses of language on particular occasions' (Turner 1987: 14).
28. This notion is also found in other narrative traditions of Rajasthan (Pābūjī, etc.). In fact, it would be worth while to examine the notion of speaker and respondent in other performative traditions relating not only to narratives but also to music and dance. A comparative study would perhaps reveal the centrality of 'dialogue' in Indian expressive traditions and the arts. It may also reveal something about the way in which 'reality' is constructed.
29. This results in a kind of 'inner' intertextuality. There exists, therefore, also at the level of text (*qua* the notion of an inter/intratext) a notion of dialogue—of telling and responding—that interrelates the first and second singers' texts with each other.
30. On reported speech and code-switching see, for example, Gumperz (1982).
31. Listening is in this sense distinguishable from Bakhtin's notion of dialogic response. Whereas listening is certainly a crucial element of all dialogue, it is not manifest in the form of a response. It is the

pretext, so to speak, of speech, the attentive field within which all speech arises. On the idea and consequences of listening, see, Fuimara (1990) and Malik (1995).

REFERENCES

Bakhtin, M.M., 1986, 'The Problem of Speech Genres', in *Speech Genres and Other Late Essays,* Trans. V.W. McGee, Austin: University of Austin Press.

Binford, M.R., 1976, 'Mixing in the Colour of Ram of Ranuja', in *Hinduism: New Essays in the History of Religions,* B.L. Smith (ed.), Leiden: E.J. Brill.

Blackburn, S.H. et al. (eds.), 1989, *Oral Epics in India,* Berkeley: University of California Press.

Bolle, K.W., 1969, 'Speaking of a Place', in *Myths and Symbols: Studies in honour of Mircea Eliade,* C.H. Long and J. Kitagawa (eds.), Chicago: University of Chicago Press.

Finnegan, R., 1992, *Oral Traditions and the Verbal Arts,* London: Routledge.

Fuimara, G.C., 1990, *The Other Side of Language: A Philosophy of Listening,* London: Routledge.

Gold, A.G., 1992, *A Carnival of Parting,* Berkeley: University of California Press.

Goodwin, C., 1981, *Conversational Organization,* New York: Academic Press.

Gumperz, J. 1982, *Discourse Strategies,* Cambridge: University of Cambridge Press.

Jardine, M., 1996, 'Sight, Sound, and Epistemology: The Experiential Sources of Ethical Concepts', in *Journal of the American Academy of Religion,* LXIV: 1-26.

Kersenboom, S., 1995, *Word, Sound, Image*, Oxford: Berg Publishers.

Lapoint, E.G., 1978, 'The Epic of Guga: A North Indian Oral Tradition', in *American Studies in the Anthropology of India,* S. Vatuk (ed.), Delhi: Manohar.

Mair, V., 1988, *Painting and Performance,* Honolulu: University of Hawaii Press.

Malik, A., 1993, 'Avatara, Avenger, and King: Narrative Themes in the Oral Epic of *Devnārāyaṇ*', in H. Brückner, L. Lutze, A. Malik (eds.), *Flags of Fame: Studies in South Asian Folk Culture,* Delhi: Manohar.

Malik, A., 2005, *Nectar Gaze and Poison Breath: An Analysis and*

Translation of the Rajasthani Oral Narrative of Devnārāyaṇ, New York: Oxford University Press.

Malik, S.C., 1995, *Reconceptualizing the Sciences and the Humanities: An Integral Approach*, Delhi: Manohar.

Miles, M.R., 1985, *Image as Insight*. Boston: Beacon Press.

Miller, J.C., 1994, 'The Twenty-four Brothers and Lord Devnārāyaṇ: The Story and Performance of a Folk Epic of Rajasthan', Ph.D. dissertation, University of Pennsylvania.

Ong, W., 1982, *Orality and Literacy*, London: Methuen.

Piatigorsky, A., 1985, 'Some Phenomenological Observations on Indian Religion', in *Indian Religion*, R. Burghart and A. Cantlie (eds.), London: Curzon Press.

Ricoeur, P., 1981, *Hermeneutics and the Human Sciences: Essays on Language, Action and Interpretation*, Cambridge: Cambridge University Press.

Singh, B., 1993, 'The Episode of the Golden Śiva Image', in H. Brückner, L. Lutze, A. Malik (eds.), *Flags of Fame: Studies in South Asian Folk Culture*, Delhi: Manohar.

Smith, J.D., 1991, *The Epic of Pābūjī*, Cambridge: Cambridge University Press.

Sontheimer, G.D., 1989, 'The Myth of the God and his Two Wives', in *Living Texts from India*, M. Thiel-Horstmann and R. Barz (eds.), Wiesbaden: Harrassowitz.

Tannen, D., 1994, *Talking Voices: Repetition, Dialogue, and Imagery in Conversational Discourse*, Cambridge: Cambridge University Press.

Thiel-Horstmann, M., 1985, *Nächtliches Wachen*, Bonn: Indica et Tibetica Verlag.

Turner, G.W., 1987, *Stylistics*, Harmondsworth: Penguin.

Wardough, R., 1985, *How Conversation Works*, Oxford: Basil Blackwell.

Contributors

MARZIA BALZANI is a senior lecturer in social anthropology. She conducted fieldwork in India among the Rajput elite and is currently researching diasporic Muslim South Asians in the UK and Pakistan.

HEIDRUN BRÜCKNER is professor of Indology and South Asian Studies at the University of Würzburg, Germany. Her areas of research are Sanskrit drama, Hinduism and the history of Indology.

HANNE M. DE BRUIN conducted research for her Ph.D. on 'Kattaikkuttu: The Flexibility of a South Indian Theatre Tradition'. She has published extensively about popular theatre in South India and the position of rural women performers on the Tamil stage. Since 2002 she works full-time for the Kattaikkuttu Sangam, an NGO promoting the interests of rural professional performers in Kanchipuram District, Tamil Nadu.

JOAN L. ERDMAN (Ph.D., University of Chicago, 1980) is professor of anthropology and cultural studies at Columbia College, Chicago, and associate member of the Committee on Southern Asian Studies at University of Chicago. Her research and writing focus on performance and cultural policy in India.

SASKIA KERSENBOOM is at present Associate Professor of Theatre Studies at University of Amsterdam. She has published widely on Hindu ritual arts in monographs, multimedia and performs regularly.

MIRELLA LINGORSKA, (Ph.D., Humboldt University of Berlin, Germany 1996), is teaching at the Department of Indology and Comparative Religious Studies, Tübingen, Germany. She has worked and published on Sanskrit rhetoric and poetics.

ADITYA MALIK is Senior Lecturer in Indian Religions in the School of Philosophy and Religious Studies, University of Canterbury in Christchurch, New Zealand. He is the author of *Nectar Gaze and Poison Breath: An Analysis and Translation of the Rajasthani Oral Narrative of Devnarayan*, Oxford University Press, 2005.

HEIKE MOSER completed her Ph.D. at Würzburg University and currently works in the Indological departments of the universities of Würzburg and Tübingen. From 1995 to 2001 she studied and performed Kutiyattam and Nangiar Kuttu at the Academy of Kerala Kaḷamandalam. At present she performs and gives lecture-demonstrations in universities, theatres and schools.

ELISABETH SCHÖMBUCHER teaches Social Anthropology at the Universities of Heidelberg and Würzburg. She has conducted extensive fieldwork and published widely on the performative aspects of spirit possession and spirit mediumship in India. Her present research focuses on death and dying among Hindus in the West.

BOŻENA ŚLIWCZYŃSKA, Institute of Oriental Studies, Warsaw University, Poland, specializes in Sanskrit and Bengali Studies. Her particular areas of interest are Kutiyattam theatre, Vedic and post-vedic ritual and popular (mass) culture.

KARIN STEINER lectures Indology at the Universities of Würzburg and Heidelberg. She specialises in Vedic religion and literature, in Sanskrit drama, and in Hindusim.

PHILLIP B. ZARRILLI is internationally known for training actors through Asian martial/meditation arts and as a director. He is currently Professor of Performance Practice within the Drama Department, University of Exeter. He has published numerous books and essays on Kathakali dance drama and Kalarippayattu.